Lecture Notes in Computer Science   10679

Commenced Publication in 1973
Founding and Former Series Editors:
Gerhard Goos, Juris Hartmanis, and Jan van Leeuwen

More information about this series at http://www.springer.com/series/7408

Manjunath Gorentla Venkata · Neena Imam
Swaroop Pophale (Eds.)

OpenSHMEM and Related Technologies

Big Compute and Big Data Convergence

4th Workshop, OpenSHMEM 2017
Annapolis, MD, USA, August 7–9, 2017
Revised Selected Papers

 Springer

Editors
Manjunath Gorentla Venkata ⓘ
Oak Ridge National Laboratory
Oak Ridge, TN
USA

Swaroop Pophale ⓘ
Oak Ridge National Laboratory
Oak Ridge, TN
USA

Neena Imam ⓘ
Oak Ridge National Laboratory
Oak Ridge, TN
USA

ISSN 0302-9743 ISSN 1611-3349 (electronic)
Lecture Notes in Computer Science
ISBN 978-3-319-73813-0 ISBN 978-3-319-73814-7 (eBook)
https://doi.org/10.1007/978-3-319-73814-7

Library of Congress Control Number: 2017963768

LNCS Sublibrary: SL2 – Programming and Software Engineering

Printed on acid-free paper

This Springer imprint is published by Springer Nature
The registered company is Springer International Publishing AG
The registered company address is: Gewerbestrasse 11, 6330 Cham, Switzerland

Preface

OpenSHMEM is a Partitioned Global Address Space (PGAS) library specification. The main abstractions of the programming model are execution contexts called processing elements (PEs) and symmetric memory objects. The programming model also provides explicit mechanisms to access and transfer data between the symmetric memory objects of different PEs. The key factors that make OpenSHMEM an excellent choice for parallel, communicating HPC applications is its simple application programming interface (API), support for remote direct memory access (RDMA), and constant innovation in the library API to keep abreast with the current scientific and hardware changes. Over the past few years there is a growing momentum behind the development and usage of the OpenSHMEM programming model.

The OpenSHMEM Workshop is the premier venue for presenting new and innovative PGAS research in the context of OpenSHMEM. OpenSHMEM 2017, held in Annapolis, Maryland, was the fourth event in the OpenSHMEM and Related Technologies workshop series. The workshop was organized by Oak Ridge National Laboratory and sponsored by ORNL, DoD, Cray, Nvidia, Mellanox, ARM, and HPE. The workshop was attended by participants from across academia, industry, and private and federal research organizations.

This year, the workshop focused on "OpenSHMEM and the Big Compute and Big Data Convergence." The workshop included two days of technical presentations followed by one day dedicated to the OpenSHMEM Specification discussions and development. The technical segment commenced with a keynote from Dr. William Carlson. Apart from being a member of the research staff at the IDA Center for Computing Sciences since 1990, he also leads the UPC language effort. The title of his talk was "Shared Memory HPC Programming: Past, Present, and Future?".

The paper session discussed a variety of concepts, including extending the OpenSHMEM API for future architectures, new applications using OpenSHMEM, evaluation and implementation of OpenSHMEM for new architectures, novel use of OpenSHMEM for the heterogeneous environments, and new development in the tools eco-system for OpenSHMEM. All papers submitted to the workshop were peer-reviewed by the Program Committee (PC) which included members from universities, industry, and research labs. Despite the short turnaround, each paper was reviewed by at least three reviewers. In all, 11 full papers were selected to be presented at the workshop.

This proceedings volume is a collection of papers presented at the workshop. The technical papers provided a variety of ideas for extending the OpenSHMEM specification and making it efficient for current and next-generation systems. This includes new research for communication contexts in OpenSHMEM, different optimizations for OpenSHMEM on shared memory machines, exploring the implementation of Open-SHMEM and its memory model on Intel's KNL architecture, and implementing new applications and benchmarks with OpenSHMEM.

The third day of the workshop was focused on developing the OpenSHMEM specification. This year, 2017, like the year before, has been a very exciting year for the OpenSHMEM committee. Thanks to the active participation at the workshop, the committee is in the process of ratifying OpenSHMEM Specification 1.4. The Open-SHMEM meeting at the workshop is an annual face-to-face OpenSHMEM committee meeting making it an important and impactful venue.

The general and technical program Chairs would like to thank everyone who contributed to the organization of the workshop. Particularly, we would to thank all authors, PC members, reviewers, session chairs, participants, and sponsors. We are grateful for the excellent support we received from our ORNL administrative staff and Daniel Pack, who helped maintain and update our workshop website.

December 2017   Neena Imam
Manjunath Gorentla Venkata
Swaroop Pophale

Organization

General Co-chairs

Neena Imam   Oak Ridge National Laboratory, USA
Manjunath Gorentla   Oak Ridge National Laboratory, USA
  Venkata
Nick Park   Department of Defense, USA

Technical Program Co-chairs

Manjunath Gorentla   Oak Ridge National Laboratory, USA
  Venkata
Swaroop Pophale   Oak Ridge National Laboratory, USA

Technical Program Committee

Ferrol Aderholdt   Oak Ridge National Laboratory, USA
Matthew Baker   Oak Ridge National Laboratory, USA
Pavan Balaji   Argonne National Laboratory, USA
Swen Boehm   Oak Ridge National Laboratory, USA
Bob Cernohous   Cray Inc., USA
Zheng Cui   VMWare, USA
Tony Curtis   Stony Brook University, USA
James Dinan   Intel Corporation, USA
Jeff Hammond   Intel Labs, USA
Bryant Lam   Department of Defense, USA
Arthur Maccabe   Oak Ridge National Laboratory, USA
Dhabaleswar (DK) Panda   Ohio State University, USA
Nick Park   Department of Defense, USA
Stephen Poole   OSSS, USA
Sreeram Potluri   NVIDIA, USA
Michael Raymond   SGI, USA
Gilad Shainer   Mellanox Technologies, USA
Pavel Shamis   ARM, USA
Sameer Shende   University of Oregon, USA
Min Si   Argonne National Laboratory, USA
Weikuan Yu   Florida State University, USA

Sponsors

Diamond Sponsors

Silver Sponsors

Bronze Sponsors

Contents

OpenSHMEM Extensions

Symmetric Memory Partitions in OpenSHMEM: A Case Study with Intel KNL

Naveen Namashivayam[1]([✉]), Bob Cernohous[1], Krishna Kandalla[1], Dan Pou[1], Joseph Robichaux[2], James Dinan[2], and Mark Pagel[1]

[1] Cray Inc., Seattle, USA
nravi@cray.com
[2] Intel Corp., Mountain View, USA

Abstract. To extract best performance from emerging tiered memory systems, it is essential for applications to use the different kinds of memory available on the system. OpenSHMEM memory model consists of data objects that are private to each *Processing Element* (PE) and data objects that are remotely accessible by all PEs. The remotely accessible data objects are called *Symmetric Data Objects* and are allocated on a memory region called as *Symmetric Heap*. Symmetric Heap is created during program execution on a memory region determined by the Open-SHMEM implementation. This paper proposes a new feature called *Symmetric Memory Partitions* to enable users to determine the size along with other memory traits for creating the symmetric heap. Moreover, this paper uses Intel KNL processors as an example use case for emerging tiered memory systems. This paper also describes the implementation of symmetric memory partitions in Cray SHMEM and use ParRes Open-SHMEM microbenchmark kernels to show the benefits of selecting the memory region for the symmetric heap.

1 Introduction

Emerging systems support multiple kinds of memory with different performance and capacity characteristics. Systems with multiple kinds of memory are seen in recent architectures such as AMD Fiji, NVIDIA Pascal, and Intel Knights Landing. The latest Many Integrated Core (MIC) processor, the Intel Xeon Phi, code-named Knights Landing (KNL) [9], combines the traditional off-package DDR memory with the increased high bandwidth on-package memory called as the Multi-Channel DRAM [10] (MCDRAM). To identify and manage different kinds of memory, vendors provide their own programming approaches using external libraries like CUDA [14] and Memkind [6]. Applications can also use low level programming approaches. Irrespective of the selection, these approaches limit application portability. To address this problem, programming libraries such as OpenSHMEM [7] must provide a more consistent and portable interface for accessing different kinds of memory on tiered memory systems.

© Springer International Publishing AG 2018
M. Gorentla Venkata et al. (Eds.): OpenSHMEM 2017, LNCS 10679, pp. 3–18, 2018.
https://doi.org/10.1007/978-3-319-73814-7_1

In this paper, we define a set of OpenSHMEM runtime changes and routines to support different kinds of memory for the symmetric heap. During program execution, the current OpenSHMEM memory model creates the symmetric heap with specific memory characteristics that are determined by the implementation. The runtime changes described in this paper would allow users to determine a region on which the symmetric heap can be created. We call this user-determined region as *Symmetric Memory Partition*. To define their characteristics, each memory partition features a list of traits, with memory kind being one of those featured traits.

The major contributions of this work are:

- proposing a set of new runtime changes and routines in OpenSHMEM to support different kinds of memory on tiered memory systems;
- implementation of the proposed changes in Cray SHMEM [12] for Intel KNL processors as an example use-case for memory partitions on emerging systems;
- performance regression analysis on creating multiple symmetric partitions; and
- performance analysis of the proposed changes using Parallel Research Kernels (ParRes) [8].

This paper is organized as follows. Section 2 provides a brief overview for Cray SHMEM and Sect. 3 describes Intel KNL architecture with its different modes of memory configuration. Section 4 illustrates the current OpenSHMEM memory model and necessitates the need for changes in the existing memory model. In Sect. 5 we propose the new symmetric memory partition feature and in Sect. 6 we follow up with the implementation of the proposed features in Cray SHMEM. Section 7 provides details of the performance regression analysis and in Sect. 8 we use ParRes OpenSHMEM kernels to present the performance benefits on determining the kind of memory for creating the symmetric heap. We discuss related work in Sect. 9 and conclude in Sect. 10.

2   Background

This section provides a brief introduction to Cray SHMEM.

2.1   Cray SHMEM

OpenSHMEM is a Partitioned Global Address Space [5] (PGAS) library interface specification. With a chief aim of performance and portability, OpenSHMEM provides an Application Programming Interface (API) for SHMEM libraries to support one-sided point-to-point data communication.

Cray SHMEM [12] is a vendor-based closed source OpenSHMEM implementation from Cray Inc. It is available as part of Cray Message Passing Toolkit [1] (MPT) software stack. It is OpenSHMEM specification version-1.3 [3] compliant and implemented over DMAPP [16]. DMAPP is an optimized communication library to support logically shared, distributed memory programming model on

Cray architectures. Apart from the OpenSHMEM standard specific features, it provides support for the following features:

- thread-safety in Cray SHMEM;
- put with signal communication;
- PE subsets called as Teams; and
- Team-based collective communication routines.

3 Intel KNL Architecture

Intel's popular Many Integrated Core (MIC) architectures are marked under the name Xeon Phi and the second generation processors are code named Knights Landing (KNL). In this paper, Intel KNL processors are used as an example for emerging architectures with tiered memory systems. This section provides a brief introduction to KNL processor architecture.

Intel KNL offers at least 68 compute cores per chip with four threads per core. The 68 compute cores are organized in 34 tiles with each tile having 2 compute cores. These 34 tiles are placed in a 2D mesh and connected through an on-chip interconnect. In addition to traditional DDR[1], KNL offers an on-package high bandwidth memory technology called Multi-Channel DRAM (MCDRAM). It offers high bandwidth up to 4X more than DDR, but with limited capacity (up to 16 GB) when compared to DDR (up to 384 GB).

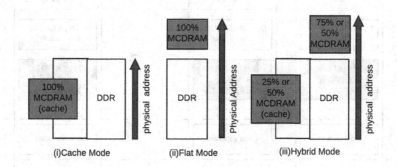

Fig. 1. Intel KNL memory configuration modes

3.1 Memory Modes

As shown in Fig. 1, MCDRAM can be configured in the following modes.

- **Cache mode** - in Cache mode MCDRAM acts as a last-level cache and it is completely used to cache the DDR data.

---

[1] Intel KNL supports double data rate fourth-generation (DDR4) synchronous dynamic random-access memory.

- **Flat mode** - in Flat mode the complete MCDRAM is available as an address-able memory and share the physical address space with DDR. With respect to Non Uniform Memory Access (NUMA), it is exposed as a separate NUMA node without cores.
- **Hybrid mode** - as the name suggests, in Hybrid mode a portion of MCDRAM is configured as addressable memory and the rest as cache.

3.2   NUMA Cluster Modes

As specified previously, the 68 compute cores are arranged in a 2D mesh and connected using on-chip interconnect. With NUMA some memory on the node has different latency or bandwidth to the core. There are two important types of NUMA modes: Quadrant and Sub-NUMA Clustering (SNC).

In quadrant mode the chip is divided into four different quadrants, but it is exposed as a single NUMA domain. In SNC mode each quadrant is available as a separate NUMA domain. Based on the number of quadrants it is further divided into SNC2 and SNC4 modes.

4   OpenSHMEM Memory Model

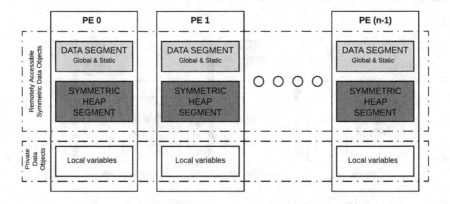

Fig. 2. OpenSHMEM memory model

As shown in Fig. 2, an OpenSHMEM program consists of two types of data objects: private and remotely accessible data objects. The private data objects are local to a particular PE and are accessible by only that PE. It follows the same memory model of the base programming language[2] (C or C++). The remotely accessible data objects are called *Symmetric Data Objects* and are

---

[2] With the proposed deprecation of Fortran support in OpenSHMEM, in this paper there is no reference to Fortran routines.

accessible by all PEs. Each symmetric data object has a corresponding object on all PEs with same name, size and data type. The following variables are considered Symmetric Data Objects:

- global or static variable on C/C++ and not defined in a DSO; and
- data allocated by shmem_malloc OpenSHMEM routines

The data allocated by shmem_malloc collective OpenSHMEM routines are placed on a special memory region called *Symmetric Heap*. There is one symmetric heap on every PE, created during the program execution on a memory region determined by the OpenSHMEM implementation. Users control only the size of the symmetric heap using SMA_SYMMETRIC_SIZE environment variable.

4.1   Need for Changes in OpenSHMEM Memory Model

As mentioned in Sect. 3.1, MCDRAM in Intel KNL can be configured either as cache or as addressable memory. While configuring as cache is a convenient way to port existing applications on to KNL based systems, it is more suitable only for applications that are optimized for cache utilizations and with small memory

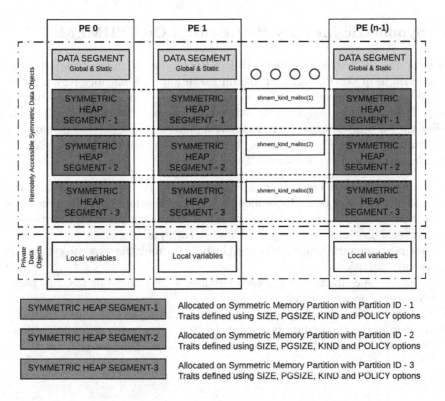

Fig. 3. OpenSHMEM memory model with symmetric memory partitions

```
SMA_SYMMETRIC_PARTITION <ID>=SIZE=<size>[:PGSIZE=<pgsize>]
                              [:KIND=<kind>:POLICY=<policy>]
```

Fig. 4. Environment variable to define the partition characteristics

footprint. As cache utilization depends specifically on the application, it is not for OpenSHMEM to handle anything for cache mode.

The flat mode configuration is suitable for memory bandwidth bound applications. Taking advantage of the high bandwidth offered by MCDRAM by making it available as a distinct NUMA node and re-designing an application can significantly improve the performance. Based on the MCDRAM utilization, memory bandwidth bound applications are of two types:

– the entire application memory fits in the MCDRAM; and
– applications capable of identifying specific bandwidth bound buffers and data access patterns, with the bandwidth critical part allocated on MCDRAM

The current OpenSHMEM memory model does not handle both the above mentioned application categories for the flat mode.

5   Symmetric Memory Partitions in OpenSHMEM

As mentioned in Sect. 4, the OpenSHMEM memory model allows creation of one symmetric heap per PE during program execution on a memory region determined by the implementation. The user controls only the size of the symmetric heap. This paper proposes a new feature called Symmetric Memory Partitions to define the runtime changes and routines to support different kinds of memory for the symmetric heap. Figure 3 shows the modified OpenSHMEM memory model and the proposed changes are as follows:

– symmetric heap is created on a single memory region determined by the implementation or on multiple memory regions determined by the users. The user-determined memory regions are called Symmetric Memory Partitions;
– only a single symmetric heap is created at each partition;
– multiple symmetric heaps are created by defining multiple separate symmetric memory partitions;
– to define the characteristics of each partition each symmetric memory partition have their own memory traits;
– each symmetric memory partition is identified using its *Partition ID* label;
– apart from the name, data type, and size attributes, symmetric data objects stored on symmetric heap segments have Partition ID as an extra attribute.

```
void *shmem_kind_malloc(size_t size, int partition_id);
void *shmem_kind_align(size_t alignment, size_t size,
                       int partition_id);
```

Fig. 5. New routines for symmetric heap management

5.1 Memory Partition Traits

The characteristics of each symmetric memory partition is uniform across all PEs and is defined using the environment variable SMA_SYMMETRIC_PARTITION. One, two, or more partitions can be defined using this environment variable. Figure 4 shows the representation of the environment variable with all its optional and required traits.

The characteristics of the partitions are established using the following features and traits.

ID, ID represents Partition ID. It is a required feature. It is a label to identify a partition and is represented as an integer. SHMEM_MAX_PARTITIONS and SHMEM_MAX_PARTITION_ID are the library constants to define the maximum number of partitions and the usable range of the ID values respectively.

SIZE. SIZE is the only required trait. It represents the number of bytes used for allocating the symmetric heap. The total size of the symmetric heap per PE is the sum of SIZE traits in all the defined partitions.

PGSIZE. PGSIZE is an optional trait to represent the number of bytes used to specify the size of the page used by the partition.

KIND. KIND is another optional trait. It is identified with a string constant. It is used to specify the kind of memory used by the partition. On systems supporting multiple different kinds of memory, each memory that is identified and documented by the implementation can be used as input.

POLICY. POLICY is an optional trait and is identified using string constants to represent the memory allocation policy for the other optional traits. It determines the strictness level to be honored by the implementation while creating the symmetric heap in the defined partition.

5.2 Memory Partition Routines

shmem_malloc, shmem_free, shmem_realloc, and shmem_align are the existing symmetric heap management routines. Apart from these existing routines, to support symmetric heap partitions, we propose the following two new routines: `shmem_kind_malloc` and `shmem_kind_align` (Fig. 5).

The functional semantics and the requirements of `shmem_kind_malloc` and `shmem_kind_align` are very similar to `shmem_malloc` and `shmem_align`. The only difference is that the new routines allows users to determine the symmetric heap using the `partition_id` argument. `shmem_realloc` and `shmem_align` routines should reallocate within the same partition and release resources respectively. This proposal does not include routines for reallocating data across partitions.

5.3 Meaning of Partition with ID:1

Symmetric memory partition with ID:1 is considered as the default partition and it has a special meaning. Using the existing `SMA_SYMMETRIC_SIZE` environment variable is still legal. But using `SMA_SYMMETRIC_SIZE` is mutually exclusive with the environment variable `SMA_SYMMETRIC_PARTITION1`. Hence, to provide backward compatibility in existing legacy applications, the symmetric heap created from the default partition is used for `shmem_malloc` and `shmem_align` routines.

6 Symmetric Memory Partitions in Cray SHMEM

The symmetric memory partition features introduced in Sect. 5 are available as `SHMEMX` prefixed features in Cray SHMEM. Table 1 provides information on the library constants used in Cray SHMEM to determine the range of usable partition ID values and the maximum number of partitions per job.

Table 1. Memory partition specific library constants in Cray SHMEM

Library Constants	Values
SHMEMX_MAX_PARTITION_ID	127
SHMEMX_MAX_PARTITIONS	7

User-defined `SIZE` and `PGSIZE` traits are any appropriate symmetric heap size and available page size in the system represented as bytes. Table 2 refers the values for `KIND` and `POLICY` traits.

On Intel KNL systems, `NORMALMEM` refers to DDR and `FASTMEM` refers to MCDRAM. If the requested kind if unavailable, based on the allocation policy Cray SHMEM either aborts or looks for other alternate kind. `INTERLEAVED` is used to shift allocation across different NUMA domains. As mentioned in Sect. 3.2, number of NUMA domains depends on the cluster configuration modes. On quadrant mode, since MCDRAM is available as a single NUMA domain, `INTERLEAVED` will allocate on a single NUMA domain. On SNC2 and SNC4 modes, allocation interleaves across 2 and 4 NUMA domains respectively.

Table 2. Available partition traits in Cray SHMEM

Traits	Values	Explanation
KIND	NORMALMEM	Primary memory kind for the node
	FASTMEM	Faster memory in addition to NORMALMEM
	SYSDEFAULT	System defined memory
POLICY	MANDATORY	Abort if requested memory kind not available
	PREFERRED	Use other memory kinds if requested kind fails
	INTERLEAVED	Page allocation interleaved across NUMA domains
	SYSDEFAULT	System defined policy

All the available kinds of memory are identified and the environment variables are queried during shmem_init operation. On NUMA policy aware kernels, numactl controls the NUMA policy for processes. Memory kind identification in Cray SHMEM is performed using numactl. There are no implementation defined default values. SYSDEFAULT refers to the system defined memory use based on numactl system calls.

7   Performance Regression Analysis

As there are no restrictions on the number of allowed partitions per memory kind, it is legal to create SHMEM_MAX_PARTITIONS on a single kind of memory. This section details the performance regression analysis on the following two scenarios using Cray SHMEM version 7.6.0:

- Using symmetric heap created on default partition instead of the existing SMA_SYMMETRIC_SIZE environment variable; and
- Creating SHMEM_MAX_PARTITIONS number of partitions.

For these tests we created multiple partitions on NORMALMEM (DDR) memory kind.

7.1   Using Default Partition Instead Of SMA_SYMMETRIC_SIZE

As mentioned in Sect. 5.3 the default partition has a special functionality. To provide backward compatibility in existing legacy applications, the symmetric heap created from the default partition is used for shmem_malloc and shmem_align routines. Hence, in this section we analyzed the performance regression specifically on using the default partition.

Figures 6 and 7 shows the performance of OSU put microbenchmark on using the source and destination buffers with symmetric heaps created from the following three options on Intel Broadwell and Intel KNL processor based Cray XC systems respectively:

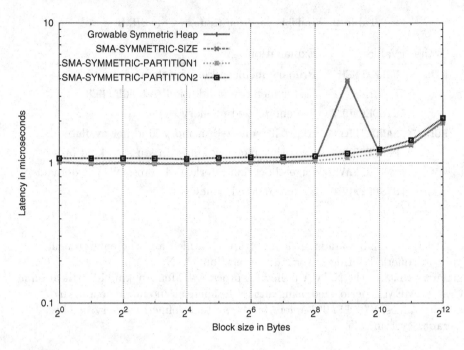

Fig. 6. Performance of OSU put microbenchmark on Cray XC system with intel broadwell processors using source and destination buffers allocated on symmetric heaps created from different options

- Symmetric heap created with the size determined from SMA_SYMMETRIC_SIZE environment variable;
- Symmetric heaps on partitions defined using SMA_SYMMETRIC_PARTITION environment variable; and
- By default in Cray SHMEM, if both SMA_SYMMETRIC_SIZE and a default partition is not defined, the symmetric heap grows dynamically as needed to a maximum of 2 GB per PE. We call this Cray specific feature as Growable Symmetric Heap.

We used 2 PEs with 1 PE per node for this test. From Figs. 6 and 7, we see that the performance of shmem_putmem operation on symmetric heaps created using the environment variables is almost identical to the growable symmetric heap in both Intel Broadwell and KNL processor based systems. But, the performance on using symmetric heaps from partitions (SMA_SYMMETRIC_PARTITION2) other than the default partition (SMA_SYMMETRIC_PARTITION1) is 5% less on Intel Broadwell based systems and 7% less on Intel KNL based systems. This performance difference can be attributed to the missing optimizations specific in controlling the maximum number of memory registrations. These optimizations can be added and the performance improved on all partitions in future Cray SHMEM versions.

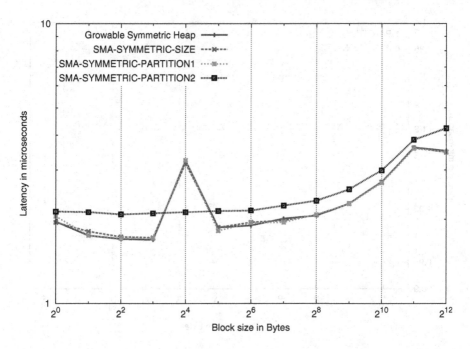

Fig. 7. Performance of OSU put microbenchmark on Cray XC system with intel KNL processors using source and destination buffers allocated on symmetric heaps created from different options

7.2   Creating SHMEM_MAX_PARTITIONS partitions

Creating multiple symmetric memory partitions results in multiple symmetric heaps on each PE. Identifying the correct symmetric segment is essential before performing an underlying communication operation. Algorithm 1 shows the introduction of lookup logic trying to match the correct symmetric heap segment on the shmem_putmem operation. Similar, lookups are introduced on all OpenSHMEM RMA and AMO operations. USER_SEGMENT refers to the symmetric heaps created on user-defined memory partitions.

We measured the performance regression behind this additional lookup operation using a modified OSU microbenchmark [4] on a Cray XC system with Intel KNL processors. We used 2 PEs with 1 PE per node for this test. The normal OSU microbenchmark selects the buffer from either DATA_SEGMENT or SHEAP_SEGMENT per job. We modified the benchmark by creating unique destination buffer for N partitions and randomly selected the destination buffer from different partitions for every iteration. We timed the average performance of all the iterations.

Figure 8 shows the performance difference between using 1 and 6 partitions on very small data sizes. The average performance variations is around 2% to 3%. This can be attributed as noise. If we increase the number of partitions to 127, we could see variations as high as 6%. But, we expect users to create

14 N. Namashivayam et al.

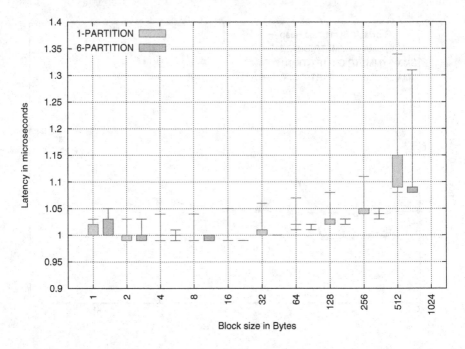

Fig. 8. Performance difference on using destination buffers from 1 partition against 6 partitions in the modified OSU Put microbenchmark on Intel KNL based Cray XC system using 2 PEs with 1 PE per node

only one partition per memory kind. Moreover, as mentioned in Table 1 the `SHMEMX_MAX_PARTITIONS` library constant in Cray SHMEM is 7.

We observe similar performance variations for small data sizes on other RMA and AMO operations. For larger message sizes, the segment lookup does not contribute for any performance variations.

8 Performance Analysis

In Sect. 7, we analyzed the performance impact of creating multiple partitions. This section provides details on the performance impact of creating partitions on different kinds of memory. On a Cray XC system, we used a maximum of 64 KNL nodes with 32 PEs per node for this test using Cray SHMEM version 7.6.0. All the KNL nodes are configured with quad-flat mode.

We used ParRes 2D-Stencil SHMEM kernel and analyzed the performance of defining partitions on different kinds of memory and different page sizes. The symmetric heap in the 2D-Stencil kernel can fit inside a single kind of memory. Hence, we just used the default partition with the following configurations:

– NORMALMEM(DDR) with page size 4K;
– NORMALMEM(DDR) with page size 64M;

ALGORITHM 1. Lookup logic with N symmetric memory partitions per PE

---

procedure `shmem_putmem`(void *dest, const void *src, size_t nblks, int pe_id);

    `dmapp_seg_desc_t` *target_seg = `NULL`;

    `dmapp_type_t` type = `DMAPP_BYTE`;

    if (dest.segment ≡ `DATA_SEGMENT`) **then**

        target_seg = `DATA_SEGMENT`;

        // verify if dest buffer is a static or global variable

    else if (dest.segment ≡ `SHEAP_SEGMENT`) **then**

        target_seg = `SHEAP_SEGMENT`;

        // verify if dest buffer is in default symmetric heap

    else

        segment_identified = *false*;

        for (int i = 1; i ≤ N; i++) **do**

            if (dest.segment ≡ `USER_SEGMENT_i`) **then**

                target_seg = `USER_SEGMENT_i`);

                segment_identified = *true*;

        if (segment_identified ≡ *false*) **then**

            abort();

        // search through all partitions to match the symmetric heap

    `dmapp_put`(dest, target_seg, pe_id, src, nelems, type);

    return;

end procedure

- `FASTMEM(MCDRAM)` with page size 4K; and
- `FASTMEM(MCDRAM)` with page size 64M

From Fig. 9, we see that using MCDRAM provides around 23% better performance compared against using DDR. But, for this particular benchmark there is no performance impact on using different page sizes.

9 Related Work

The need for utilizing different kinds of memory in upcoming system architectures is not specific to OpenSHMEM. OpenMP [15] Affinity subcommittee proposes changes for memory management [2] support for future architectures. Similarly Cray MPICH, an optimized MPI implementation for Cray systems have improvised the functionality of `MPI_Alloc_mem` routine for allocating the requested memory size on user-determined memory kind. Kandalla et al. [11] provides detailed explanation on the performance benefits of using different memory kinds with `MPI_Alloc_mem` on real world applications WOMBAT and SNAP.

Similarly, the concept of creating multiple symmetric heaps in OpenSHMEM is not unique to the proposal introduced in this paper. Welch et al. [17] proposes **Teams** and **Memory Spaces** in OpenSHMEM. OpenSHMEM Teams are PE

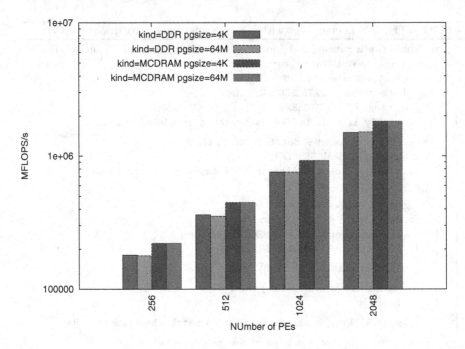

Fig. 9. Performance difference on using different kinds of memory and different hugepages on ParRes 2D-Stencil SHMEM kernels

subsets and Memory Spaces are team-specific symmetric heaps. Cray SHMEM already supports OpenSHMEM Teams [13] as `SHMEMX` prefixed features. With the introduction of symmetric memory partitions, it is logical to understand the possibilities of combining memory partitions as part of OpenSHMEM Teams and introduce multiple symmetric heaps on each partition in the form of Memory Spaces.

10   Conclusion

In this paper, we described our study on the need for changes in the existing OpenSHMEM memory model to enable users in utilizing the different available kinds of memory on emerging tiered memory architectures. We motivated this change by illustrating the missing features in OpenSHMEM for supporting Intel KNL processors with different memory configurations. Using a new feature in OpenSHMEM called `Symmetric Memory Partitions`, we then proposed the runtime changes with its associated new routines for supporting different kinds of memory. We implemented symmetric memory partitions on Cray SHMEM as `SHMEMX` prefixed features without breaking backward compatibility and creating performance regression. We validated our implementation with ParRes kernels on Intel KNL processors, for which we received a close to 23% improvements on using MCDRAM compared to using DDR for the symmetric heap.

The basic traits proposed in this paper for symmetric memory partitions are based on our best estimate for supporting emerging tiered memory systems. In future work, we will build on the proposed feature to support systems with heterogeneous memory and include other additional types of memory like persistent memory and constant memory. Moreover, our early analysis are performed on kernels with the entire memory fitting into one single kind. In future, we will also test our implementation on bandwidth bound applications with requirement for more than one kind of memory.

Acknowledgment. The authors wish to dedicate this paper to deceased Cray Inc., employee - David Charles Knaak for his contributions in the design of symmetric memory partitions to Cray SHMEM. Any opinions, findings, and conclusions or recommendations expressed in this material are those of the authors and do not necessarily reflect the views of associated organizations.

References

1. Cray - Message Passing Toolkit. http://goo.gl/Cts1uh
2. OpenMP TR5 - Memory Management Support. https://goo.gl/74yS2C
3. OpenSHMEM specification version-1.3. http://goo.gl/YK2JKD
4. OSU Micro-benchmarks. http://goo.gl/LgMc8e
5. Almasi, G.: In: Padua, D.A. (ed.) Encyclopedia of Parallel Computing (2011)
6. Cantalupo, C., Venkatesan, V., Hammond, J., Czurlyo, K., Hammond, S.D.: Memkind: An Extensible Heap Memory Manager for Heterogeneous Memory Platforms and Mixed Memory Policies, March 2015
7. Chapman, B., Curtis, T., Pophale, S., Poole, S., Kuehn, J., Koelbel, C., Smith, L.: Introducing OpenSHMEM: SHMEM for the PGAS community. In Proceedings of the Fourth Conference on Partitioned Global Address Space Programming Model, PGAS 2010 (2010)
8. Van der Wijngaart, R.F., Mattson, T.G.: The parallel research kernels. In: 2014 IEEE High Performance Extreme Computing Conference (HPEC), pp. 1–6, September 2014
9. Intel Knights Landing. https://goo.gl/QdAG68
10. Intel Xeon Phi Processor "Knights Landing" Architectural Overview. https://goo.gl/7UfuW2
11. Kandalla, K., Mendygral, P., Radcliffe, N., Cernohous, B., Namashivayam, N., McMahon, K., Sadlo, C., Pagel, M.: Current state of the cray MPT software stacks on the cray XC series supercomputers. In: Cray User Group (CUG) meeting 2017 (2017)
12. Knaak, D., Namashivayam, N.: Proposing OpenSHMEM extensions towards a future for hybrid programming and heterogeneous computing. In: Gorentla Venkata, M., Shamis, P., Imam, N., Lopez, M.G. (eds.) OpenSHMEM 2014. LNCS, vol. 9397, pp. 53–68. Springer, Cham (2015). https://doi.org/10.1007/978-3-319-26428-8_4
13. Knaak, D., Namashivayam, N.: Proposing OpenSHMEM Extensions Towards a Future for Hybrid Programming and Heterogeneous Computing. In: Gorentla Venkata, M., Shamis, P., Imam, N., Lopez, M.G. (eds.) OpenSHMEM 2014. LNCS, vol. 9397, pp. 53–68. Springer, Cham (2015b). https://doi.org/10.1007/978-3-319-26428-8_4

14. NVIDIA Corporation: NVIDIA CUDA C programming guide. Version 3.2 (2010)
15. OpenMP Architecture Review Board: OpenMP application program interface version 4.5, November 2015. http://goo.gl/MLcVTD
16. ten Bruggencate, M., Roweth, D.: DMAPP: An API for One-Sided Programming Model on Baker Systems. Technical report, Cray Users Group (CUG), August 2010
17. Welch, A., Pophale, S., Shamis, P., Hernandez, O., Poole, S., Chapman, B.: Extending the OpenSHMEM memory model to support user-defined spaces. In: Proceedings of the 8th International Conference on Partitioned Global Address Space Programming Models, PGAS 2014 (2014)

Implementation and Evaluation of OpenSHMEM Contexts Using OFI Libfabric

Max Grossman[1(✉)], Joseph Doyle[2], James Dinan[3], Howard Pritchard[4], Kayla Seager[3], and Vivek Sarkar[1]

[1] Rice University, Houston, USA
jmg3@rice.edu
[2] Carnegie Mellon University, Pittsburgh, USA
[3] Intel Corporation, Santa Clara, USA
[4] Los Alamos National Laboratory, Los Alamos, USA

Abstract. HPC system and processor architectures are trending toward increasing numbers of cores and tall, narrow memory hierarchies. As a result, programmers have embraced hybrid parallel programming as a means of tuning for such architectures. While popular HPC communication middlewares, such as MPI, allow the use of threads, most fall short of fully-integrating threads with the communication model. The Open-SHMEM contexts proposal promises thread isolation and direct mapping of threads to network resources; however, fully realizing these potentials will be dependent upon support for efficient threaded communication through the underlying layers of the networking stack. In this paper, we explore the mapping of OpenSHMEM contexts to the new OpenFabrics Interfaces (OFI) libfabric communication layer and use the libfabric GNI provider to access the Aries interconnect. We describe the design of our multithreaded OpenSHMEM middleware and evaluate both the programmability and performance impacts of contexts on single- and multi-threaded OpenSHMEM programs. Results indicate that the mapping of contexts to the Aries interconnect through libfabric incurs low overhead and that contexts can provide significant performance improvements to multithreaded OpenSHMEM programs.

1 Introduction

Over the past decade, the degree of parallelism within high performance computing (HPC) system nodes has increased dramatically through the introduction of accelerators, such as general purpose graphics processing units (GPGPUs), and many-core processors, such as the Intel® Xeon Phi™ processor. Such nodes are often able to achieve peak performance and resource efficiency only when programmed using a node-level programming model, such as OpenACC [12] and OpenMP [15]. At the same time, HPC networking interfaces have also been provisioned to handle communication operations for these large numbers of cores. These drastic shifts in node-level architecture have left conventional, networking-centric HPC programming models, such as OpenSHMEM [16] and MPI [10],

© Springer International Publishing AG 2018
M. Gorentla Venkata et al. (Eds.): OpenSHMEM 2017, LNCS 10679, pp. 19–34, 2018.
https://doi.org/10.1007/978-3-319-73814-7_2

scrambling to provide APIs that are thread-safe, use resources efficiently, and are scalable enough to support hundreds of threads per process.

A first step, taken by MPI 2.0 in 2003 and soon to be adopted by OpenSH-MEM, is to make existing HPC communication libraries thread safe. While this addresses the first-order need for threads to perform communication, this approach presents significant challenges, as interference between threads within the middleware and within the semantics of the communication model can lead to significant overheads. For example, in OpenSHMEM's unordered communication model, the *fence* and *quiet* operations are used to ensure ordering and remote completion for operations issued by an OpenSHMEM processing element (PE). When PEs are multithreaded, a fence or quiet performed by any thread will affect operations performed by all threads. Thus, a deeper level of threading integration with the communication middleware is needed to provide thread isolation, enable overlap across threads, and achieve more intelligent resource mapping.

In this work, we focus on the OpenSHMEM communication middleware and the proposed contexts extension for threading integration [3]. In this paper, we present an implementation of the proposed OpenSHMEM contexts extension using the OpenFabrics Interfaces libfabric [14] communication layer and use this as a vehicle to evaluate the above requirements. We utilize the libfabric generic networking interface (GNI) provider to interface with the high performance Aries[1] interconnect. We evaluate our implementation's performance using several representative benchmarks and discuss our experiences developing applications with this new interface, commenting on its programmability and usability characteristics.

2 Background

The SHMEM programming model was first created by Cray Research for the Cray (See footnote 1) T3D machine and has subsequently been supported by a number of vendors across many platforms. The OpenSHMEM specification was created in an effort to improve the consistency of the library across implementations and, more importantly, to provide a forum for the user and vendor communities to discuss and adopt extensions to the SHMEM API.

The OpenSHMEM library provides a single program, multiple data (SPMD) execution model in which N instances of the program are executed in parallel.

---

[1] Other names and brands may be claimed as the property of others.
Intel and Xeon are trademarks of Intel Corporation in the U.S. and/or other countries. Software and workloads used in performance tests may have been optimized for performance only on Intel microprocessors. Performance tests, such as SYSmark and MobileMark, are measured using specific computer systems, components, software, operations and functions. Any change to any of those factors may cause the results to vary. You should consult other information and performance tests to assist you in fully evaluating your contemplated purchases, including the performance of that product when combined with other products. For more information go to http://www.intel.com/performance.

Listing 1.1. Proposed OpenSHMEM Contexts API, including examples of contexts version of point-to-point routines and interprocess synchronization routines.

```
int shmem_ctx_create(long options, shmem_ctx_t *ctx);
int shmem_ctx_destroy(shmem_ctx_t ctx);
void shmem_ctx_putmem(shmem_ctx_t ctx, void *dest, const void *source,
                      size_t nelems, int pe);
void shmem_ctx_quiet(shmem_ctx_t ctx);
void shmem_sync_all(void);
void shmem_sync(int PE_start, int logPE_stride, int PE_size, long *pSync);
```

Each instance is referred to as a processing element (PE) and is identified by its integer ID in the range from 0 to $N-1$. PEs exchange information through one-sided *get* (read) and *put* (write) operations that access remotely accessible *symmetric objects*. Symmetric objects are objects that are present at all PEs and they are referenced using the local address to the given object. By default, all objects within the data segment of the application are exposed as symmetric; additional symmetric objects are allocated through OpenSHMEM API routines. OpenSHMEM's communication model is unordered by default. Point-to-point ordering is established through *fence* operations, remote completion is established through *quiet* operations, and global ordering is established through *barrier* operations.

Recently, thread safety extensions have been proposed for OpenSHMEM [17]. These extensions provide a shmem_init_thread routine that can be used to initialize the library with thread safety enabled. Several thread safety levels are provided, with the most notable being SHMEM_THREAD_SINGLE, which disables thread safety, and SHMEM_THREAD_MULTIPLE, which enables full thread safety. The thread safety extension further defines the behavior of the existing API when used by multiple threads within a PE. In this model, all threads are logically part of the same PE and synchronization actions, such as fence, quiet, and barrier, are performed at the level of the PE. Thus, when any thread performs one of these operations, communication operations performed by all threads are affected.

2.1   OpenSHMEM Contexts

Contexts have been proposed as a means of isolating communication streams, isolating threads from each other, and improving the mapping of threads to underlying network resources [3]. The proposed API extension is summarized in Listing 1.1. Contexts introduce a shmem_ctx_t object that is passed to communication and synchronization operations. Thus, operations performed on a given context can be treated separately from those performed on a different context, enabling isolation and overlap across contexts. In effect, each context represents a separate ordering and completion environment, enabling the middleware to efficiently map the communication of different contexts to different communication resources (e.g. transmit engines, command interfaces, or rails). While a single PE can utilize multiple contexts, the PE still represents a single destination (i.e. PE ID) for SHMEM communication operations. Thus, contexts extend the existing $1 : N$ communication model, where each PE can generate one stream of accesses to N targets in the OpenSHMEM global address space, to an $M : N$ model, where each PE can generate M independent streams of accesses to N targets.

Contexts versions of the shmem_putmem and shmem_quiet routines are shown to illustrate the extension to the point-to-point API. The full proposal adds contexts version of all point-to-point operations, including put, get, quiet, fence, and atomic memory operations (AMOs).

2.2   Libfabric

Libfabric (OFI) is a vendor-neutral, open interface for high-performance networking applications requiring low latency and high message throughput. The interface was designed by the OpenFabrics Alliance (OFA) Interfaces Working Group (OFWIG), with one of the primary goals of this working group being to define a fabric interface that has a tight semantic map to various applications that use it, including PGAS programming models.

The initial libfabric API and internal design of libfabric has been previously described [7]. Libfabric was designed to provide a vendor-neutral client API that is mapped to a set of *providers* that implement the communication interfaces for a particular fabric hardware. In this paper, we take advantage of key libfabric API features, such as the fine grain transmission context support, to enhance performance and scalability. The latest version of the API and documentation are available online [13]. Libfabrics is freely available on Github [14] and is also distributed via the OpenFabrics Enterprise Distribution (OFED).

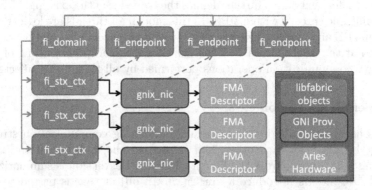

Fig. 1. Relationship of libfabric fi_domain, fi_endpoint, and fi_stx_context objects to GNI provider internal gnix_nic objects and underlying Aries hardware. Solid blue lines indicate libfabric objects which are instantiated from a fi_domain, while dashed blue lines indicate objects which are associated via an fi_bind operation. Black lines indicate associations between libfabric upper level objects and lower-level GNI-provider internal objects and network hardware. (Color figure online)

2.3   Aries and the GNI Libfabric Provider

The Aries interconnect and the GNI libfabric provider have attributes that lend themselves to the investigation of performance gains possible using OpenSH-MEM contexts. The Aries interface supports a large number of fast memory access (FMA) descriptors that can be used to enable independent issue of RDMA requests from multiple threads using the same Aries interface. One of the design goals of the GNI provider is to ensure that threads within a multi-threaded process can access the FMA descriptor resources with as little contention as possible [2]. In addition, the Aries interconnect has additional attributes that make it well suited to investigating extensions to the OpenSHMEM API including its ability to offload RDMA transactions and support for an extensive set of 32- and 64-bit atomic memory operations.

For this work, the GNI provider was enhanced to support the libfabric *shared transmission (TX) context* (fi_stx_context) construct. The shared context enables multiple endpoints to share an FMA descriptor if transmission resources become scarce. Figure 1 depicts the relationship between libfabric endpoints, shared TX contexts, and the underlying Aries network hardware.

3   Implementation of Contexts over Libfabric

In our previous work, we described an implementation of OpenSHMEM using the OpenFabrics Interfaces libfabric communication layer [19]. This implementation is available as part of the open source Sandia OpenSHMEM (SOS) library [18] and is referred to as the OFI transport layer. The current OFI transport layer was designed to support the single-threaded OpenSHMEM 1.3 programming model; in this work, we extend this layer to support both the proposed thread safety and contexts extensions.

3.1   Middleware Extensions to Support Contexts

The design of the OFI transport layer with threading and contexts support is shown in Fig. 2. The fabric domain represents a handle to the fabric and is the first object created. The OFI transport layer queries libfabric for a domain that can support the required features, including support for the one-sided FI_RMA and FI_ATOMICS capabilities. Thread safety for libfabric routines is provided by enabling the FI_THREAD_SAFE attribute on the fabric domain. Libfabric provides several threading modes; FI_THREAD_SAFE was selected because it provides the greatest opportunity for communication parallelism. This mode requests the provider to ensure thread safety, providing the greatest opportunity for fine-grain synchronization at the lower levels of the networking stack. Any other libfabric threading mode would have required SOS to protect calls to the libfabric API with additional locks. Thread safety for internal state in the SOS middleware was implemented using POSIX (See footnote 1) mutexes and separate mutexes are used for each context. Synchronization overheads can be

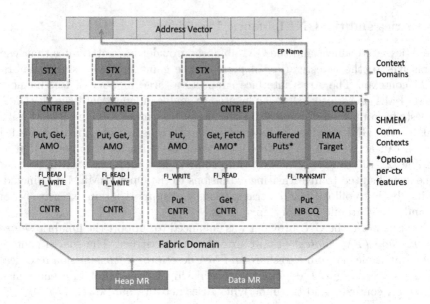

Fig. 2. Architecture of the multithreaded OFI transport layer with contexts support.

further reduced by replacing mutexes with atomic operations, and we plan to investigate this as part of future performance tuning.

From the domain, fabric endpoints (EPs) are created. Endpoints can be used for sending and receiving messages, and the corresponding completion events can be captured as full events in a completion queue (CQ) or as lightweight counting events in an event counter (CNTR). The heap and data segments are registered on the domain and are exposed for remote access through the CQ EP endpoint. The fabric addresses of the RMA target endpoints are queried and exchanged using the process manager in order to populate the libfabric address vector (AV) to provide efficient and scalable translation between OpenSHMEM PE IDs and fabric addresses. Finally, shareable transmit contexts (STX) are created and bound to the endpoints, enabling them to be used for transmitting messages. The STX is "shareable" in the sense that it can be bound to more than one endpoint.

OFI defines its threading model on a domain basis, which forces all EPs on a domain to conform to the same threading model. This model can be restrictive in cases where multiple EPs are bound to an STX, but the application can guarantee that the EPs are not shared by multiple threads (e.g., by setting the SHMEM_CTX_PRIVATE flag on the corresponding contexts). From this work we have identified this as a potential performance optimization and are investigating the addition of a synchronization hint on the STX to improve the OFI threading model.

We introduce *context domains* as a means for managing the mapping between OpenSHMEM contexts and fabric resources. Context domains contain the set of resources needed to support a context; minimally, a context domain contains an

STX, but it could also be extended to include resources such as bounce buffer pools, CQs, etc. The maximum number of context domains that can be created is bounded by the `tx_ctx_cnt` attribute on the fabric domain. The maximum number of contexts per context domain is bounded by the `max_ep_stx_ctx` limit. In our current implementation, context domains are created as-needed and the mapping to contexts is controlled manually. In future work, we plan to more deeply explore methods for automatic and efficient mapping of context domains to contexts.

In Fig. 2, we show three context domains each mapped to one context. The rightmost context represents the default (i.e., `SHMEM_CTX_DEFAULT`) context. Optimizations, such as splitting get/put counting events and bounce buffering are optional features that can be enabled on a context. For the backwards compatibility, these optimizations are all made available on the default context. For all other contexts, these optimizations are disabled by default to improve resource utilization. Thus, most contexts are implemented as an EP/CNTR pair that is bound to the STX of the corresponding context domain.

4   Results

In this section, we present quantitative performance evaluation of the OpenSH-MEM Contexts implementation described in Sect. 3 and qualitative programmability evaluation of the proposed Contexts API.

4.1   Evaluation Platform

All experiments presented were collected on the NERSC Edison machine. Edison is a Cray (See footnote 1) XC30 with 2×12-core Intel® Xeon® Processors E5-2695 v2 and 64 GB DDR3 in each node. Edison nodes are connected by the Aries interconnect. All experiments are run on the libfabric-based implementation of Contexts in Sandia OpenSHMEM, as described in Sect. 3. All baseline MPI experiments are run using Cray MPICH 7.4.4. Unless otherwise noted, all tests with hybrid parallelism are run with one PE per socket and 12 threads per PE. All tests with flat parallelism are run with one PE per core.

4.2   Micro-benchmarks

As part of this work, we extended Sandia OpenSHMEM's suite of performance micro-benchmarks to include multi-threaded, contexts-based implementations of all existing micro-benchmarks. For simplicity and platform agnosticism, these multi-threaded benchmarks were written using POSIX (See footnote 1) threads (referred to as pthreads). The benchmarks implemented measure uni-directional and bi-directional bandwidth/message rate for blocking and non-blocking puts and gets. They also measure latencies for blocking and non-blocking puts and gets.

Figure 3 shows the uni-directional put and get rates achieved by contexts-less and contexts-based microbenchmarks using 1 or 12 pthreads. Contexts-less multi-threaded tests rely on libfabric for thread safety. Tests were run using two PEs on two neighboring Edison nodes, with each PE pinned to 12 cores. The rates for non-blocking puts at transfer sizes where an Aries FMA descriptor is utilized show similar improvements to those reported when the libfabric API is used directly [2]. The results obtained for blocking puts are similar owing to a buffering mechanism used by SOS for puts up to 512 bytes. Transfer sizes of 8 KB and higher show little improvement over the single threaded case as these are off-loaded to the Aries RDMA block transfer engine (BTE), which introduces a serialization point.

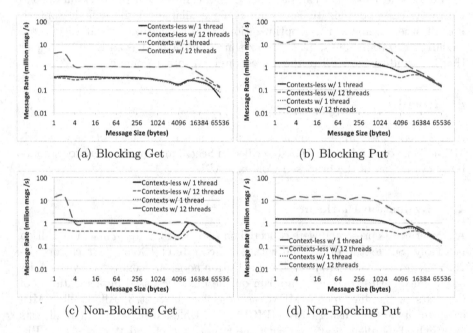

(a) Blocking Get

(b) Blocking Put

(c) Non-Blocking Get

(d) Non-Blocking Put

Fig. 3. Uni-directional get and put rate micro-benchmark results, comparing single-threaded performance with and without contexts with multithreaded performance with contexts. X-axes show message sizes in bytes and Y-axes show achieved message rate in messages per second.

The situation is more complicated for get operations as the target buffer of each get operation must be registered with the Aries device. For very small transfers of 1 to 3 bytes, the GNI libfabric provider uses a mechanism that bypasses its internal memory registration cache and the associated lock. Thus the speedup using contexts for these small transfers is similar to that achieved for put operations. For four byte and larger transfers, the memory registration lock must be taken as the libfabric consumer does not supply a local memory descriptor as part of the call to the libfabric fi_read function. To conserve Aries I/O MMU resource usage, the GNI provider's memory registration cache is associated with a libfabric domain object, rather than the underlying gnix_nic objects depicted in Fig. 1. The need to acquire this lock significantly limits speedup when using multiple contexts. Note for the single threaded case, performance is significantly better for non-blocking gets owing to the ability to take advantage of pipelining requests to the Aries FMA descriptor.

Figure 4 shows the latencies observed for blocking gets and puts, with and without contexts. In general we observe that using contexts with one thread shows the same latency as not using contexts at all, which is desirable. The put latency remains roughly constant as function of thread count, up to the largest transfer size where bandwidth limitations of the Aries FMA mechanism result in an increase in latency when using 12 threads and contexts. When using 12 threads and no contexts, contention for locks protecting shared endpoints and counter resources leads to large increases in latency.

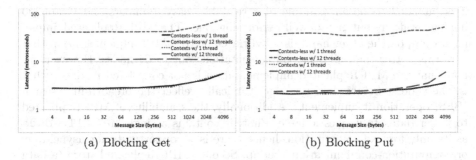

(a) Blocking Get   (b) Blocking Put

Fig. 4. Latency micro-benchmark results, comparing single-threaded performance with and without contexts with multithreaded performance with contexts. X-axes show message size in bytes and Y-axes show latency in microseconds.

These micro-benchmark results illustrate the performance benefits of contexts that previous work [3] has also shown: contexts significantly improve network utilization at small and medium transfer sizes, particularly for put operations. Get transfer rates could be improved either by enhancements to the GNI libfabric provider or by modifying Sandia OpenSHMEM to use pre-registered temporary buffers as the destination for small gets to avoid registration overheads.

4.3   Graph500

Graph500 is an end-to-end benchmark intended to stress the ability of computing systems to support irregular accesses. In this work, we focus specifically on the breadth-first search kernel of the Graph500 benchmark, which traverses a large and randomly generated directed graph. We evaluate two implementations of the BFS kernel using OpenSHMEM Contexts:

1. **Put-Based:** The Put-Based Graph500 implementation partitions vertices of the graph evenly across PEs. A logically global vertex array is partitioned across PEs in their symmetric heaps, where each slot in this global array is an integer that indicates whether the corresponding vertex has been traversed. At each wavefront of the BFS, vertices in the next wavefront are signaled by performing individual puts to the PE that owns those vertices.
2. **Atomics-Based:** The Atomics-Based G500 implementation is similar to Put-Based. However, the global vertex array is instead a bit vector. Signals are sent using atomic bitwise OR operations, rather than puts. This has the benefit of reducing total number of bytes sent, but has the downside of requiring atomic operations.

Figure 5 compares the Put-Based and Atomics-Based G500 implementations against existing OpenSHMEM baselines [6] and reference MPI implementations, performing weak scaling experiments from 8 to 64 Edison nodes. The reference MPI Simple implementation fails to scale to 16 nodes. This is expected, as it is intended to be an example of a readable, easy-to-understand Graph500 implementation, but not a well-performing one. The MPI Replicated implementation, on the other hand, is a hybrid OpenMP+MPI implementation that performs better than all other implementations out to 64 nodes. However, we note that the MPI Replicated implementation is not considered readable; that is, the code structure does not algorithmically reflect the breadth-first search (BFS) operation it implements. Additionally, the scalability of MPI Replicated to larger datasets is questionable. First, it contains a single `MPI_Allreduce` as its only form of computation, hence there is no opportunity for asynchrony or computation-communication overlap. Second, MPI Replicated stores a data structure in each rank whose size scales linearly with the number of vertices in the graph. Larger graphs would hence trigger out-of-memory errors. It is also important to note that as the MPI implementations are run using Cray MPICH 7.4.4, this is not entirely an apples-to-apples comparison.

As described in previous work [6], the OpenSHMEM Checksummed implementation is message-based and to some extent inspired by the MPI Simple implementation. While it outperforms both the Put-Based and Atomics-Based

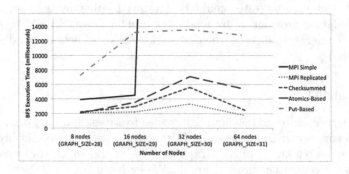

Fig. 5. Graph500 BFS kernel execution time

implementations, it suffers from similar maintainability, readability, and programmability issues as the MPI Replicated implementation.

On the other hand, the code structure of Put-Based and Atomics-Based
implementations is much more faithful to the algorithmic structure of BFS. As
a result, the RDMAs performed are more fine grain because they model communication along individual edges in the graph. This is exactly the type of
communication pattern that generally leads to drastic underutilization of networks. Without OpenSHMEM Contexts, these algorithmically-elegant but generally inefficient communication patterns would not be feasible.

To demonstrate this, we ran two additional experiments. First, we compare running the Atomics-Based implementation with one PE per socket and
12 threads per PE vs. 2 PEs per socket and 6 threads per PE, to see how a
reduction in intra-PE parallelism affects performance. We found that using 1
PE per socket ran ~1.5–2× faster as a result of having more state stored in each
PE, reducing redundant cross-PE atomics. Hence, hybrid parallelism enables
higher performing Graph500 implementations through the elimination of redundant communication.

Second, we ran the multi-threaded Atomics-Based implementation while relying on runtime-managed thread safety. We keep 1 PE per socket and 12 threads
per PE, and compare between giving each thread its own private context vs.
simply configuring the runtime as SHMEM_THREAD_MULTIPLE. In these tests,
we observed that relying on runtime-managed thread-safety led to a slowdown
of up to 4×, relative to using contexts.

Therefore, we desire hybrid parallelism in Graph500 and similar benchmarks
that exhibit large amounts of small or medium sized communication. However,
without contexts, contention between multiple threads within the OpenSHMEM
runtime prevents this performance improvement from being realized.

4.4 HPC Challenge Random Access Benchmark

The HPC challenge random access benchmark [9], referred to as the Giga-
Updates Per Second (GUPS) benchmark, stresses the ability of a system to
perform random memory accesses by performing atomic bitwise XOR updates
on a distributed hash table. OpenSHMEM implementations of GUPS that are
compliant with the latest ratified specification (OpenSHMEM v1.3) use a get-
modify-put pattern to imprecisely emulate bitwise atomic XORs.

In this work, we contribute an OpenSHMEM GUPS implementation based on
the APIs in the recently ratified bitwise atomics proposal and show how hybrid
programming with OpenSHMEM Contexts improves its performance. We compare two implementations of GUPS: one which is compliant with OpenSHMEM
v1.3 and uses a GET, a local bitwise XOR, and a PUT to emulate bitwise atomics, and another which uses the recently ratified bitwise atomics APIs to natively
perform the atomic operation.

For both versions of GUPS, we perform three experiments:

1. Flat OpenSHMEM: We run one OpenSHMEM PE per core.
2. Hybrid OpenSHMEM w/Pthreads: We run one OpenSHMEM PE per socket, and run one pthread per core. Each pthread issues atomic updates, gets, or puts (depending on the implementation of GUPS being executed). The OpenSHMEM runtime is configured in thread-safe mode.
3. Hybrid OpenSHMEM w/Pthreads and Contexts: Same as the above, but each pthread has a private context to which it issues OpenSHMEM operations.

Our GUPS experiments are run with a total main table size of ~500 M words on 16 nodes.

Table 1 demonstrates that the newly ratified bitwise atomics produce a drastic jump in performance, yielding a 2.80× performance improvement when running Flat OpenSHMEM compared to the Gets/Puts-based implementation (rows 1 and 4). When using pthreads without contexts we see the performance cost of purely runtime-managed thread safety with a 14× slowdown when moving from Flat OpenSHMEM with Bitwise Atomics to Hybrid OpenSHMEM with Bitwise Atomics. This slowdown can be attributed primarily to the serialization of accesses to the Aries network AMO hardware when only a single libfabric endpoint is used. However, using contexts allows us to regain that performance plus an additional 1.27× improvement over flat parallelism with bitwise atomics, resulting in a speedup of 3.55× over the baseline.

Table 1. GUPS execution time and speedup relative to the shmem_long_g/p-based implementation.

API used	Pthreads used?	Contexts used?	Time (s)	Speedup
Gets/Puts	No	No	60.31	1.00×
Gets/Puts	Yes	No	1042.66	0.06×
Gets/Puts	Yes	Yes	330.08	0.18×
Bitwise atomics	No	No	21.58	2.80×
Bitwise atomics	Yes	No	306.23	0.20×
Bitwise atomics	Yes	Yes	16.97	3.55×

4.5 Mandelbrot

Mandelbrot is a multithreaded benchmark that computes the complex-plane points that are members of the Mandelbrot set. The Mandelbrot implementation used in this paper allows the user to either disable the use of contexts, use contexts for multi-threading, or use contexts in a pipeline. It is also possible to select between blocking and non-blocking OpenSHMEM APIs. We will explore all of these parameters and their effect on performance.

Table 2 shows the performance of Mandelbrot at various runtime configurations, varying whether blocking or non-blocking APIs are used and how contexts are used in the application. In particular, we note that going from no contexts to using contexts for multi-threading generally yields a $\sim 2\times$ performance improvement, with pipelining yielding another incremental improvement in performance.

Table 2. Mandelbrot Performance

Blocking APIs?	Contexts?	Execution time (sec)	Speedup
Yes	No	$1,285.27$	$1.00\times$
Yes	For multithreading	612.13	$2.10\times$
Yes	Pipelined	592.56	$2.17\times$
No	No	$1,487.10$	$0.86\times$
No	For multithreading	635.34	$2.02\times$
No	Pipelined	608.20	$2.11\times$

4.6 Pipeline Example

We take this benchmark from the OpenSHMEM Contexts proposal itself. This benchmarks demonstrates the use of contexts in a single-threaded C program that performs a summation reduction where the data contained in input arrays on all PEs is reduced into the output arrays on all PEs. The buffers are divided into segments and processing of the segments is pipelined. Contexts are used to overlap an all-to-all exchange of data for segment p with the local reduction of segment $p - 1$.

For these experiments, we perform a reduction on a 16 M element array with staging segments of 4 K elements, using 4 Edison nodes. When running the single-threaded pipeline example without contexts we observed a mean execution time of 7.80 s, versus 6.94 s with contexts (a 12.4% improvement).

4.7 Application Development Discussion

It is important to consider the programmability and usability of any new API being considered for inclusion in the OpenSHMEM specification. While achieving high network utilization is important, the fact is that without usable abstractions it would not be possible to develope large scientific and analytics applications using OpenSHMEM. In our experiences developing these benchmarks on Open-SHMEM we noted several items of interest.

First, contexts enable programmers to write multi-threaded applications with less boilerplate and fine-tuning by making higher network utilization possible at smaller packet sizes. This ability to send data at the natural algorithmic granularity rather than having to manually aggregate and chunk at the application level leads to significant improvement in the clarity of application code.

Second, because contexts facilitate the use of OpenSHMEM in multi-threaded applications, an ancillary benefit is that more state is stored in each PE (assuming some global domain is decomposed across PEs). This low latency, zero copy access to a larger segment of the data domain often leads to improved performance, even relative to OpenSHMEM implementations that support fast on-node data movement.

Third, in our experience working with these benchmarks we did not find that creating and managing contexts added any significant developer burden. Admittedly, these are not large applications and so our experiences may not apply to development of million-line projects. However, we did not find passing an extra object to communicating routines to be overly burdensome. Additionally, the improvement in composability and network resource partitioning would particularly benefit large applications and libraries.

5 Related Work

The contexts extension to OpenSHMEM was initially proposed in [3], along with an implementation of the API using Sandia OpenSHMEM [18] for the Portals 4 networking layer. They reported performance improvement for two single-threaded OpenSHMEM applications using contexts to avoid unnecessary completion of pending operations and to pipeline OpenSHMEM data transfers. Namashivayam et al. have also presented an implementation of the context extensions for the Aries network using Cray DMAPP as the underlying network API [11].

An alternative approach to OpenSHMEM threading support was proposed by ten Bruggencate et al. [1]. This approach registers thread with the OpenSH-MEM runtime in order provide thread isolation and enhance throughput (see [3] for a detailed comparison of contexts and thread registration). Weeks et al. [21] presented results for a set of multi-threaded OpenSHMEM kernels and mini-apps (SHMEM-MT) using these Cray thread safety extensions. Jost et al. [8] have presented a more general discussion of multi-threaded OpenSHMEM applications, including benefits to applications when using a hybrid program model and enhancements to OpenSHMEM to better support such hybrid applications.

Related work in the Message Passing Interface (MPI) community includes the MPI endpoints extension [4,20]. MPI endpoints are conceptually similar to OpenSHMEM contexts in that they allow an MPI implementation to more readily associate individual threads within an MPI process with network resources. Unlike OpenSHMEM contexts however, endpoints are individually addressable so as to allow for sending a message to a particular thread in a target MPI process. There have also been investigations of the performance of MPI-3 RMA operations using multi-threaded MPI applications and micro-benchmarks [5].

6 Conclusion

Contexts extend OpenSHMEM with a programmable abstraction for low-latency, high-throughput access to modern HPC networks. Such programming model primitives are critical as the trend toward multi- and many-core platforms drives applications to utilize hybrid parallelism. This work described a new and portable implementation targeting the OFI libfabric networking layer. Performance results demonstrated that this API extension maps well to libfabric and can provide significant communication efficiency improvements both for single- and multi-threaded OpenSHMEM applications.

Acknowledgments. This research was funded in part by the United States Department of Defense, and was supported by resources at Los Alamos National Laboratory. This publication has been approved for public, unlimited distribution by Los Alamos National Laboratory, with document number LA-UR-17-26416.

References

1. ten Bruggencate, M., Roweth, D., Oyanagi, S.: Thread-safe SHMEM extensions. In: Poole, S., Hernandez, O., Shamis, P. (eds.) OpenSHMEM 2014. LNCS, vol. 8356, pp. 178–185. Springer, Cham (2014). https://doi.org/10.1007/978-3-319-05215-1_13

2. Choi, S.E., Pritchard, H., Shimek, J., Swaro, J., Tiffany, Z., Turrubiates, B.: An implementation of OFI libfabric in support of multithreaded PGAS solutions. In: Proceedings of the 9th International Conference on Parititioned Global Address Space Programming Models, September 2015

3. Dinan, J., Flajslik, M.: Contexts: a mechanism for high throughput communication in OpenSHMEM. In: Proceedings of the 8th International Conference on Partitioned Global Address Space Programming Models, pp. 10:1–10:9. ACM, New York (2014). http://doi.acm.org/10.1145/2676870.2676872

4. Dinan, J., Grant, R.E., Balaji, P., Goodell, D., Miller, D., Snir, M., Thakur, R.: Enabling communication concurrency through flexible MPI endpoints. Int. J. High Perform. Comput. Appl. **28**(4), 390–405 (2014)

5. Dosanjh, M.G.F., Groves, T., Grant, R.E., Brightwell, R., Bridges, P.G.: RMA-MT: a benchmark suite for assessing MPI multi-threaded RMA performance. In: 2016 16th IEEE/ACM International Symposium on Cluster, Cloud and Grid Computing (CCGrid), pp. 550–559, May 2016

6. Grossman, M., Pritchard Jr., H.P., Budimlic, Z., Sarkar, V.: Graph 500 on Open-SHMEM: using a practical survey of past work to motivate novel algorithmic developments. Technical report, Los Alamos National Laboratory (LANL) (2016)

7. Grun, P., Hefty, S., Sur, S., Goodell, D., Russell, R., Pritchard, H., Squyres, J.: A brief introduction to the openfabrics interfaces-a new network API for maximizing high performance application efficiency. In: Proceedings of the 23rd Annual Symposium on High-Performance Interconnects, August 2015

8. Jost, G., Hanebutte, U.R., Dinan, J.: Multi-threaded OpenSHMEM: a bad idea? In: Proceedings of the 8th International Conference on Partitioned Global Address Space Programming Models, PGAS 2014, pp. 21:1–21:4. ACM, New York (2014). http://doi.acm.org/10.1145/2676870.2676890

9. Luszczek, P., Dongarra, J.J., Koester, D., Rabenseifner, R., Lucas, B., Kepner, J., Mccalpin, J., Bailey, D., Takahashi, D.: Introduction to the HPC challenge benchmark suite. Technical report LBNL-57493, Lawrence Berkeley National Laboratory, March 2005

10. MPI Forum: MPI: A message-passing interface standard version 3.1. Technical report, University of Tennessee, Knoxville, June 2015

11. Namashivayam, N., Knaak, D., Cernohous, B., Radcliffe, N., Pagel, M.: An evaluation of thread-safe and contexts-domains features in cray SHMEM. In: Gorentla Venkata, M., Imam, N., Pophale, S., Mintz, T.M. (eds.) OpenSHMEM 2016. LNCS, vol. 10007, pp. 163–180. Springer, Cham (2016). https://doi.org/10.1007/978-3-319-50995-2_11
12. OpenACC Standards Committee: OpenACC: Directives for Accelerators (2011). http://www.openacc.org/About_OpenACC
13. OpenFabrics Interfaces Working Group: Libfabric Programmer's Manual. https://ofiwg.github.io/libfabric
14. OpenFabrics Interfaces Working Group: OFIWG libfabric repository. https://github.com/ofiwg/libfabric
15. OpenMP Application Program Interface, Version 3.0, May 2008. http://www.openmp.org/mp-documents/spec30.pdf
16. OpenSHMEM application programming interface, version 1.3, February 2016. http://www.openshmem.org
17. OpenSHMEM Redmine Issue #218 - Thread Safety Proposal. http://www.openshmem.org/redmine/issues/218
18. Sandia OpenSHMEM. https://github.com/Sandia-OpenSHMEM/SOS
19. Seager, K., Choi, S.-E., Dinan, J., Pritchard, H., Sur, S.: Design and implementation of OpenSHMEM using OFI on the aries interconnect. In: Gorentla Venkata, M., Imam, N., Pophale, S., Mintz, T.M. (eds.) OpenSHMEM 2016. LNCS, vol. 10007, pp. 97–113. Springer, Cham (2016). https://doi.org/10.1007/978-3-319-50995-2_7
20. Sridharan, S., Dinan, J., Kalamkar, D.D.: Enabling efficient multithreaded MPI communication through a library-based implementation of MPI endpoints. In: Proceedings of the International Conference for High Performance Computing, Networking, Storage and Analysis, SC 2014, pp. 487–498. IEEE Press (2014)
21. Weeks, H., Dosanjh, M.G.F., Bridges, P.G., Grant, R.E.: SHMEM-MT: a benchmark suite for assessing multi-threaded SHMEM performance. In: Gorentla Venkata, M., Imam, N., Pophale, S., Mintz, T.M. (eds.) OpenSHMEM 2016. LNCS, vol. 10007, pp. 227–231. Springer, Cham (2016). https://doi.org/10.1007/978-3-319-50995-2_16

Merged Requests for Better Performance and Productivity in Multithreaded OpenSHMEM

Swen Boehm$^{(\boxtimes)}$, Swaroop Pophale, Matthew B. Baker,
and Manjunath Gorentla Venkata

Computer Science and Mathematics Division, Oak Ridge National Laboratory,
Oak Ridge, TN, USA
boehms@ornl.gov

Abstract. A merged request is a handle representing a group of Remote Memory Access (RMA), *Atomic* or Collective operations. The merged request can be created either by combining multiple outstanding merged request handles or using the same merged request handle for additional operations. We show that introducing such simple yet powerful semantics in *OpenSHMEM* provides many productivity and performance advantages. In this paper, we first introduce the interfaces and semantics for creating and using merged request handles. Then, we demonstrate with a merge request that we can achieve better performance characteristics in multithreaded *OpenSHMEM* application. Particularly, we show one can achieve higher message rate, a higher bandwidth for smaller message, and better computation-communication overlap. Further, we use merged request to realize multithreaded collectives, where multiple threads co-operate to complete the collective operation. Our experimental results show that in a multithreaded *OpenSHMEM* program, the merged request based RMA operations achieve over 100 Million Messages Per Second (MMPS). It achieves over 10 MMPS compared to 4.5 MMPS with default RMA operations in a single threaded environment. Also, we achieve higher bandwidth for smaller message sizes, close to 100% overlap, and reduce the latency by 60%.

Keywords: PGAS · Shared memory · Interoperability

This manuscript has been authored by UT-Battelle, LLC under Contract No. DE-AC05-00OR22725 with the U.S. Department of Energy. The United States Government retains and the publisher, by accepting the article for publication, acknowledges that the United States Government retains a non-exclusive, paid-up, irrevocable, worldwide license to publish or reproduce the published form of this manuscript, or allow others to do so, for United States Government purposes. The Department of Energy will provide public access to these results of federally sponsored research in accordance with the DOE Public Access Plan (http://energy.gov/downloads/doe-public-access-plan).

M. Gorentla Venkata et al. (Eds.): OpenSHMEM 2017, LNCS 10679, pp. 35–49, 2018.
https://doi.org/10.1007/978-3-319-73814-7_3

1   Introduction

With the evolution of hardware technology and the trend towards fewer but more capable nodes with thousands of cores and hundreds of hardware threads per core, applications need to be multithreaded to take advantage of the capabilities. The *OpenSHMEM* specification committee is discussing various abstractions, which enables performance for *OpenSHMEM* program on many threaded architectures. The thread safety proposal, which defines the safe invocation of *OpenSHMEM* interfaces from multiple threads is the first step towards that goal and is close to be ratified.

The thread safety proposal defines the interaction between threads and *OpenSHMEM* interfaces. To provide the necessary semantics for thread safety, four thread levels are being proposed: SHMEM_THREAD_SINGLE, SHMEM_THREAD_FUNNELED, SHMEM_THREAD_SERIALIZED, and SHMEM_THREAD_MULTIPLE. SHMEM_THREAD_SINGLE allows for one thread per process and does not define thread safety on the OpenSHMEM API. The next level SHMEM_THREAD_FUNNELED permits processes to have multiple threads but only one of the threads can make OpenSHMEM calls. Since all calls are expected to be funneled through a single thread it is the programmer's responsibility to make certain that all the Open-SHMEM calls by a process are executed by the same thread. The next level of thread support is SHMEM_THREAD_SERIALIZED, which allows processes to have multiple threads that issue OpenSHMEM calls, but only one OpenSHMEM call per process can be active at any given time. Since simultaneous calls from two threads belonging to the same process are not allowed, it limits concurrency available through the multithreading approach. Finally, the SHMEM_THREAD_MULTIPLE level allows processes to have multiple threads and any thread may issue an OpenSHMEM call at any time, subject to a few restrictions.

Though these semantics enable *OpenSHMEM* programs to use multiple threads and thread packages, it does not necessarily translate into performance advantages and does not provide enough abstractions to take advantage of the capabilities in the network. Particularly, the modern High-Performance Computing (HPC) networks provide high message rate and bandwidth with low latency, often exposing multiple resources to the software stack. To utilize these resources and parallelism in an optimal way, we need to give the application programmer a way to provide *hints* to the communication library, or to provide a way to expose the available resources in a portable way to the programmer.

To address these bottlenecks, we propose to use merged requests introduced in [3]. The merged request handle can represent a group of RMA or *Atomic* operations. Each of these handles can be progressed and completed independently. The operations are non-blocking and can be progressed asynchronously; the operations are posted using a post operation and completed with a wait operation. The wait operation completes all operations represented by the merge request handle.

This approach adds minimal complexity to the *Application Programming Interface* (API) and the implementation, while providing various advantages for OpenSHMEM applications. Grouping related RMA operations into a single request offers the ability to isolate different sets of operations, which can be progressed and completed independently. The requests can be used to assign independent communication resources to the operations for the merged request, and thus take advantage of multiple network resources available in modern HPC networks. Further, this provides the flexibility to achieve a varying granularity of synchronization. The OpenSHMEM programs can achieve fine-grained completion and ordering and do not have to rely on the coarse-grained synchronization provided by quiet, fence, and barrier operations where fine-grained synchronization are required. The merge request abstraction also gives the programmer the flexibility to implement user defined collectives. For example, OpenSHMEM is still limited to an *active set* and log of 2 based *stride*. By using *merged requests*, a programmer may achieve a collective communication pattern that may have an irregular active set. This is different from defining a collective with a loop as the *OpenSHMEM* program can achieve communication and computational overlap, in addition to the simplicity of completing the related operations of the collective with a single handle.

Our contributions in this paper:

- Define the interfaces and semantics of RMA and *Atomic* operations with merge request handle
- Demonstrate that RMA and *Atomic* operations using merge requests can achieve higher message rate
- Demonstrate that the merged request abstraction can be used to realize custom collectives
- Demonstrate that merged requests can be used to achieve performance and productivity in multithreaded OpenSHMEM
- An in-depth analysis of the implementation of *merged requests* on a portable and scalable low level communications library UCX

In Sect. 2, we introduce the non-blocking API with merged handles. In Sect. 3, we discuss our implementation and the different considerations that had to be made to make the implementation thread safe. In Sect. 4, we discuss results of the different micro benchmarks. Related work in this context is covered in Sect. 5. The highlights of our analysis and our next steps are discussed in Sect. 6.

2 API for RMA and Atomic Operations with Merged Requests

The proposal for merged requests adds new API functions for explicit non-blocking RMA to OpenSHMEM. They follow the OpenSHMEM naming convention for RMA operations and add a _nbe postfix. These functions return a handle to request objects. In the case of a merged request, multiple RMA operations can share the same request. Additionally, operations to test and wait for completion of the request are added to the OpenSHMEM API.

The new functions for the non-blocking interfaces are explained below.

```
shmem_NAME_put_nbe (TYPE *target, const TYPE *source,
                    size_t nelems, int pe,
                    shmem_request_h *request);

shmem_put_SIZE_nbe (TYPE *target, const TYPE *source,
                    size_t nelems, int pe,
                    shmem_request_h *request);
```

Just like the regular blocking and implicit non-blocking functions, the put operations for the explicit non-blocking operations share the same interface, with the exception that they take a pointer to a request handle as the last parameter.

```
shmem_NAME_get_nbe (TYPE *target, const TYPE *source,
                    size_t nelems, int pe,
                    shmem_request_h *request);

shmem_get_SIZE_nbe (TYPE *target, const TYPE *source,
                    size_t nelems, int pe,
                    shmem_request_h *request);
```

The get functions follow the same pattern as the put functions.

Additionally we introduce explicit non-blocking functions for the following atomic operations:

```
shmem_NAME_swap_nbe (TYPE *target, TYPE value,  int pe,
                     shmemx_request_h *request)

shmem_NAME_cswap_nbe (TYPE *target, TYPE cond, Type value,
                      int pe, shmemx_request_h *request)

shmem_NAME_fadd_nbe (TYPE *target, TYPE value, int pe,
                     shmemx_request_h *request)
```

The following two functions are to manage outstanding requests:

```
shmem_request_test (shmem_request_h *request, int *flags);
```

The request handle is passed in as the first parameter, The second parameter is an integer pointer and is set according to the status to the outstanding operation. It is set to 0 is the operation is still in progress, and to 1 if the operation is finished. In the case that the operation is completed, the handle is freed internally and the handle is set to NULL.

```
shmem_request_wait (shmem_request_h *request);
```

The wait function takes a pointer to the request handle as its argument and blocks the execution of the calling context until the operation is completed. In the case of a multi threaded Processing Element (PE), only the calling thread is blocked. Before the function returns, the request object is freed and the handle is set to NULL, ready to be used again.

```
shmem_request_alloc (shmem_request_params_t params,
                     shmem_request_h *request);
```

This function can be used to explicitly allocate a request object. The flags argument that can be used to pass hints to the runtime. After the successful allocation, the pointer is not NULL.

```
shmem_request_free (shmem_request_h *request);
```

A request can be freed using this function.

```
shmem_merge_request (size_t count,
                     shmem_request_h **requests,
                     shmem_request_h *request);
```

This function can be used to merge multiple requests into a single request. The input parameters are the number of requests in the input array, a pointer to the input array and a pointer to the merged request.

3 Implementation

To evaluate the Merge request extensions, we extended *OpenSHMEM-X* to support RMA and *Atomic* operations with merge requests.

OpenSHMEM-X supports the functionality specified by the *OpenSHMEM* specification, as well as several extensions. The extensions include support for thread safety, merge requests, contexts, nonblocking RMA operations and several collectives. It is derived from the open source reference implementation [1]. The components in *OpenSHMEM-X* are shown in the Fig. 1.

OpenSHMEM-X can use Unified Communication X (UCX) [2], Universal Common Communication Substrate (UCCS), or GASNet as a communication abstraction. For this work, we leverage UCX and extend it as required. UCX provides different sets of APIs. UC-Protocols (UCP) is the high level API and is used by *OpenSHMEM-X*. Additionally, UCX provides the UC-Transports (UCT) API, which abstracts the differences of various hardware architectures. Finally, the service API UC-Services (UCS), provides functionality to write a portable networking framework.

3.1 Network and Resource Abstraction in UCX

UCX provides two different levels of network abstractions to the applications. The lower level abstraction, UCT, abstracts a single network device, memory, and provides basic data transfer primitives. The higher level abstraction, UCP, combines multiple UCT abstractions, defines the higher level message transfer protocols, and also provides wire-up and connection management. The details of the these layers can be found in our previous paper [2,3].

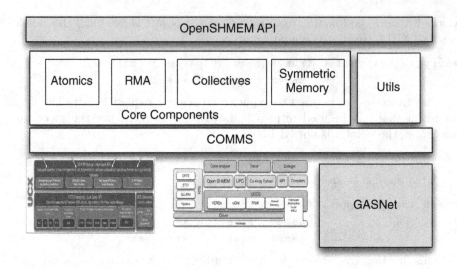

Fig. 1. Various components in the *OpenSHMEM* reference implementation

UCP Contexts: The UCP context defines a memory domain and memory allocation methods for use with the network interface. A UCT memory domain represents the memory mapped to a single device. It represents and co-ordinates the memory allocation, registration, and cleanup of the memory required for the communication buffers. The UCP context combines multiple UCT memory domains as required for the programming model. Typically, a single UCP context is used by a programming model instance. For example, if application is using both Message Passing Interface (MPI) and OpenSHMEM in the program, there is one UCP context for *Message Passing Interface* (MPI) and other for OpenSH-MEM. This allows each programming model to manage it's own memory without interfering with the other.

UCP Worker: The UCP and UCT Worker abstracts the network resources, which include network endpoints and the interface the endpoint attaches to. The UCT Worker represents a particular network interface and its attached end points. The UCP Worker represents a collection of interfaces. It abstracts the selection of the most efficient interface for the new endpoint and starts the wire-up of the endpoint. Each UCP Worker can be independently progressed and the operations on the Worker can be completed independently. If the communication operations from an application thread are mapped onto a Worker, there is no need for inter-thread synchronization for completing the communication operations of the thread. To communicate between the Workers, the UCP Worker creates the UCP endpoint using UCT endpoints attached to UCT interfaces. The UCT endpoints represent the connection endpoints of a single device, and UCP endpoints represents the endpoints of multi device instances used by the programming models.

3.2   Mapping Merged Requests to Resources

As described above, the merged request represents a group of either RMA or *Atomic* operations. In *OpenSHMEM-X*, we provide independent network resources to the merged requests as available by mapping each merged request to a separate UCP worker. To reduce the overhead, the UCP Workers are created during initialization and maintained in a pool. Workers are mapped to the merged request, when a merged request is created, and are removed from the pool. When the merged request is completed by calling shmem_request_wait(), the Worker is returned back to the pool. When the network resources (Workers) on the pool are exhausted, the runtime will start sharing Workers.

3.3   Threads and Merged Requests

By using merged requests higher communication performance can be achieved in a multithreaded *OpenSHMEM* program. In our experiments, we map the communication operations on a thread to a single merged request. Mapping merged request to independent network resource in *OpenSHMEM-X*, translates into a higher message rate and bandwidth (as shown in the results). Further, the communication operations on the thread can be completed without the need for inter-thread synchronization.

The mapping between the operations from a thread to a merged request and a UCP worker is managed through Thread Local Storage (TLS). TLS is not dependent on library and thus can be used regardless of the programming model chosen by the application developer. A reference to the Worker associated with a thread is stored in a thread local variable. This can be one Worker shared by all threads, a dedicated Worker per thread, or threads can be grouped together and the thread group shares a Worker. The number of Workers can be controlled through environment variables. The decision to use TLS adds additional overhead. The overhead introduced by the additional indirection was measured and is shown in Fig. 2.

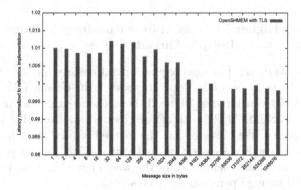

Fig. 2. Shows the difference in the put latency between the vanilla and the TLS implementation

The data in the graph is normalized to the latency of the reference implementation. There is a small overhead of less then 2% associated with using TLS, when the message size is below 8 kB. After this threshold, our experiments show a reduced latency compared to the standard implementation (without TLS). For larger messages, the indirection does not play a critical role with respect to adding latency and we can observe benefits from storing resources local to the thread.

4   Experimentation and Results

The section evaluates the merged request abstraction and presents the results. First, we evaluate the message rate, and bandwidth achieved by RMA operations with merged request. We compare the message rate achieved with multiple threads and compare it with the messaged rate achieved by multiple PEs. Then, we evaluate the implementation with Giga Updates Per Second (GUPS) benchmark to understand the performance impact on the application benchmark.

Testbed: The experiments were conducted on Turning, a 16-node institutional cluster at Oak Ridge National Laboratory (ORNL). Each node has two $Intel^{\circledR} Xeon^{\circledR}$ E5-2660 processors with 10 physical cores and hyper threading and 12 GB RAM. The nodes are connected by a InfiniBand network with Mellanox ConnectX-4 EDR IB. For these experiments, the communication does not cross the switch.

Benchmarks: To measure the latency, bandwidth, and message rate, we used the extended versions of Ohio State University (OSU) OpenSHMEM Benchmarks. The extensions include converting the benchmarks to use merged request API, make *OpenSHMEM* calls from multiple threads, and use OpenMP threads.

To measure the overlap between communication and the computation, we modified the MPI benchmark developed to measure the overlap achieved by nonblocking MPI operations [7]. This benchmark was modified to use *OpenSH-MEM* and the merged request API.

4.1   Achieving Higher Message Rate with Merged Request RMA Operations and Multiple Threads

To establish the overhead of merged request operations, we compare the message rate of merged request based RMA operations with the default RMA operations using modified OSU benchmarks. Figure 3 shows the message rate achieved with single-thread *OpenSHMEM* PE with merged request and Non-Blocking Implicit (NBI) put semantics. We observe that the merged request does have a performance advantage over RMA operations without explicit request per operation. This is due to the relaxed semantics of the wait operation, that can return as soon as the outstanding operation completes.

In the experiment shown in the Fig. 4, we configure the *OpenSHMEM* program with multiple OpenMP threads. The *OpenSHMEM* program was initialized

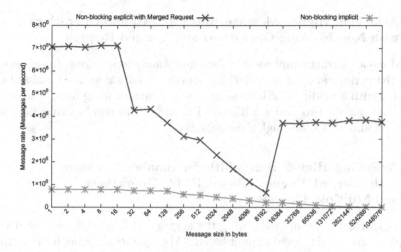

Fig. 3. Average message rate for a single thread.

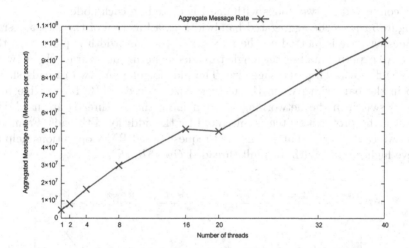

Fig. 4. Aggregated message rate for a multi threaded PE with increasing no. of threads

with *SHMEM_THREAD_MULTIPLE*. The RMA operations on each thread was mapped to a merged request, and merged request was completed with a wait operation. To measure the message rate, we modified the OSU put benchmark for this setup.

Figure 4 shows the aggregated message rate of a PE increasing with the number of threads. For 40 threads, we can observe in the figure, the merged request achieves over 100 MMPS. Also, we observed in the experiments the higher message rate could be achieved with the availability of more threads. Unfortunately, the maximum number of threads on this system was 40 threads per node.

4.2   Achieving Higher Message Rates for Atomic Operations with Non-blocking Operations and Merged Request

Merged requests where implemented for some *Atomic* operations. In this experiment the performance of non-blocking semantics for `shmem_long_fadd_nbe` is evaluated with a modified OSU message rate benchmark using fadd. The experiment was run on two nodes with one PE each. The non-blocking functions achieve an almost 4 times higher message rate.

4.3   Achieving Higher Bandwidth for Smaller Messages with Merged Request Based RMA Operations and Multiple Threads

In this experiment, we are measuring the aggregated bandwidth achieved with multiple threads and merged request based RMA operations. Also, for the experiments a modified version of the OSU OpenSHMEM benchmarks, that was extended to support multi-threading with OpenMP, was used. The experiments where conducted on two nodes with one PE placed on each node.

Figure 5 shows the aggregated bandwidth as a function of the message size. The message size is plotted on the x-axis, and the bandwidth is plotted on the y-axis. All experiments but the single threaded experiment saturate the network with a sufficiently large message size. The plot for one and two threads shows a dip in the bandwidth when the message size exceeds 8 kB. This is due to a protocol switch in the networking layer. If more than 2 threads are used, the impact of the protocol switch is mitigated by the additional threads. From the figure, we can observe that the merged request based RMA operations help to achieve higher bandwidth for multithreaded *OpenSHMEM*.

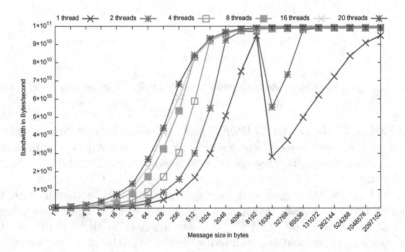

Fig. 5. Bandwidth for a single thread as a function of the message size (in bytes)

4.4   Communication/Computational Overlap

In the experiment, we measure the overlap achieved by the merged request based RMA operations using a modified version of the COMB benchmark [7]. The modifications include support for *OpenSHMEM* and merged request based RMA operations. The benchmark supports two modes, Post-Work-Wait and Post-Work-Poll modes of operation. The Post-Work-Wait is used to measure the largest uninterrupted computation-communication overlap duration, and we use this mode for the experiments in the paper.

The benchmark has three steps:

- Compute the communication time for a given message size.
- Estimate the work loop which is equivalent to the communication time. The work loop in our experiments is a busy loop.
- Post the communication operation. Upon return from the communication operation, the computation/work loop is started. After completion of computation/work loop, the wait is called for the completion of communication operation.

The overlap is measured by comparing the time to complete step 3 and step 2, while repeating the step (3) by incrementing the work done until the work in step 3 is equal to work in step 2.

Figure 6 shows the overlap achieved for small (64 Bytes) and large message (6 MB) as the work is increased. We can observe that as we increase the work, the merged request based RMA operations achieve close 100% overlap. For large message, the experiment measured 99.89% with a computation to communication ratio of 1.01. For smaller message sizes, the overlap is still close to 90%.

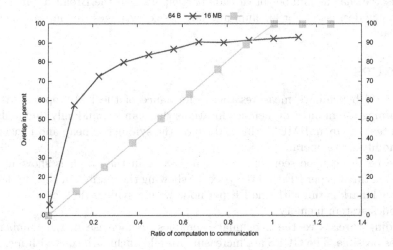

Fig. 6. Overlap between communication and computation using non-blocking put operations.

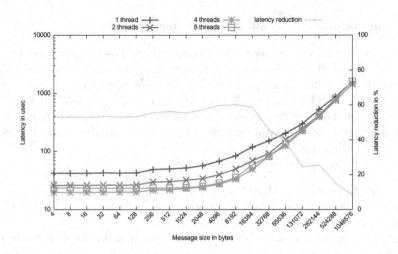

Fig. 7. Latency for put based broadcast using 32 PEs

4.5 Custom Collectives

This section measures the latency of multithreaded collective. In this collective, multiple threads participate in the same collective. The latency for the multi-threaded Broadcast is shown in Fig. 7. Here, each thread participating in the Broadcast sends a part of the buffer. Besides the latency advantages, these custom collectives are expected to be useful for many-threaded systems such as Graphical Processing Unit (GPU) based extreme-scale systems [10].

Figure 7 shows the latency of Broadcast as we increase the message size. We can observe that as number of threads participating in the Broadcast increase, the latency decreases. For medium and larger size messages the improvement is significant.

4.6 GUPS

The GUPS benchmark measures the performance of the RMA operations by determining the number of memory locations that can be randomly updated. In the context of OpenSHMEM, this is done on the symmetric heap and is using a read-modify-write operation.

The results can be seen in Fig. 8. The x-axis in the graph is showing the number of threads per PE, and the y-axis is showing the number of Giga updates. The benchmark is run with one PE per node with a symmetric heap size of half of a nodes system memory.

Adding threads to the benchmarks enables an increase in the number of updates possible. The GUPS are increasing for all benchmark runs with increasing numbers of threads.

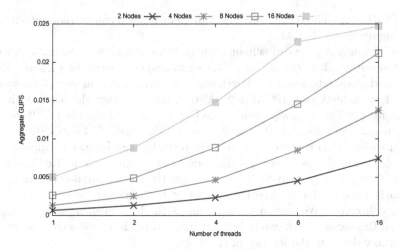

Fig. 8. Results for GUPS benchmark using OpenMP and OpenSHMEM with merged requests

5   Related Work

Other Partitioned Global Address Space (PGAS) low level libraries like GAS-Net [4] and ARMCI [9] provide similar ways to aggregate non-blocking communication as we do with *merged requests*. Making it available at the OpenSHMEM level gives more control to the application programmer to exploit concurrency at a much finer level. The Message Passing Interface (MPI) 1.0 [6] utilizes communicators which are a logical stream for two-sided communication. For interoperability amongst programming models that use threads MPI community has explored *endpoints* [5,11] for MPICH that relax the one-to-one relationship between processes and threads by generating additional MPI ranks that can be assigned to threads used in the execution of such models. The MPI *endpoints* are similar to the merged request to the extent that it can be used to identify set of resources that will support independent execution of communication operations. The MPI 2.0 [8] one-sided mechanisms achieve the same using *windows*. All ranks in the group have to call MPI_Win_allocate that returns a window object that can be used by all processes in the communicator to perform RMA operations. One significant difference from the approach proposed for OpenSHMEM is that the *endpoints* and *windows* created in MPI are a collective call, which is not the case for *merged requests*.

6   Conclusion

In this paper, we demonstrated how merged request abstraction can be used to achieve productivity and performance for multithreaded *OpenSHMEM* programs. The abstractions were implemented in high-performing experimental

OpenSHMEM-X. The results show that implementation can be realized without incurring overhead (Fig. 4).

The simple yet powerful semantics help achieve higher performance in the case of multithreaded *OpenSHMEM*, which we can observe in the various results shown in the evaluation section. Particularly, we can observe in the results shown in Fig. 4, we achieve over 100 MMPS. Also, it helps improve the bandwidth utilization for small messages as seen in the Fig. 5. The results of the GUPS benchmark are another indicator, that multithreaded OpenSHMEM applications with merged request operations can greatly improve the performance of applications (see Fig. 8). Finally, we measured the overlap of computation and communication, and see that especially for large messages the computation-communication overlap is close to 100%. Another benefit is the ability to utilize threads in custom collectives. We demonstrate its use with the implementation of multithreaded Broadcast. As shown in Fig. 7 utilizing threads for collective operations can notably decrease the latency of the operation.

Acknowledgment. This work is supported by the United States Department of Defense and used resources of the Extreme Scale Systems Center located at the Oak Ridge National Laboratory.

References

1. OpenSHMEM reference implementation. https://github.com/openshmem-org/openshmem. Accessed 26 June 2017
2. Baker, M., Aderholdt, F., Venkata, M.G., Shamis, P.: OpenSHMEM-UCX: evaluation of UCX for implementing OpenSHMEM programming model. In: Venkata et al. [12], pp. 114–130. https://doi.org/10.1007/978-3-319-50995-2_8
3. Boehm, S., Pophale, S., Venkata, M.G.: Evaluating OpenSHMEM explicit remote memory access operations and merged requests. In: Venkata et al. [12], pp. 18–34. https://doi.org/10.1007/978-3-319-50995-2_2
4. Bonachea, D.: Gasnet specification, v1.1. Technical report, Berkeley, CA, USA (2002)
5. Dinan, J., Balaji, P., Goodell, D., Miller, D., Snir, M., Thakur, R.: Enabling MPI interoperability through flexible communication endpoints. In: EuroMPI 2013, Madrid, Spain (2013)
6. Forum, M.P.: MPI: A message-passing interface standard. Technical report, Knoxville, TN, USA (1994)
7. Lawry, W., Wilson, C., Maccabe, A.B., Brightwell, R.: COMB: a portable benchmark suite for assessing MPI overlap. In: 2002 IEEE International Conference on Cluster Computing (CLUSTER 2002), Chicago, IL, USA, 23–26 September 2002, pp. 472–475. IEEE Computer Society (2002). https://doi.org/10.1109/CLUSTR.2002.1137785
8. Li, G., Palmer, R., DeLisi, M., Gopalakrishnan, G., Kirby, R.M.: Formal specification of MPI 2.0: case study in specifying a practical concurrent programming API. Sci. Comput. Program. **76**(2), 65–81 (2011). https://doi.org/10.1016/j.scico.2010.03.007

9. Nieplocha, J., Carpenter, B.: ARMCI: a portable remote memory copy library for distributed array libraries and compiler run-time systems. In: Rolim, J., et al. (eds.) IPPS 1999. LNCS, vol. 1586, pp. 533–546. Springer, Heidelberg (1999). https://doi.org/10.1007/BFb0097937

10. Potluri, S., et al.: Exploring OpenSHMEM model to program GPU-based extreme-scale systems. In: Venkata, M.G., Shamis, P., Imam, N., Lopez, M.G. (eds.) Open-SHMEM 2014. LNCS, vol. 9397, pp. 18–35. Springer, Cham (2015). https://doi.org/10.1007/978-3-319-26428-8_2

11. Sridharan, S., Dinan, J., Kalamkar, D.D.: Enabling efficient multithreaded MPI communication through a library-based implementation of MPI endpoints. In: SC 2014: International Conference for High Performance Computing, Networking, Storage and Analysis, pp. 487–498 (2014)

12. Venkata, M.G., Imam, N., Pophale, S., Mintz, T.M. (eds.): OpenSHMEM 2016. LNCS, vol. 10007. Springer, Cham (2016). https://doi.org/10.1007/978-3-319-50995-2

Evaluating Contexts in OpenSHMEM-X Reference Implementation

Aurelien Bouteiller[2], Swaroop Pophale[1(✉)], Swen Boehm[1],
Matthew B. Baker[1], and Manjunath Gorentla Venkata[1]

[1] Oak Ridge National Laboratory, Computer Science and Mathematics Division,
Oak Ridge, USA
`pophaless@ornl.gov`
[2] Innovative Computing Laboratory, The University of Tennessee, Knoxville, USA

Abstract. Many-core processors are now ubiquitous in supercomputing. This evolution pushes toward the adoption of mixed models in which cores are exploited with threading models (and related programming abstractions, such as OpenMP), while communication between distributed memory domains employ a communication *Application Programming Interface* (API). OpenSHMEM is a partitioned global address space communication specification that exposes one-sided and synchronization operations. As the threaded semantics of OpenSHMEM are being fleshed out by its standardization committee, it is important to assess the soundness of the proposed concepts. This paper implements and evaluate the "context" extension in relation to threaded operations. We discuss the implementation challenges of the context and the associated API in *OpenSHMEM-X*. We then evaluate its performance in threaded situations on the Infiniband network using micro-benchmarks and the Random Access benchmark and see that adding communication contexts significantly improves message rate achievable by the executing multi-threaded PEs.

Keywords: PGAS · Shared memory · Interoperability

A. Bouteiller and S. Pophale—Contributed equally.

This manuscript has been authored by UT-Battelle, LLC under Contract No. DE-AC05-00OR22725 with the U.S. Department of Energy. The United States Government retains and the publisher, by accepting the article for publication, acknowledges that the United States Government retains a non-exclusive, paid-up, irrevocable, worldwide license to publish or reproduce the published form of this manuscript, or allow others to do so, for United States Government purposes. The Department of Energy will provide public access to these results of federally sponsored research in accordance with the DOE Public Access Plan (http://energy.gov/downloads/doe-public-access-plan).

M. Gorentla Venkata et al. (Eds.): OpenSHMEM 2017, LNCS 10679, pp. 50–62, 2018.
https://doi.org/10.1007/978-3-319-73814-7_4

1   Introduction

OpenSHMEM [5] library specification aims at providing a standard API for SHMEM libraries to aid portability across different vendor implementations on different architectures. With behavior and semantics defined for the library API, OpenSHMEM programs are expected to provide consistent behavior across multiple platforms. Many high-performance implementations from vendors such as HPE, Cray, and Intel along with open source implementations by University of Houston (reference implementation over GASNet) and ORNL (reference implementation over UCX, *OpenSHMEM-X*) exist.

As we march towards the exascale era, the new trend in hardware is to have more capable nodes with multiple levels of concurrency and parallelism. To utilize these complex systems OpenSHMEM programming model has to evolve to include support for heterogeneous architectures and hybrid programming. The first step towards it is to have thread safety as part of the OpenSHMEM specification that will allow threads representing a PE to make OpenSHMEM calls.

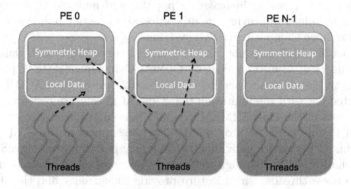

Fig. 1. Multi-threaded OpenSHMEM memory model

Figure 1 shows the logical evolution of the OpenSHMEM memory model, where each PE may spawn a number of threads. Since the OpenSHMEM programming model does not recognize individual threads as separate entities, any OpenSHMEM operation initiated by a thread is considered an action of the PE as a whole. Like the single-threaded PE, threads of a multi-threaded PE may access the local memory of the PE and the *symmetric* memory of its PE and that of any other PE participating in the OpenSHMEM application but cannot access the local memory of any other PE. The threading model itself is outside the scope of this work.

The most recent version, 1.3 of the OpenSHMEM specification, does not define a thread safe API, but the community is having a productive discussion about the appropriate interfaces and semantics that can effectively support concurrently communicating threads. Multiple designs have been proposed in recent years, and in this paper we evaluate the *Contexts* proposal by providing an implementation over IB using the UCX communication library. The paper also explores the possibility of a multi-threaded PE where individual threads can, within the bounds of the OpenSHMEM semantics, add another level of concurrency to the application thus increasing overlap not only between operations of the different PEs but also that of the same PE.

In Sect. 2, we give the background on thread safety in OpenSHMEM and details about the *Context* proposal as presented to the OpenSHMEM community. In Sect. 3, we discuss our implementation and the different considerations made to make the implementation thread safe. In Sect. 4, we discuss the different benchmarks used to evaluate the implementation and discuss our results. Related work in this context is covered in Sect. 5. The highlights of our analysis and our next steps are discussed in Sect. 6.

2   Background

Accompanying the evolution toward many-core architectures, hybrid programming models are becoming increasingly popular and multiple threads play an ever increasing role in improving the utilization and programmability of modern High-Performance Computing (HPC) systems.

The OpenSHMEM does not currently have a threading model, thus hybrid programming (e.g. using OpenMP or OpenACC in OpenSHMEM programs) is not directly supported. Nonetheless, successful use of OpenACC has been demonstrated [2], with the limitation that OpenACC calls are restrained to isolated segments in the OpenSHMEM program between *shmem_barrier_all* calls. In contrast to this work, we propose to study the support of threaded Processing Elements (PEs) where individual threads may participate in OpenSHMEM calls on behalf of a PE. Through the context proposal, hardware resources are exposed to these threads, which in turn provide concurrency and the ability to synchronize on a per thread basis.

2.1   Thread Safe API

An earlier proposal from Cray [4] introduced OpenSHMEM extensions for thread safety which include different levels of threading support similar to those used in MPI. This proposal has not been incorporated by the OpenSHMEM specification community as of version 1.3, but the OpenSHMEM standardization committee is working on integrating these concepts in the standard.

These thread support levels are hierarchical. In lower support levels, the programmer is responsible for restraining access to authorized threads, or serializing access to the OpenSHMEM library, according to the supported semantics in that level. Higher levels expand on the capabilities of the lower levels by relaxing the allowed concurrency between OpenSHMEM calls. In the highest thread support level, multithreaded programs may issue concurrent calls to the otherwise unchanged OpenSHMEM routines.

The first level of thread support is SHMEM_THREAD_SINGLE and it allows for one thread per process. The next level SHMEM_THREAD_FUNNELED , permits processes to have multiple threads but only one of the threads can make OpenSHMEM calls, and it is the programmer's responsibility to enforce that all OpenSHMEM calls in a process are executed by that thread. The next level of thread support is SHMEM_THREAD_SERIALIZED, which permits multiple threads to issue OpenSH-MEM calls in a PE, but only one OpenSHMEM call per process can be active at any given time. Since simultaneous calls from two threads belonging to the same process are not allowed, it limits concurrency available through the multithreading approach. Finally, in the SHMEM_THREAD_MULTIPLE level, processes may have multiple threads and any thread may issue a OpenSHMEM call at any time, subject to a few restrictions. In this latest mode, the OpenSHMEM Specification would enable hybrid programming with OpenSHMEM, but it would still overlook other performance important factors such as network resource management. Modern HPC networks have sophisticated network adapters, often exposing multiple resources to the software stack. To utilize these resources in a optimal way, the application programmer needs to be able to provide a "hint" to the communication library about the intended, and potentially exclusive, usage of the OpenSHMEM interfaces, and the OpenSHMEM interface needs to be expanded to expose the available resources in a portable way to the programmer.

2.2 Communication Contexts

The context proposal, first fleshed out by Dinan et al. [7], seeks to alleviate the aforementioned issue with resource allocation, mapping, and sharing. The context proposal which expands on top of the thread safe API discussed in Sect. 2.1, introduces a set of new API functions to map contexts onto resources, and to issue Remote Memory Access (RMA) operations and synchronizations on a specific context.

Additional RMA operations from the context proposal take the context as an explicit parameter. They follow OpenSHMEMs API for the function names and add a ctx_ qualifier to the function name (e.g., shmem_ctx_putmem corresponds to shmem_putmem). Finally, there are supplementary API functions for memory ordering using contexts (shmem_ctx_fence and shmem_ctx_quiet). The full semantics of the proposal are outside the scope of the paper; the interested reader will find details on the proposed API in [7].

Contexts are created using the shmem_ctx_create function. The user may indicate at creation time if the context is intended for shared, or exclusive use. When the context is shared, multiple threads may issue operations concurrently on the context. In addition to context synchronization targeting explicitly the context, non-context synchronizations (e.g., shmem_quiet, which does not have a context argument) will synchronize the default context (i.e., the implicit context in which operations without a context argument operate). When the context is exclusive, only the calling thread may issue operations on the context, and only synchronization operations that explicitly target the context affect the ordering, visibility and completion of posted communication on the context.

Thanks to these additional API calls, the context proposal enables several advantageous usage patterns. Regardless of the number of threads in an application, contexts provide the opportunity to finely control and pipeline overlap of multiple communication. Contexts can in effect be used to provide a fine control on completion ordering while maintaining the performance benefit of implicit operations (*i.e.*, sparring the overhead associated with request-based approaches).

Additionally, RMA operations in one thread can be issued on a separate context, and thereby isolated from RMA operations issued by a different thread on another context. As we will further discuss in the rest of this paper, supporting thread safe access to shared network queues and resources can have a significant impact on communication performance, most notably on latency and injection rate as locks, atomic operations and memory barriers must be added to the critical path to ensure consistency across multiple threads. If a context is exclusive, although the application may issue operations from multiple threads, there is no need to lock or ensure memory consistency between these threads, therefore opening an alley for lock-free multithreaded operations.

Last, given the information about the number and nature (private or shared) of the contexts requested by the application threads, and the number of underlying hardware communication channels, the OpenSHMEM implementation has an opportunity for optimizing the mapping between contexts and resources to again minimize the need for serialization and locking. If sufficient hardware resources are available, locking can be eliminated completely.

3   Implementation

Early evaluation versions of the context proposal have been implemented targeting specific hardware such as Portals, and Cray DMAPP [14]. In this work, we implement the concepts in a generic fashion in the OpenSHMEM reference implementation, with the intent of stressing the portability implications of the proposal when facing a generic interface to access network resources.

To test the proposed extensions to OpenSHMEM, we implemented the context proposal in the OpenSHMEM reference implementation. The reference implementation can use different conduits to map OpenSHMEM calls onto network operations. The University of Houston (UH) reference implementation employs GASNet [3], but the OpenSHMEM reference implementation has recently been adapted to use UCX as the networking conduit [1].

UCX is a community effort to implement a portable and scalable high performance network API framework. UCX supports different HPC networking architectures and supports RMA operations, active messages, as well as tag matching. UCX provides different sets of APIs. UCP is the high level API, and is used by our *SHMEM* implementation. Additionally, UCX provides the UCT API, which abstracts, at a low level, the differences of various hardware architectures. Finally, the service API, UCS, provides functionality to write a portable networking framework. One of the strong design points in UCX is its emphasis in providing a close to the metal, yet portable access to network technology. In addition, a significant effort has been made to make UCX API thread-scalable [11].

The UCP layer provides communication resources called UCP workers. A worker object has methods for synchronizing and ordering (similar to those provided by `shmem_quiet` and `shmem_fence`), as well as methods for waiting on events or memory locations (similar to `shmem_wait_int`). Multiple workers can be created in a process, thereby providing separated access to low level communication resources. Communication operations are posted in an UCP endpoint; An endpoint is a local queue for posting operations into a peer to peer channel between a local and a remote worker. Workers at a target can be individually addressed by creating different endpoints.

3.1 Per-Context Endpoints

The major difference between the context-extended OpenSHMEM and the regular UCX OpenSHMEM is the way UCP endpoints are managed. In the regular OpenSHMEM, one UCP endpoint is created between two PEs. That endpoint is used to issue all communication and synchronization targeting that PE. With this design, when multiple thread issue OpenSHMEM calls simultaneously, all operations are serialized in that unique UCP endpoint; and the cost of thread consistency (*i.e.,* atomic operations and memory barriers) must be paid on performance critical operations (like `shmem_int_put`). In addition, a single UCP progress entity (a UCP Worker) is created. All threads requiring progress, ordering, and synchronization then issue a call to the same Worker object, which again needs to ensure internal thread safety, and enforces ordering between events that are not in a deterministic order. For example, a fence issued by one thread may enforce the order between messages issued in another thread, but without further user-level thread synchronization, that order is nondeterministic, and enforcing it is spurious overhead.

In contrast, the context extended implementation creates a supplementary worker for each calling thread. Every time a thread creates a context, a thread-specific UCP worker is instantiated on which context synchronization operations are posted. In addition, supplementary thread-specific endpoints are created to issue communication operations. All context communication calls (*e.g.,* `shmem_ctx_int_put`) are then simply remapped to the corresponding UCX call on the context-specific UCP endpoint. Similarly, synchronization calls are remapped to the context-specific UCP worker.

The context object contains a reference to the associated worker and array of context-specific endpoints. Because the context is then passed as an explicit parameter to all communication and synchronization functions, retrieving the thread-appropriate worker and endpoints can be implemented without relying on perhaps expensive thread-local storage (TLS).

3.2   Thread/Context Mapping

As of this writing the OpenSHMEM Threads sub-committee is still fleshing out the context proposal and parts of the interface are still under development. One such aspect of the proposal that remains a work in progress is the mapping interface to attach contexts to threads.

The context proposal itself does not necessarily binds contexts and threads. A single thread may create and use multiple contexts, or a context can be created shareable, in which case it may be used by multiple threads concurrently, or transitioned from thread to thread for serial accesses. However, one of the most promising aspect in terms of performance optimization is for thread-exclusive contexts, that is, contexts created for the exclusive use of the thread calling the context creation function.

Our implementation of the proposal uses OpenMP runtime functions to gather information of the number of threads the application is using. Shared contexts are mapped onto the default UCX level network resource, *i.e.*, the thread-safe worker that handles operations posted on the default context, or using the non-context interfaces. For thread-exclusive contexts, UCX level network resources are allocated on a per thread basis. If the current thread has no resources assigned to it, when that thread first creates a context, a new UCX worker is created, and the reference to the worker is stored in both the new context, and in a global table indexed per thread. Note however that during communication operations, the appropriate worker resource is obtained from the context itself, unlike in Cray's thread hot implementation, thereby sparing the potentially costly identification of the calling thread and the global lookup in the shared table.

With this policy, if a thread creates multiple contexts, they will share the same resource object. This mapping policy may result in under-utilizing available hardware network resources, if the number of available network hardware queues is larger than the number of threads in the application. It also results in over-synchronizing operations issued on multiple context from the same thread, thereby limiting pipelining opportunities. An alternate strategy would be to allocate a new UCX worker for every created context, resulting in a workers potentially outnumbering the available network hardware queues. In this case, without additional information on the intended usage pattern for the context, determining which context should share a worker, so that the total number of created workers is commensurate with the available hardware resources becomes a difficult problem. A particularly stringent problem arises when one threads creates many contexts, thereby exhausting exclusive resources and leaving all other threads to suffer from the performance penalty of using shared resources. A companion proposal to the context interface adds the concept of *domains*. Domains represent a way for application codes to express preferences for the bundling of contexts on the same physical network resources, when sharing becomes necessary. In the current work, contexts are implicitly bundled by calling threads, as identified by calling OpenMP routines. Using the explicit domain interface would remove the runtime dependency to OpenMP and support arbitrary thread libraries (including full-user threads that would not register in system calls). The domain proposal is currently evaluating exposing to the end-user the number of available hardware queues, or on the opposite, obtain from the user the desired number of logical queues and their sharing dependencies, which would then inform the communication driver mapping (such a feature is available in UCX).

4   Experimentation and Results

The experiments were conducted on a 16 node cluster at Oak Ridge National Laboratory (ORNL). Each node has two $Intel^{\circledR} Xeon^{\circledR}$ E5-2660 processors with 10 physical cores and hyper threading, a Mellanox ConnectX-4 VPI adapter card, EDR IB (100 Gb/s) and 12 GB RAM.

To evaluate the implementation of *Contexts* in OSH-X we use three benchmarks. These benchmarks create a communication context per thread and all RMA and atomic operations use an additional parameter to identify the context used as discussed in Sect. 2.2. This isolates the different threads form each other and enables efficient resource sharing between threads. These benchmarks are:

1. Message Rate benchmark
   We modified the Ohio State University (OSU) [13] OpenSHMEM message rate benchmark to use communication contexts and OpenMP. Adding support for OpenMP enabled the benchmark to run in a threaded environment. The benchmark measures the message rate using put operations with an increasing number of PEs per compute node.
2. Bandwidth benchmark
   This benchmark has been derived by adding per thread bandwidth measurement to OSU [13] OpenSHMEM bandwidth benchmark. We measure the aggregate bandwidth across all threads of a PE, as well as the average bandwidth for individual threads across runs. The benchmark is run with two PEs on two nodes and records bandwidth of put operations with an increasing number of OpenMP threads per PE.
3. Random Access benchmark
   This benchmarks gives the Giga Updates per second (GUPs) [8] for a given number of PEs. The problem size (number of updates) is directly proportional to the number of PEs. The OpenSHMEM random access benchmark is modified such that all updates are made to remote PEs. We run different problem sizes with increasing number of OpenMP threads per PE with one PE per node.

4.1   Message Rates

We measure the message rate using shmem_put operations. Figure 2 shows the message rate with an increasing number of threads for PEs using communication contexts for a one byte transfer size. The overall message rate increases but the

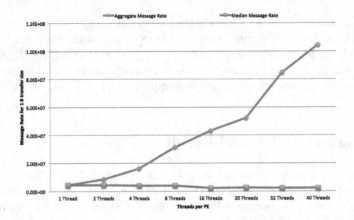

Fig. 2. Aggregate and median message rate with increasing threads per PE

aggregated message rate does not level off with the maximum number of threads, showing potential for an increasing number of threads to achieve higher message rate. Figure 3 shows the message rate change with increasing message size for different threads per PE.

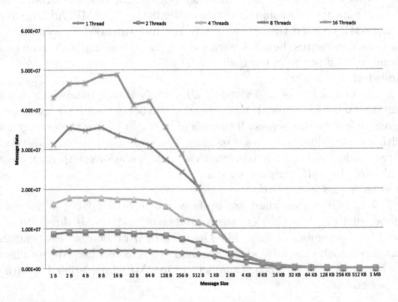

Fig. 3. Aggregate message rate (messages per second) with increasing message size for increasing threads per PE

4.2 Bandwidth

In Fig. 4, we show the median bandwidth achieved across the thread team and the aggregate bandwidth for increasing number of threads per PE for large messages (1 MB). From the graph it is evident that it is not difficult to saturate the network using large message sizes with fewer threads per PE. Figure 5 shows the bandwidth utilization as a function of transfer size. The graph shows that the

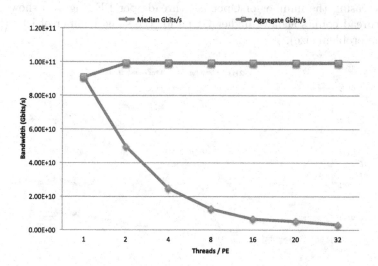

Fig. 4. Bandwidth for the context implementation for a transfer size of 1 MB with increasing number of threads per PE

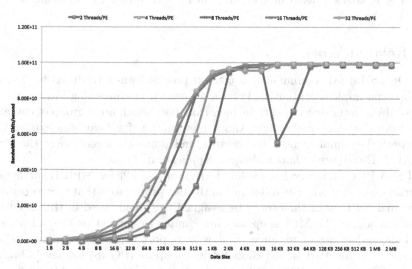

Fig. 5. Bandwidth of different threads per PE as a function of the message size

benefits of having a multiple threads with independent contexts dwindle as the transfer size increases. At this point the network becomes the bottleneck.

4.3 Random Access

The OpenSHMEM Random Access benchmark allocates a large remotely accessible table data structure on each PE and updates are made to random locations at each iteration. We test this benchmark by allocating one PE per node and then increasing the number of OpenMP threads per PE. Figure 6 shows that, higher thread counts achieve higher GUPs for the same number of PEs (hence the same problem size).

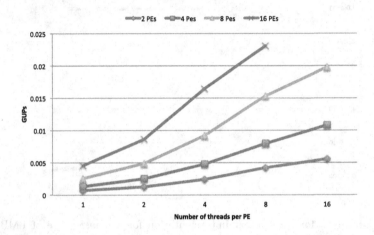

Fig. 6. GUPs measurement for different PE and threads/PE combination

5 Related Work

The OpenSHMEM communication context proposal was introduced by [7] with a prototype implementation on Portals 4 network programming interface. The proposal was later developed to include Domains; which are a group of contexts that have the same properties. Another evaluation for Cray was explored in [9] where they implemented the context and domain concepts over the Cray DMAPP (Distributed Shared Memory Application) library.

The MPI community has explored *endpoints* [6,12] for MPICH for hybrid programming support. The difference in the two proposals is that they generated additional MPI ranks that could be assigned to threads used in the execution of such models. The MPI *endpoints* are similar to context as they also identify independent set of resources that will support concurrent communication operations. Other Partitioned Global Address Space (PGAS) low level libraries like GASNet [3] and ARMCI [10] provide ways to aggregate non-blocking communication. These aggregations can then, by the library, provide independent resources without user intervention.

6 Conclusions and Future Work

We have implemented the context proposal with a hardware neutral interposition layer (UCX) in the reference OpenSHMEM implementation. This implementation creates separate resource pools on a per-thread basis, thereby eliminating the cost of serializing accesses from multiple threads to a single shared resource. Our experimental evaluation demonstrates that the design can scale with the number of threads concurrently issuing communication. Notably, the random access benchmark performs significantly faster with more threads per PE.

In future works, given the significant advantage shown in the micro-benchmarks and Random Access benchmark, we expect the performance gain to permeate to the applications; we would therefore like to extend the evaluation to more application benchmarks. As we stated in the implementation section, the mapping of contexts to hardware resources remains an open problem at this point. Given our experience with UCX, we would like to experiment with the concept of domains to drive the context mapping onto hardware resources in an efficient and portable way.

Acknowledgment. This work is supported by the United States Department of Defense and used resources of the Extreme Scale Systems Center located at the Oak Ridge National Laboratory.

References

1. Baker, M., Aderholdt, F., Venkata, M.G., Shamis, P.: OpenSHMEM-UCX: evaluation of UCX for implementing OpenSHMEM programming model. In: Gorentla Venkata, M., Imam, N., Pophale, S., Mintz, T.M. (eds.) OpenSHMEM 2016. LNCS, vol. 10007, pp. 114–130. Springer, Cham (2016). https://doi.org/10.1007/978-3-319-50995-2_8
2. Baker, M., Pophale, S., Vasnier, J.-C., Jin, H., Hernandez, O.: Hybrid programming using OpenSHMEM and OpenACC. In: Poole, S., Hernandez, O., Shamis, P. (eds.) OpenSHMEM 2014. LNCS, vol. 8356, pp. 74–89. Springer, Cham (2014). https://doi.org/10.1007/978-3-319-05215-1_6
3. Bonachea, D.: Gasnet specification, v1.1. Technical report, Berkeley, CA, USA (2002)
4. ten Bruggencate, M., Roweth, D., Oyanagi, S.: Thread-safe SHMEM extensions. In: Poole, S., Hernandez, O., Shamis, P. (eds.) OpenSHMEM 2014. LNCS, vol. 8356, pp. 178–185. Springer, Cham (2014). https://doi.org/10.1007/978-3-319-05215-1_13
5. Chapman, B., Curtis, T., Pophale, S., Poole, S., Kuehn, J., Koelbel, C., Smith, L.: Introducing OpenSHMEM: SHMEM for the PGAS community. In: Proceedings of the Fourth Conference on Partitioned Global Address Space Programming Model, PGAS 2010, pp. 2:1–2:3. ACM, New York (2010). http://doi.acm.org/10.1145/2020373.2020375
6. Dinan, J., Balaji, P., Goodell, D., Miller, D., Snir, M., Thakur, R.: Enabling MPI interoperability through flexible communication endpoints. In: EuroMPI 2013, Madrid, Spain (2013)

7. Dinan, J., Flajslik, M.: Contexts: a mechanism for high throughput communication in OpenSHMEM. In: Proceedings of the 8th International Conference on Partitioned Global Address Space Programming Models, PGAS 2014, pp. 10:1–10:9. ACM, New York (2014). http://doi.acm.org/10.1145/2676870.2676872

8. Lawry, W., Wilson, C., Maccabe, A.B., Brightwell, R.: COMB: a portable benchmark suite for assessing MPI overlap. In: 2002 IEEE International Conference on Cluster Computing (CLUSTER 2002), 23–26 September 2002, Chicago, IL, USA, pp. 472–475 (2002). https://doi.org/10.1109/CLUSTR.2002.1137785

9. Namashivayam, N., Knaak, D., Cernohous, B., Radcliffe, N., Pagel, M.: An evaluation of thread-safe and contexts-domains features in cray SHMEM. In: Gorentla Venkata, M., Imam, N., Pophale, S., Mintz, T.M. (eds.) OpenSHMEM 2016. LNCS, vol. 10007, pp. 163–180. Springer, Cham (2016). https://doi.org/10.1007/978-3-319-50995-2_11

10. Nieplocha, J., Carpenter, B.: ARMCI: a portable remote memory copy library for distributed array libraries and compiler run-time systems. In: Rolim, J., et al. (eds.) IPPS 1999. LNCS, vol. 1586, pp. 533–546. Springer, Heidelberg (1999). https://doi.org/10.1007/BFb0097937

11. Shamis, P., Venkata, M.G., Lopez, M.G., Baker, M.B., Hernandez, O., Itigin, Y., Dubman, M., Shainer, G., Graham, R.L., Liss, L., Shahar, Y., Potluri, S., Rossetti, D., Becker, D., Poole, D., Lamb, C., Kumar, S., Stunkel, C., Bosilca, G., Bouteiller, A.: UCX: an open source framework for HPC network APIs and beyond. In: 2015 IEEE 23rd Annual Symposium on High-Performance Interconnects, pp. 40–43, August 2015

12. Sridharan, S., Dinan, J., Kalamkar, D.D.: Enabling efficient multithreaded MPI communication through a library-based implementation of MPI endpoints. In: SC14: International Conference for High Performance Computing, Networking, Storage and Analysis, pp. 487–498 (2014)

13. The Ohio State University: OSU micro-benchmarks (2016). http://mvapich.cse.ohio-state.edu/benchmarks/

14. Gorentla Venkata, M., Imam, N., Pophale, S., Mintz, T.M. (eds.): OpenSHMEM 2016. LNCS, vol. 10007. Springer, Cham (2016). https://doi.org/10.1007/978-3-319-50995-2

OpenSHMEM Applications

Parallelizing Single Source Shortest Path with OpenSHMEM

Ferrol Aderholdt[1]([⊠]), Jeffrey A. Graves[2], and Manjunath Gorentla Venkata[1]

[1] Computer Science and Mathematics Division,
Oak Ridge National Laboratory (ORNL), Oak Ridge, USA
aderholdtwf1@ornl.gov
[2] Tennessee Tech University (TTU), Cookeville, USA

Abstract. Single Source Shortest Path (SSSP) is one of the widely occurring graph problems where the paths are discovered from an origin vertex to all other vertices in the graph. In this paper, we discuss our experience parallelizing SSSP using OpenSHMEM. We start with the serial *Dijkstra* and *Bellman-Ford* algorithms, parallelize these algorithms, and adapt them to the Partitioned Global Address Space (PGAS) programming model. We implement the parallel algorithms using OpenSHMEM and introduce a series of optimizations to achieve higher scaling and performance characteristics. The implementation is evaluated on Titan with various graphs including synthetic Recursive Matrix (R-MAT) and small-world network graphs as well as real-world graphs from Facebook, Twitter, LiveJournal, and the road maps of California and Texas.

1 Introduction

The SSSP problem is a well-studied graph theory problem that is widely used in many applications across various domains, and has been applied successfully by many in industry, including Facebook, Google, and others. With its importance and the value of delivering efficient high performance SSSP results over billions of documents and locations, fully adapting the algorithms to High Performance Computing (HPC) systems with a performant communication library is imperative.

Recently, HPC system architectures have been evolving towards both HPC-centric (i.e., BigCompute) and data-centric (i.e., BigData) workloads. This evolution is directly realized through the use of multiple highly threaded *Central Processing Units* (CPUs), multiple compute accelerators, high performing networks, and large amounts of hierarchical and heterogeneous memories. By making use of system architectures with this composition, HPC systems will be able to provide fast and accurate results to many data-analytic applications at increasing scales.

This work focuses on the adaptation of popular SSSP algorithms to the PGAS programming model with OpenSHMEM. OpenSHMEM is a PGAS programming library interface suitable for implementing graph-based algorithms.

M. Gorentla Venkata et al. (Eds.): OpenSHMEM 2017, LNCS 10679, pp. 65–81, 2018.
https://doi.org/10.1007/978-3-319-73814-7_5

This is because of its lightweight semantics and simple interfaces to the underlying communication library, which leads to fast communication and *Atomic Memory Operations* (AMO). These properties are necessary for deploying a high performance implementation of graph-based algorithms due to the irregular structure and poor locality of graphs [1].

The algorithms to be adapted in this work include both the *label-setting* approach employed by Dijkstra's algorithm [2] and the *label-correcting* approach used in Bellman-Ford [3,4]. Label-setting algorithms, such as Dijkstra's algorithm, will calculate a correct minimum distance value and set this to a particular vertex before moving to the next vertex. That is to say, once a path from the source vertex to a particular vertex has been found, it is guaranteed to be the shortest path, and so, these algorithms can be thought of as only visiting a vertex once. With respect to label-correcting algorithms, such as Bellman-Ford, vertices may be visited iteratively while continually updating distance values until convergence has been reached. These algorithms give us two primary and differing methodologies to explore. While parallelizing these algorithms for OpenSHMEM, we have identified and demonstrated multiple optimizations that can be made to these algorithms to further their scalability.

This paper is organized as follows: Sect. 2 presents related work. The necessary background to this work is presented in Sect. 3, which includes a discussion on the serial version of Dijkstra's algorithm and the Bellman-Ford algorithm. We discuss our parallelization of these algorithms in Sects. 4 and 5, respectively, and follow this discussion with an experimental evaluation in Sect. 6. Finally, we offer our conclusions in Sect. 7.

2   Related Work

There has been a considerable amount of work on the parallelization of both Dijkstra's algorithm and the Bellman-Ford algorithm for solving the SSSP problem. The majority of this work is (i) Message Passing Interface (MPI)-based or (ii) Graphics Processing Unit (GPU)-based.

With respect to (i), there are multiple works focusing on either Dijkstra's or Bellman-Ford's SSSP algorithm in MPI. Edmonds et al. [5] adapted multiple versions of Dijkstra's algorithm including the modifications by Crauser et al. [6] and Eager Dijkstra [7] into the Parallel Boost Graph Library (Parallel BGL). In [8], the authors developed a MapReduce library using a thin-MPI layer and adapted the Bellman-Ford algorithm for their library. Cahkaravarthy et al. [9] derived a hybrid algorithm for SSSP that is a combination of Bellman-Ford and the Delta-Stepping SSSP algorithm [10], where the algorithm initially uses Bellman-Ford for several iterations before switching to a Delta-Stepping approach. This approach was used in order to lower the required amount of relaxations per iteration, which increased performance. In [11], the authors developed an algorithm called Dijkstra Strip-Mined Relaxation (DSMR), which partitions graphs based on a set of vertices and their remote adjacent vertices called halo vertices. The subgraph partitions are then taken through three stages of updates: (1) local vertices, (2) halo vertices, and (3) any local vertices that were updated by halos vertices.

For (ii), there are several works focused on adapting the SSSP algorithms to the GPU. Martín et al. [12] took an initial look at parallelizing Dijkstra's for CUDA while taking into account the synchronization requirement between CUDA threads. Davidson et al. [13] developed three general optimizations for SSSP algorithms, but show the effectiveness of these optimizations with Dijkstra's and Bellman-Ford. The optimizations include Workfront Sweep to determine the next vertices to execute in an iteration, Near-Far piles in order to separate near vertices from far vertices, and the bucketing of both near and far vertices. *H-BF* [14] is a hybridization of Bellman-Ford that makes use of frontier propagation as well as edge classification to increase the algorithm's efficiency on GPUs.

Our work is different from those listed here as we do not limit the effectiveness of our implementations to smaller scales (i.e., GPU-based solutions) and, because we make use of OpenSHMEM, our algorithms are capable of taking advantage of the high performance implementations of OpenSHMEM and its one-sided communication, allowing us to create both optimized synchronous and asynchronous implementations.

3 Background

In this section, we review the serial versions of both Dijkstra's algorithm and Bellman-Ford.

3.1 Dijkstra's Algorithm

Dijkstra's algorithm is one of the best-known solutions to the SSSP problem for undirected and directed graphs with non-negative weights. It is a greedy algorithm that identifies the nth vertex nearest to the source on the nth iteration, with ties broken arbitrarily; when a path to a vertex is identified, it is guaranteed to be the shortest path. It is for this reason that Dijkstra's algorithm is often referred to as a label-setting algorithm.

The algorithm begins by marking the source with a distance of zero and an initial distance of infinity to all other vertices. On each iteration, the algorithm identifies the vertex with the smallest marked distance that has not been previously visited and, after marking it as visited, sets it as the current vertex. Then, all of the neighbors of the current vertex are considered and a temporary distance is calculated; the temporary distance is taken to be the distance marked on the current vertex plus the weight of the edge to the neighbor under consideration. If the temporary distance is less than that of the currently marked distance, the marked distance is updated to the temporary distance. The algorithm proceeds until all vertices have been visited, or all unvisited vertices have a marked distance of infinity. If an efficient heap data structure is used to identify the next current vertex on each iteration of the algorithm, Dijkstra's algorithm can be one of the most efficient algorithms for solving the SSSP problem. The pseudocode for this algorithm is shown in Algorithm 1.

Require: G, a weighted graph
Require: src, a source vertex
1: **function** DIJKSTRA(G, src)
2:     **for** v in $V(G)$ **do**
3:         $distance[v] \leftarrow \infty$
4:         $path[v] \leftarrow null$
5:         $Queue.push(v, dst)$
6:     **end for**
7:     $Queue.decrease(src, 0)$
8:     **while** $Queue$ is not empty **do**
9:         $v \leftarrow Queue.pop()$
10:        **for** u in $\Gamma(v)$ **do**
11:            RELAX($v, u, \text{edge}(v, u)$)
12:        **end for**
13:    **end while**
14:    **return** $distance$, $path$
15: **end function**

1: **function** RELAX(v, u, e)
2:     $tmp \leftarrow distance[v] + \text{weight}(e)$
3:     **if** $distance[u] > tmp$ **then**
4:         $distance[u] \leftarrow tmp$
5:         $path[u] \leftarrow v$
6:         $Queue.decrease(u, distance[u])$
7:     **end if**
8: **end function**

Algorithm 1. Serial Dijkstra's Algorithm

3.2   Bellman-Ford

The Bellman-Ford algorithm discovers the shortest path between a source and destination vertex on a weighted graph, which may contain positive and negative edges. The algorithm uses two data structures, which are: (i) a tentative distance array, *distance*, and (ii) a predecessor array, *path*. The tentative distance array contains the current distance value for a particular vertex. The predecessor array contains the vertex label of the vertex to be visited prior to this vertex. The algorithm operates by iterating over each vertex and its edges, relaxing the edges to adjacent vertices, which may update the distance and predecessor values. This update occurs if the distance of the vertex and the weight of the edge is less than the distance of the adjacent vertex. This algorithm can be seen in Algorithm 2.

Require: G, a weighted graph
Require: src, a source vertex
1: **function** BELLMANFORD(G, src)
2:     **for** v in $V(G)$ **do**
3:         $distance[v] \leftarrow \infty$
4:         $path[v] \leftarrow null$
5:     **end for**
6:     $distance[src] \leftarrow 0$
7:     **for** $k = 1$ to $|V| - 1$ **do**
8:         **for** v in $V(G)$ **do**
9:             **for** u in $\Gamma(v)$ **do**
10:                RELAX($v, u, \text{edge}(v, u)$)
11:            **end for**
12:        **end for**
13:    **end for**
14:    **return** $distance$, $path$
15: **end function**

1: **function** RELAX(v, u, e)
2:     $tmp \leftarrow distance[v] + \text{weight}(e)$
3:     **if** $distance[u] > tmp$ **then**
4:         $distance[u] \leftarrow tmp$
5:         $path[u] \leftarrow v$
6:     **end if**
7: **end function**

Algorithm 2. Serial Bellman-Ford

4   Parallelization of Dijkstra's

Each iteration of the main loop of Dijkstra's algorithm, which identifies the next closest vertex to the source, must be done in serial. Thus, only the portion of the algorithm responsible for updating the marked distances on the neighbors of the current vertex can be parallelized. When mapping Dijkstra's algorithm to OpenSHMEM, we have chosen to store only a portion of the priority queue on the symmetric heap, rather than storing the graph on the symmetric heap. This enables the number of reads/writes to symmetric memory to be determined ahead of time, as will be shown shortly. While not all communication networks are the same, communication is generally an expensive operation, and knowing the amount of communication ahead of time can be useful for predicting performance.

In order to partition the work for Dijkstra's algorithm, each Processing Element (PE) will be assigned a contiguous partition of vertices from the graph. Each PE will store, in local memory, only those edges in the graph that have end points within its assigned partition of the vertices. In addition, each PE will maintain a local priority queue containing only those vertices in its assigned partition. On each iteration of the main loop of Dijkstra's algorithm, every PE will write its locally assigned vertex of minimum marked distance to the symmetric heap on some master process (e.g., PE 0). The master process will then determine and broadcast the vertex with the absolute minimum marked distance to every PE. At this point, every PE will know the current vertex and the PE responsible for the current vertex can remove it from its local priority queue. Then, every PE can continue to execute Dijkstra's algorithm as normal with respect to its locally assigned partition of vertices. These modifications can be seen in Algorithm 3.

It is easy to place an upper bound on the number of times that the PEs must communicate in our OpenSHMEM version of Dijkstra's algorithm. It is

Require: G, a weighted graph
Require: src, a source vertex
1: **function** PARALLELDIJKSTRA(G, src, v_{start}, v_{end})
2:    **for** $v_{start} \leq v \leq v_{end}$ in $V(G)$ **do**
3:       $distance[v] \leftarrow \infty$
4:       $path[v] \leftarrow null$
5:       $Queue.push(v, dst)$
6:    **end for**
7:    $Queue.decrease(src, 0)$
8:    **while** $Queue$ is not empty **do**
9:       $v \leftarrow$ FINDMIN($rank$)
10:      **for** u in $\Gamma(v)$ **do**
11:         RELAX(v, u, edge(v, u))
12:      **end for**
13:   **end while**
14:   **return** $distance$, $path$
15: **end function**

1: **function** RELAX(v, u, e)
2:    $tmp \leftarrow distance[v] + weight(e)$
3:    **if** $distance[u] > tmp$ **then**
4:       $distance[u] \leftarrow tmp$
5:       $path[u] \leftarrow v$
6:       $Queue.decrease(u, distance[u])$
7:    **end if**
8: **end function**

1: **function** FINDMIN($rank$)
2:    $p, v \leftarrow Queue.peek()$
3:    PUT(shared[$rank$], (p, v), MASTER)
4:    **if** $rank =$ MASTER **then**
5:       $p, v \leftarrow$ MIN($shared$)
6:    **end if**
7:    BCAST(p, v)
8:    **if** $v = Queue.peek()$ **then**
9:       $Queue.pop()$
10:   **end if**
11:   **return** v
12: **end function**

Algorithm 3. Parallel Dijkstra's Algorithm

clear that the maximum number of times that each PE must write its locally marked vertex of minimum distance to the master process (as well the number of times that the master process must broadcast the globally marked vertex of minimum distance) is equal to the number of times that the main loop of Dijkstra's algorithm is executed. In the case that all vertices are reachable from the source vertex, this is precisely equal to the number of vertices in the graph.

4.1 Communication Optimization

A non-trivial amount of communication is required in order to determine the globally marked vertex of minimum distance. We have found that the most efficient way of accomplishing this is to have every PE inform a master PE of their locally marked vertex of minimum distance through the use of symmetric memory using a non-blocking *Put*. The master PE then determines the globally marked vertex of minimum distance, which is then broadcasted to all other PE. It is possible that, on some PEs, the locally marked vertex of minimum distance will not change during an iteration of Dijkstra's algorithm. And so, a PE need only update the master when the root of the priority queue changes in some way, hence reducing total communication and related resource contention. From this point forward, the naive approach shall be referred to as the broadcast (or BCAST) version, and the attempt to minimize communication will be referred to as the broadcast with update (or BCAST w/ Update) version.

5 Parallelization of Bellman-Ford

In this section, we will discuss the parallelization of the Bellman-Ford algorithm, the optimizations that may be made, and the realization of the algorithm with optimizations in OpenSHMEM.

5.1 Parallel Bellman-Ford Algorithm

Parallelizing the Bellman-Ford algorithm in Algorithm 2 is simplistic due to the iterative updates of the distance and predecessor values for the graph's vertices. Because the algorithm allows for iterative update operations on these values, each PE can simply iterate over its local set of vertices. Thus, for the parallelization of the algorithm, we need to focus on two components: (i) the partitioning of the graph dataset to determine the local set of vertices and (ii) ensuring the correctness of remote operations. For (i), because the workload is not known prior to execution, a simple approach to partitioning is to uniformly partition vertices between PEs. With respect to (ii), ensuring the correctness of local and remote update operations can be accomplished with OpenSHMEM's AMOs (i.e., *compare-and-swap*). This algorithm can be seen in Algorithm 4.

```
Require: G: a weighted partitioned graph          1: function RELAX(v, u, e)
Require: src: a source Vertex                     2:    du ← GET(distance[u])
 1: function PARALLELBELLMANFORD(G, src)          3:    tmp ← distance[v] + weight(e)
 2:    for v ∈ local V(G) do                      4:    if du > tmp then
 3:       distance[v] = ∞                          5:       ATOMIC_CSWAP(distance[u], tmp)
 4:       path[v] = null                           6:       ATOMIC_CSWAP(path[u], v)
 5:    end for                                     7:    end if
 6:    if src is local then                        8: end function
 7:       distance[src] = 0
 8:    end if
 9:    for k = 1 to |V| − 1 do
10:       for v in local V(G) do
11:          for u in Γ(v) do
12:             RELAX(v, u, edge(v, u))
13:          end for
14:       end for
15:       BARRIER
16:    end for
17:    return distance, path
18: end function
```

Algorithm 4. Parallel Bellman-Ford

5.2 Optimizations

In order to further improve the efficiency and scalability of Algorithm 4, we consider three areas of optimizations: the algorithm, the implementation, and the load balancing between PEs.

5.2.1 Algorithmic Optimizations

Common algorithmic optimizations include: (i) the removal of self-loops from the graph, (ii) the determination of required work for the next iteration, and (iii) the ability to determine convergence [13, 14].

For (i), self-loop removal reduces unnecessary work performed within the shortest path calculation. This is possible because a self-loop will never result in a shorter path. Pruning this edge will reduce the amount of relaxations and decrease the required memory for the algorithm.

With respect to (ii), during an iteration, a PE is required to call the relax function on all adjacent vertices to update their distance and predecessor values if appropriate. However, after the first few iterations, the amount of relaxation calls resulting in updates decreases, which results in wasted work. Instead, the use of a distributed queue or array to maintain a list of "active" vertices can reduce the number of relaxations.

Building on (ii), (iii) allows PEs to determine if they have converged and finish execution. This is accomplished through collective communication, such as an *all-reduce* operation, at the end of an iteration. The use of an *all-reduce* also has the benefit of synchronizing the PEs, which allows it to replace the *barrier* on line 15 of Algorithm 4.

5.2.2 Implementation Optimizations

Based on Algorithm 4, the algorithm uses two atomic operations to set the distance and predecessor values. Because the relax function could be called multiple times to update the same vertex, the use of multiple atomic operations can become expensive with large datasets.

To improve the efficiency of the relax operation, the distance and predecessor arrays can be merged into a single array with each index corresponding to both values. This can be implemented with the value of an index being partitioned such that the predecessor values occupy the upper bits and the distance values occupy the lower bits. Because the distance value cannot be greater than the maximum weight of an edge in the graph, this will not greatly restrict the size of supported graphs.

5.2.3   Load Balancing Optimizations

Without prior knowledge of the possible workload, it is likely that many PEs will remain idle during the execution of the algorithm assuming a uniformly distributed graph partitioning. With a synchronous *all-reduce* operation used at the end of an iteration as suggested in Sect. 5.2.1, the amount of time a PE spends idle waiting on the completion of the *all-reduce* could be large depending on workload imbalance and the scale of the graph. However, if the PEs were allowed to operate as work is presented to them (i.e., asynchronous operation), then PEs will be able to work immediately rather than waiting for the next iteration. The difficulty with this approach stems in the agreement protocol on when convergence is achieved.

To determine convergence, a simple first approach is to inform all other PEs of convergence. More clearly, when a PE is idle, it informs all other PE it is idle by setting a *convergence flag* on a shared array. Then the PE will loop over all other PEs values in the shared array to determine if convergence has occurred. If convergence has occurred, the PE will proceed to perform the loop again in order to ensure completion.

5.3   Realizing Parallel Bellman-Ford with OpenSHMEM

To implement the Bellman-Ford algorithm described in Sect. 5.1 with the optimizations discussed in Sect. 5.2, we will discuss the data structures used for the implementation as well as the graph partitioning and realization of the algorithm.

With respect to the data structures to implement the algorithm, we made use of four distributed arrays that were allocated on the symmetric heap. The first two arrays were the tentative distance and predecessor arrays, which were explained earlier in Sect. 3.2. The last two distributed arrays were related to the determination of an active PE and active vertices discussed in Sect. 5.2.1.

To perform the graph partitioning, the graph is read in from a file and partitioned uniformly among PEs. During this process, each PE adds the vertices within its partition and their edges. Additionally, the implementation tracks the in and out edges of a vertex to determine if the vertex is a purely local vertex (i.e., all in and out edges are local to the PE), which does not require *compare-and-swap* operations on the distance or predecessor arrays in order to maintain correctness. During the relax function, operations on purely local vertices do not make use OpenSHMEM's communication library and are direct assignments. However, if a vertex has a remote edge, then atomic operations are used to guarantee correctness.

6   Experimental Evaluation

This section provides a detailed evaluation of the algorithms discussed in Sects. 4 and 5. In order to evaluate the efficiency of our algorithms, we compare them against the well-known and peer-reviewed Parallel BGL [5]. The default version of Dijkstra's algorithm in Parallel BGL is based on Crauser et al.'s work [6]. In the case of the Bellman-Ford algorithm, we compare against Parallel BGL's implementation of Delta-Stepping with delta set to the maximum weight; this reverts the Delta-Stepping algorithm to Bellman-Ford [10].

For the remainder of this section, we will discuss the datasets and testbed used to evaluate our algorithms and present our evaluation using synthetic R-MAT and small-world network graphs along with real-world graphs from Facebook, Twitter, and LiveJournal as well as road maps of California and Texas from the SNAP dataset [15].

6.1   Datasets and Testbed

In order to demonstrate the performance and scalability of the algorithms on different types of workloads, several types of graphs were selected for evaluation. To evaluate the weak scaling properties of the algorithms, R-MAT and small-world networks are used. In addition to R-MAT and small-world networks, several real-world datasets (e.g., Facebook, Twitter, LiveJournal, and road maps) were taken to explore the strong scaling properties of the algorithms.

The R-MAT graph generator uses recursive matrix partitioning in an attempt to generate real-world graphs. It is capable of generating both directed and undirected graphs, with weights if desired. Graphs with various real-world properties can be can be generated including scale-free graphs (i.e., a graph in which the degree distribution follows a power law), graphs containing communities and sub-communities, and graphs with small diameters [16].

A small-world network is a graph in which the neighbors of a vertex have a high probability of being connected by an edge, but the majority of vertices in the graph are not neighbors of each other. The (global) clustering coefficient tends to be high, implying the graph contains many cliques/near-cliques. In addition, the diameter of the graph tends to be small; small-world networks are so named as they exhibit the small-world phenomenon (i.e., six degrees of separation) [17].

We have selected several real-world graphs to further evaluate the strong scaling capabilities of our algorithm implementations. Graphs of Facebook, Twitter, and LiveJournal were selected as they represent well-known social media platforms. Graphs of the road networks of California and Texas were selected because they display characteristics contrary to what is common in many social networks; social network graphs tend to have small diameters and larger clustering coefficients, while road networks tend to have large diameters and small clustering coefficients. The details of the real-world graphs can be found in Table 1.

Table 1. Real-world graph details

	Facebook	Twitter	LiveJournal	Road-CA	Road-TX
Vertices	4,039	81,306	4,847,571	1,971,281	1,393,383
Edges	176,468	2,420,766	68,993,773	5,516,784	3,805,842
Clustering coef.	0.6055	0.5653	0.2742	0.0464	0.0470
Diameter	8	7	16	849	1054

The testbed for this evaluation was the Titan system located at the *Oak Ridge Leadership Computing Facility* (OLCF). Titan is composed of 18,688 compute nodes containing a single 2.2 GHz AMD Opteron processor and 32 GB of memory. Each compute node uses the Gemini interconnect for communication.

6.2   Evaluation with R-MAT Graphs

The R-MAT graphs used in our experiments were generated with parameters $a = 0.45$, $b = 0.22$, $c = 0.22$, $d = 0.11$. These parameters resulted in an average vertex degree of 16 for the graphs generated. We made use of the same scaling parameters for graph generation as the Graph500 benchmark [18]. More clearly, the number of vertices in the graph is 2^n where n is the scale (i.e., a scale of 20 will result in 2^{20} vertices). Strong scaling evaluations were made using R-MAT graphs with a scale of 20, while the weak scaling evaluations were made using a range from 16 to 24. Thus, with strong scaling, the algorithm is using a graph dataset with roughly 1 million vertices and 16 million edges. The weak scaling, at its largest (i.e., a scale of 24), is a dataset with over 16 million vertices and over 268 million edges.

The results of strong and weak scaling for parallel versions of Dijkstra's algorithm are shown in Fig. 1. In the case of strong scaling, it can be seen that adding more PEs tends to increase the runtime for each of the algorithms. While this may initially seem counterintuitive, it is due to the fact that there is relatively

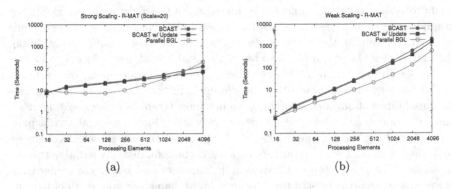

(a)   (b)

Fig. 1. Scaling for parallel Dijkstra on R–MAT graphs

little work to be carried out in the main loop of Dijkstra's algorithm. Since the degree distribution of the R-MAT graphs follow a power law, the majority of vertices have very few edges. And so, regardless of the partitioning strategy, there is not a lot of work that can be distributed to a large number of PEs. The majority of the PEs sit idle on most iterations of Dijkstra's main loop, and synchronization overhead between loop iterations causes the runtime to increase as PEs are added.

This situation is only exacerbated if the problem size per PE is held constant and additional PEs are used. As expected, this is due to the additional communication overhead required as the number of PEs increase. From the runtime results, there appears to be a significant benefit to only updating the master PE's view of the local priority queues when the data is changed. This benefit ranges from roughly 3% to 45% reduction in execution time for the strong scaling experiment when compared to blindly updating the priority queue on every iteration. Additionally, for weak scaling this benefit ranges from roughly 1% to 33%. This becomes more apparent for larger numbers of PEs as there is more opportunity to eliminate unnecessary communication.

The results show that Parallel BGL's implementation of Dijkstra's algorithm performs better than our distributed shared memory implementations, specifically when the number of PEs are between 16 and 1024 for strong scaling and 16 and 4096 for weak scaling. However, if the runtime trends continue, Parallel BGL will end up performing worse. The reason for this is most likely an unbalanced workload seen in the R-MAT graphs. As previously mentioned, we distributed the edges of the graph based on the target vertex of the edges. And so, it is possible that some PE can be assigned a larger collection of edges than others, resulting in a load imbalance. Again, this partitioning strategy was chosen in an attempt to reduce the number of reads and writes to symmetric memory. Parallel BGL uses a different partitioning strategy, and attempts to distribute the adjacency list representation of the graph evenly across PEs. This results in a more balanced workload at the expense of more communication between PEs.

With respect to the evaluation of Bellman-Ford with R-MAT graphs, we will evaluate three implementations of the algorithms presented in Sect. 5. These implementations build on each other and begin with (i) bellman-ford composed of optimizations from prior work, (ii) with the *compare-and-swap* reduction optimization, and (iii) the asynchronous execution. The result of the strong and weak scaling evaluation can be seen in Fig. 2.

With respect to the strong scaling characteristics for the Bellman-Ford modifications, the performance of both the single cswap modification and the asynchronous modification out perform Parallel BGL's Delta-Stepping algorithm as more PEs are used to solve the problem. The primary reason for this is the reduced need for synchronization between PEs. For Parallel BGL, the implementation of the algorithm that is used requires multiple barriers and all-reduce operations in order to perform label correction, while the synchronous bellman-ford with a single cswap requires only atomics and a single all-reduce. This causes Parallel BGL to decrease in performance dramatically when using more than 128 PEs.

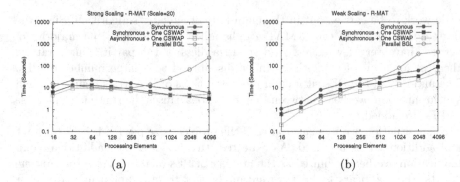

Fig. 2. Scaling for Bellman-Ford on R-MAT graphs

For the weak scaling characteristics, the amount of communication required between PEs in all evaluated versions cause the algorithm execution time to increase. This is especially true for Parallel BGL after 128 PEs. Prior to this point, Parallel BGL and the synchronous single cswap are similar with respect to performance.

Overall, the asynchronous version proves to perform the best of the various approaches. This is due to the non-uniform layout of edges within the graph as it follows the power law. This results in a graph with few vertices with many edges and many vertices with few edges. This causes an unbalanced workload for the PEs in the job. Because the asynchronous version can perform work whenever it is possible, it is able to immediately work when work is available. When compared to Parallel BGL, this results in performance improvement of between 7% up to 98% in the case of strong scaling and between 24% and 90% in the case of weak scaling.

6.3   Evaluation with Small-World Networks

We use the Watts-Strogatz model for generating small-world networks with a rewiring probability of $p = 0$, which results in a regular graph [17]. We chose to use small-world networks in addition to R-MAT graphs because small-world networks have a fixed number of edges per vertex, resulting in uniform workloads. For our experiments, we employ a scale similar to that of the R-MAT graphs, and every vertex has 1024 neighbors. Again, we evaluate the strong and weak scaling characteristics for our algorithms. For strong scaling, we created a small-world network with a scale of 15. This resulted in a graph with 32 thousand vertices, each having 1024 edges (i.e., over 33 million edges in total). The weak scaling were made using a range from 11 to 19. And so, the largest graph used for weak scaling contained half a million vertices with half a billion edges.

The scaling results for parallel Dijkstra's algorithm can be seen in Fig. 3. As with the R-MAT graphs, the addition of PEs causes an increase in runtime. Also, the BCAST w/ Update continues to perform better than the regular BCAST algorithm. Unlike the runtime results for the R-MAT graphs, the runtime for

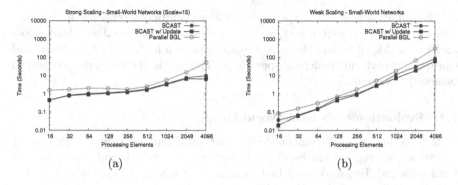

Fig. 3. Scaling for parallel Dijkstra on small-world networks

Parallel BGL's Dijkstra's algorithm is worse than our OpenSHMEM implementations. This is probably due to a more balanced workload seen in the small-world networks, allowing for more active PEs on each iteration of Dijkstra's algorithm.

The results of the Bellman-Ford experiments can be seen in Fig. 4. With respect to strong scaling, the synchronous approaches appear to perform more consistently over all, but do not scale well. This is due to the amount of relax operations per vertex. Regardless of needing to perform an update during the relaxation operation, every edge from a vertex must be checked if it is active, which requires a considerable amount of communication. This limits the scaling capabilities. However, at each amount of PEs, the Parallel BGL implementation performed worse than any of the OpenSHMEM versions. Similar results to the strong scaling experiment can be see with the weak scaling experiment. For this experiment, what can be seen, with respect to the synchronous approaches, is that the amount of communication and work stays constant as we increase the data size. This keeps the performance relatively stable. However, the asynchronous approach suffers from continually checking to determine if all of the PEs have converged or not.

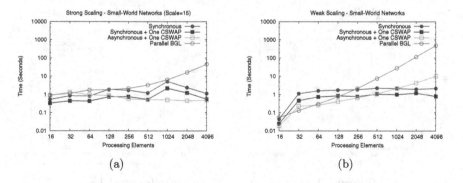

Fig. 4. Scaling for Bellman-Ford on small-world networks

Overall, in both scaling experiments, the asynchronous version suffered compared to the results seen in Sect. 6.2. This is due to the balanced workload across all PEs. In this situation, the synchronous approach has an equal workload and can quickly perform reduction operations. Thus, it is the preferred method in balanced workloads.

6.4 Evaluation with Real-World Graphs

In this section, we will present the evaluation of our algorithms with respect to real-world graphs from Facebook, Twitter, LiveJournal, and road maps for California and Texas. We will first evaluate our modified Dijkstra's algorithm and then Bellman-Ford.

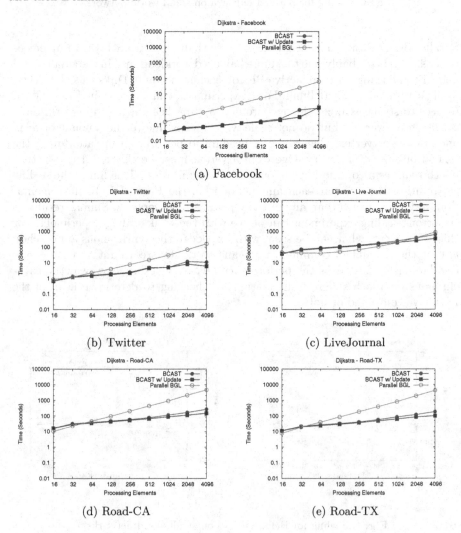

(a) Facebook

(b) Twitter   (c) LiveJournal

(d) Road-CA   (e) Road-TX

Fig. 5. Strong scaling for parallel Dijkstra on real-world graphs

The strong scaling runtime results for parallel Dijkstra's algorithm can be seen in Fig. 5. As before, the addition of PEs increases the runtime for every algorithm on each of the datasets. The only exception to this is Parallel BGL on the LiveJournal graphs, in which there is a very small initial reduction in runtime for 32 and 64 PEs. Our OpenSHMEM based approaches outperform Parallel BGL's Dijkstra's algorithm on all real-world datasets except LiveJournal. Of the real-world graphs selected, the LiveJournal graph is the most similar to the R-MAT graphs, with the performance similar to that as seen in Sect. 6.2.

With respect to our modified version of Bellman-Ford, the results of the evaluation using real-world graphs can be seen in Fig. 6. The results for the Facebook,

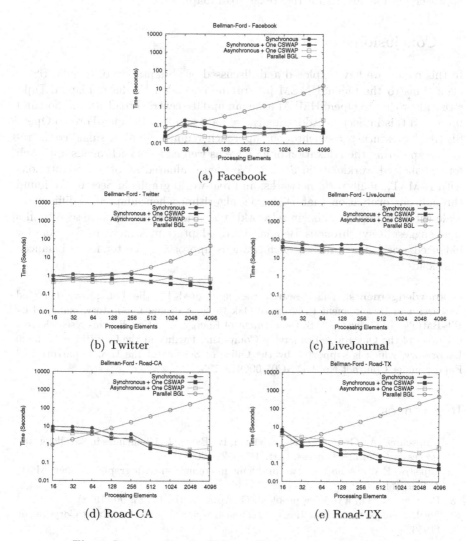

(a) Facebook

(b) Twitter

(c) LiveJournal

(d) Road-CA

(e) Road-TX

Fig. 6. Strong scaling for Bellman-Ford on real-world graphs

Twitter, and LiveJournal graphs follow the results seen in Sect. 6.2, where the workload is unbalanced due to the number of edges each individual vertex has. This causes the asynchronous approach to perform best for each graph with less than 512 PEs. With 512 and more PEs, the performance of the asynchronous approach begins to suffer due to continually checking for convergence.

Like the social media graphs were similar to the R-MAT results, so are the road maps similar to the small-world network results. In these graphs, 98% of the vertices contain between one and four edges, which results in a very balanced workload. From there, it can be seen that the single cswap optimized approach is the best performing with a 92% performance advantage over the asynchronous approach with 4096 PEs for the Texas road map.

7 Conclusions

In this paper, we have explored and discussed our adaptation of popular SSSP algorithms to the OpenSHMEM programming model. We have adapted Dijkstra's algorithm to OpenSHMEM using an update-centric broadcast method and presented this in Sect. 4. Additionally, we have adapted Bellmen-Ford to Open-SHMEM presenting a synchronous approach requiring only a single compare-and-swap during the relaxation of an edge as well as an asynchronous approach for unbalanced workloads in Sect. 5. We then evaluated all of our adaptations with R-MAT, small-world networks, and real-world graphs in Sect. 6. We found through our evaluation that Dijkstra's algorithm when adapted is difficult to scale with balanced or unbalanced workloads. Additionally, we have seen results that suggest a synchronous Bellman-Ford adaptation is more performant for balanced workloads while an asynchronous approach is better for unbalanced workloads.

Acknowledgements. This research was sponsored by the Laboratory Directed Research and Development Program of Oak Ridge National Laboratory, managed by UT-Battelle, LLC, for the U.S. Department of Energy. Additionally, this research used resources of the Oak Ridge Leadership Computing Facility at the Oak Ridge National Laboratory, which is supported by the Office of Science of the U.S. Department of Energy under Contract No. DE-AC05-00OR22725.

References

1. Lumsdaine, A., Gregor, D., Hendrickson, B., Berry, J.: Challenges in parallel graph processing. Parallel Process. Lett. **17**, 5–20 (2007)
2. Dijkstra, E.W.: A note on two problems in connexion with graphs. Numer. Math. **1**, 269–271 (1959)
3. Bellman, R.: On a routing problem. Q. Appl. Math. **16**, 87–90 (1958)
4. Ford, L.A.: Network flow theory. Technical report P-923, The Rand Corporation (1956)

5. Edmonds, N., Breuer, A., Gregor, D.P., Lumsdaine, A.: Single-source shortest paths with the parallel boost graph library. In: The Shortest Path Problem, Proceedings of a DIMACS Workshop, Piscataway, New Jersey, USA, 13–14 November 2006, pp. 219–248 (2006)
6. Crauser, A., Mehlhorn, K., Meyer, U., Sanders, P.: A parallelization of Dijkstra's shortest path algorithm. In: Brim, L., Gruska, J., Zlatuška, J. (eds.) MFCS 1998. LNCS, vol. 1450, pp. 722–731. Springer, Heidelberg (1998). https://doi.org/10.1007/BFb0055823
7. Crauser, A., Mehlhorn, K., Meyer, U., Sanders, P.: Parallelizing Dijkstra's shortest path algorithm. Technical report, MPI-Informatik (1998)
8. Plimpton, S.J., Devine, K.D.: Mapreduce in MPI for large-scale graph algorithms. Parallel Comput. **37**, 610–632 (2011)
9. Chakaravarthy, V.T., Checconi, F., Murali, P., Petrini, F., Sabharwal, Y.: Scalable single source shortest path algorithms for massively parallel systems. IEEE Trans. Parallel Distrib. Syst. **28**, 2031–2045 (2017)
10. Meyer, U., Sanders, P.: Delta-stepping: a parallelizable shortest path algorithm. J. Algorithms **49**, 114–152 (2003)
11. Maleki, S., Nguyen, D., Lenharth, A., Garzarán, M., Padua, D., Pingali, K.: DSMR: a shared and distributed memory algorithm for single-source shortest path problem. SIGPLAN Not. **51**, 39:1–39:2 (2016)
12. Martín, P.J., Torres, R., Gavilanes, A.: CUDA solutions for the SSSP problem. In: Allen, G., Nabrzyski, J., Seidel, E., van Albada, G.D., Dongarra, J., Sloot, P.M.A. (eds.) ICCS 2009. LNCS, vol. 5544, pp. 904–913. Springer, Heidelberg (2009). https://doi.org/10.1007/978-3-642-01970-8_91
13. Davidson, A., Baxter, S., Garland, M., Owens, J.D.: Work-efficient parallel GPU methods for single-source shortest paths. In: 2014 IEEE 28th International Parallel and Distributed Processing Symposium, pp. 349–359 (2014)
14. Busato, F., Bombieri, N.: An efficient implementation of the Bellman-Ford algorithm for Kepler GPU architectures. IEEE Trans. Parallel Distrib. Syst. **27**, 2222–2233 (2016)
15. Leskovec, J., Krevl, A.: SNAP datasets: Stanford large network dataset collection (2014). http://snap.stanford.edu/data
16. Chakrabarti, D., Zhan, Y., Faloutsos, C.: R-MAT: a recursive model for graph mining, pp. 442–446 (2004)
17. Watts, D.J., Strogatz, S.H.: Collective dynamics of 'small-world' networks. Nature **393**, 440–442 (1998)
18. Bader, D.A., Berry, J., Kahan, S., Murphy, R., Riedy, E.J., Willcock, J.: Graph 500 Benchmark Specification 1.2 (2017)

Efficient Breadth First Search on Multi-GPU Systems Using GPU-Centric OpenSHMEM

Sreeram Potluri[1]([✉]), Anshuman Goswami[1], Manjunath Gorentla Venkata[2], and Neena Imam[2]

[1] NVIDIA Corporation, Santa Clara, USA
spotluri@nvidia.com
[2] Computer Science and Mathematics Division,
Oak Ridge National Laboratory, Oak Ridge, USA

Abstract. NVSHMEM is an implementation of OpenSHMEM for NVIDIA GPUs which allows communication to be issued from inside CUDA kernels. In this work, we present an implementation of Breadth First Search for multi-GPU systems using NVSHMEM. We analyze the benefits and bottlenecks of moving fine-grained communication into CUDA kernels. Using our implementation of BFS, we achieve up to 75% improvement in performance compared to a CUDA-aware MPI-based implementation, in the best case.

1 Introduction

Graphs have been shown to naturally model data sources, relationship between the data sources, and interactions between them. This has led to graphs being used to model data produced by a variety of daily-life activities like social network posts and financial transactions. In addition, more voluminous data sources like sensors that observe neutron scattering or other scientific instruments that collect weather samples, are also starting to use graphs to model the captured data. As the set of applications that use graphs to model data grows, the size of graphs to be processed can vary from millions of vertices to tens of billions of vertices. Processing graphs with billions of vertices requires systems with large memory capacity, massive processing power and a high-performance network.

Some of the growing computation and memory needs of graph applications are addressed by using HPC systems. This trend will accelerate as we move towards exascale given that the architectures of these systems with petabytes of memory, processing accelerators, and high-performing networks are better equipped to efficiently run data-intensive applications. This can be seen with progressive improvement in the Graph500 results [1]. As the HPC systems with computing accelerators, particularly with GPUs, are becoming highly common, many graph algorithms have been successfully adapted for HPC systems with GPUs [2,3].

Though modern GPU-based HPC systems have been successfully used for graph applications, using traditional programming models such as MPI for graph

© Springer International Publishing AG 2018
M. Gorentla Venkata et al. (Eds.): OpenSHMEM 2017, LNCS 10679, pp. 82–96, 2018.
https://doi.org/10.1007/978-3-319-73814-7_6

applications can result in performance drawbacks. For example, [3] adapted the Breadth First Search (BFS) algorithm and parallelized it for GPU-based systems. They achieved a significant improvement by reducing the number of communication episodes between GPUs and the amount of data exchanged. However, with this programming paradigm, the graph is processed by the GPU, and data and result exchanges are handled by the CPU, resulting in serialization when there is a need for data exchange between GPUs solving different parts of the graph. This has shown to impact both performance and scalability of applications [4].

In this paper, we address the serialization and performance challenges by using NVSHMEM, an *OpenSHMEM* based GAS programming paradigm for GPU-based HPC systems. Particularly, we evaluate the effectiveness of using GPU-initiated communication for BFS.

2   Background

2.1   Current Programming Model Approach for GPU-Based Systems

Most HPC applications ported to clusters accelerated with NVIDIA GPUs currently use an MPI+CUDA hybrid programming model. The application is split into phases of communication and computation with CPU orchestrating their execution. Computation is typically offloaded onto the GPUs while MPI communication is managed from the CPU.

The existing model requires frequent synchronization between GPU and CPU. The CPU has to be running at full-speed to ensure fast synchronization and hence will stay in a high power state even though it does little useful work. The synchronization between compute and communication phases typically require the GPU to be drained before starting the next phase which reduces the utilization of the GPU and also kills any opportunity of data locality and reuse. Computation and communication phases can be overlapped using CUDA streams but this often leads to greater code complexity. Further, the benefits of such overlap diminishes as applications are strong scaled where the overhead of synchronization and kernel launches can dominate the application runtime [4].

2.2   *OpenSHMEM*

OpenSHMEM is a PGAS (Partitioned Global Address Space) library interface specification. It includes routines, environment variables, and constants to implement a PGAS programming model as a library.

OpenSHMEM presents a PGAS view of execution contexts and memory model. The execution contexts in *OpenSHMEM* is an OS process identified by integer called Processing Element (PE). An *OpenSHMEM* program has private address space and shared address space. A PE allocates and stores its private data and control structures in the private address space. The shared address space in *OpenSHMEM* is presented as symmetric objects, which are accessible by all PEs in an *OpenSHMEM* program. The symmetric objects are allocated using a collective allocation operation in *OpenSHMEM*.

OpenSHMEM provides routines for communication and synchronization with other PEs. The communication in *OpenSHMEM* is primarily one-sided. It provides many variants of Put, Get and Atomic operations to access and modify symmetric data objects that are located on remote PEs. It provides Quiet and Fence which complete communication and orders communication, respectively. It provides interfaces for collective communication and synchronization.

3   GPU-Initiated Communication Using NVSHMEM

NVSHMEM presents a programming approach using GPU-initiated communication which is motivated by the throughput oriented architecture of the GPU. The GPUs are designed to support tens of thousands of threads to achieve maximum parallel throughput. These threads are extremely light weight and thousands of threads are queued up for work (in groups called warps). If one warp must wait on a memory access, another warp can start executing in its place. As a separate set of registers is allocated for all active threads, there is no need for swapping of registers or state. As a consequence, this execution model has inherent latency hiding capabilities with minimal scheduling overheads. With the increasing amount of parallelism, GPU architectures can have enough state to hide latencies not only to local GPU device memory but also to remote GPU memory over a network. GPU-initiated communication can be used to take advantage of this inherent capability of the GPU hardware while relying on the CUDA programming paradigm that has been used for scaling within a GPU. Further, this improves programmability as developers will not have to rely on a hybrid model to orchestrate and overlap between different phases of the application.

The communication initiated and synced from within CUDA kernels will not only reduce the reliance on the CPU, additionally it also avoids existing synchronization overheads that limit the strong scaling. Also, to enhance the efficiency within a warp and reduce the pressure on the memory sub-system, the loads and stores can be coalesced by the hardware when alignment and access pattern requirements are met.

Using PGAS programming model such as *OpenSHMEM*, suits GPU-initiated communication better. The one-sided communication model of *OpenSHMEM* requires only the caller (origin) of the interface to be active, which matches the massive parallelism and dynamic scheduling model on the GPU. Further, a combination of global address space approach and semantics of *OpenSHMEM* communication interfaces such as Put and Get is a close match to load and stores on shared-memory space of GPU.

4   Baseline Multi-GPU BFS Code Using MPI

We use an MPI-based multi-GPU implementation of BFS from the work done by Bisson et al. [3] as the baseline in this paper. Their work loosely follows the

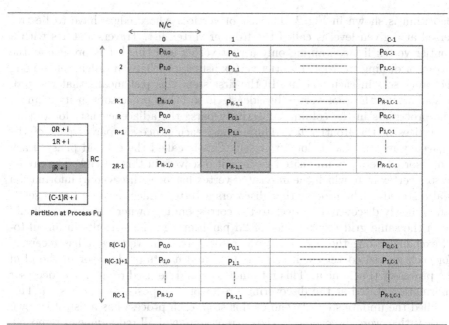

Fig. 1. Adjacency matrix decomposition among processors

Graph500 benchmark specifications. It generates in advance a list of edges with an R-MAT generator and measures the performances over 64 BFS operations started from random vertices. They do not strictly adhere to the Graph500 as they use 32bit vertices instead of the required minimum of 48bits. We make our changes based on this MPI version of BFS and compare the performance.

Graph Partitioning: The adjacency matrix that represents the graph is mapped onto a logical processor grid arranged as R rows and C columns. Partitioning is as shown in Fig. 1. The processor grid is mapped once horizontally and C times vertically, dividing the matrix in C blocks along the row and RC blocks along the column. This kind of partitioning has two key characteristics:

1. the edge lists of vertices handled by each processor are partitioned among processors in the same grid column.
2. the destination vertex on each edge is in the same grid row as the vertex owning that edge.

Such a partitioning helps limit communication within columns and rows, as explained later in this section. The adjacency matrices are stored in Compressed Sparse Column (CSC) format that allows processors to scan adjacency lists by accessing blocks of consecutive memory locations.

Parallel Implementation Using MPI: Graph traversal in the baseline version is implemented in a level-synchronous fashion. A high-level summary of the algorithm is shown in Fig. 2. The list of vertices whose edges have to be traversed at a given level is called the frontier vertex list. Traversal starts with a frontier vertex list containing only a root vertex and this list is present at the processor owning the root. Frontier vertex lists are exchanged (allgather) among the processors in each column. In the first step, this just means that the processor owning the root vertex broadcasts it to other processors in its column. The processors in the column collectively parse the adjacency lists for the set of vertices in the frontier list. This means, each processor parses part of the adjacency matrix that is local to itself. This is called the expand phase. Each processor gathers any un-visited vertices it discovers in this process. The predecessor (vertex from which the un-visited vertex has been discovered) information is also stored at the process that discovers a vertex. Each processor then sends lists of newly discovered vertices to the corresponding owner processors (should be in the same grid row because of 2d partitioning). This results in an all-to-all exchange along the row. Each processor parses the vertices it has received. For each un-visited vertex, it sets the level and it sets predecessor to the id of the processor that sent it. This information could be used to query predecessor information stored at the discovering processor as a post-processing step. This is called the update step. At end of this step, each process has a list of its own vertices that were discovered in the current step, will all redundancies removed. This list is then exchanged with the processes in the same grid column (allgather as mentioned earlier). Each step ends with a convergence check which calculates the sum of the lengths of frontier lists (Allreduce) at all the processors. The traversal goes to the next level if the aggregate length is non-zero.

That vertex lists exchanged between the processors are moved from GPU memory to CPU memory. The inter-processor exchange is then implemented using non-blocking MPI sends/recvs. The order in which MPI sends/recvs are issued is twiddled in-order to avoid congestion as is done in common implementation of MPI collectives. There are two variations in how the vertex information is exchanged. It can be exchanged as a bitmap (one bit per vertex, covering all N/RC vertices) where the bits corresponding to newly discovered vertices is set. It can also be exchanged as list of vertices (integer array). The base version used in this paper applies an optimization to use one of the two formats for different levels in a single traversal. It uses the general characteristic of RMAT graphs to statically decide which format is used in which level. The bitmap is used to exchange when large number of vertices are expected to discovered (levels 4 and 5). A vertex list is used when the number of vertices is expected to be smaller (all levels other than 4 and 5).

In Sect. 6.1, we optimize the base version using MVAPICH2, a CUDA-aware MPI library, which internally uses GPUDirect and hence uses direct PCIe/ NVLink paths between the GPUs for data movement. This provides a fair comparison between the MPI and NVSHMEM version, both using direct GPU-GPU paths over PCIe or NVLink.

```
while (frontier not empty) {
    Vertical exchange: allgather frontier list along grid columns
    Expand: local expansion
    Horizontal Exchange: exchange newly discovered vertices along grid rows
    Append: build new frontier vertex list
    Convergence check: allreduce frontier list size among all processors
}
```

Fig. 2. High-level summary of the base BFS version

5 DGX-1 GPU-Node Architecture

For one-sided communication in PGAS programming models like *OpenSHMEM* to be performant, it is helpful to have low cost fine-grained accesses across the shared global address space. When GPUs are connected through PCIe, there is significant degradation in the overall throughput that can be achieved when accessing peer GPU memory. To solve this performance bottleneck, NVIDIA recently announced the DGX-1 system shown in Fig. 3. It consists of eight Tesla P100 GPUs connected by *NVLink*, a high-speed interconnect enabling 5 to 12 times faster data sharing between the GPUs compared to PCIe. The DGX-1 system is also equipped with four EDR Mellanox ConnectX-4 InfiniBand NICs each configured with four ports and dual-socket 20-core Intel Xeon E5-2698 v4 (Broadwell) CPUs. Multiple DGX-1 systems can be connected to build a high-speed GPU cluster that can effectively balance the intra-node and the inter-node bandwidth between the GPUs.

The Tesla P100 GPUs has four *NVLink* connection points where each link offers a peak bandwidth of 20 GB/s. The DGX-1 network topology is a hybrid

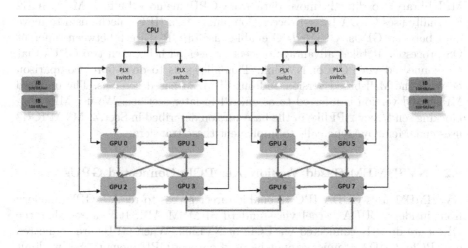

Fig. 3. System architecture of a DGX-1

cube-mesh where two groups of four GPUs are all-to-all connected and GPUs between the two groups are at most two *NVLink* hops away. The combined physical memory capacity on the GPUs in a DGX-1 system is 128 GB. To gauge how this measures up to real-world graph datasets, nearly the entire data from a month from the Google GDELT project's 2015 dataset consisting of over 1.5 billion location references can be processed in memory in a DGX-1 without sending any data over the network. As a result, the DGX-1 system makes for a very interesting platform to investigate communication libraries such as *OpenSHMEM* used in data-intensive graph algorithms like BFS.

6   Design

Here, we present an optimized base version of BFS discussed in Sect. 4, in order to provide a fair comparison between MPI and GPU-initiated SHMEM versions of the application. We then present two variations of the BFS implementation using SHMEM: one that uses peer-to-peer writes which works over PCIe or NVLink and another that uses peer-to-peer atomics that can work only over NVLink. All three versions are based on the base version described in Sect. 4. They only differ in the way communication is implemented. We compare the performance of these versions in Sect. 7.

6.1   CUDA-Aware MPI Based Version

The base version of the BFS code uses CUDA memory copy API to move frontier list data from the GPU to the CPU before using MPI to exchange data among the processors. Frontier list is copied to the GPU after it is received on the host. This would mean that NVLink is not used for data movement between the GPUs on a DGX-1. We modified the base version to use CUDA-aware MPI (MVAPICH2 MPI library) to directly move data from GPU memory buffers. MVAPICH2 internally uses CUDA Inter-Process Communication (IPC) mechanism to move data between GPUs. CUDA IPC enables use of GPUDirect between different OS processes. It takes advantage of peer-to-peer path between two GPUs that are connected via PCIe or NVLink. This allows us to do a fairer comparison between the MPI-based version and our SHMEM-based versions. The updated MPI-based version is referred to as cuMPI in later sections. We use MPI non-blocking send/recv API like in the base version described in Sect. 4. MVAPICH2 uses cudaMemcpyAsync calls to implement these transfers.

6.2   NVSHMEM-Based Version over PCIe-Connected GPUs

NVSHMEM uses CUDA IPC to enable direct access to remote GPU memory from inside a CUDA kernel via standard SHMEM API. It requires that the GPUs are directly connected via PCIe or NVLink. When GPUs are connected over PCIe, CUDA atomics cannot be used on peer-GPU memory. So, we limit ourselves to shmem_put operations (which translate to P2P writes) for this version for PCIe-connected GPUs. Each processor (PE in the context of SHMEM) maintains a remotely accessible integer map of the vertices it owns. This is allocated using shmem_malloc and hence is accessible via SHMEM API. In the expand phase, when a PE discovers an un-visited vertex, it updates the frontier map at the owner PE directly with a shmem_int_p. It writes its own PE id (incremented by 1 to differentiate from default value 0). This allows for better overlap between traversal and remote updates compared to the MPI version which waits for the traversal in the current level to complete before exchanging the list of discovered vertices. However, this results in random accesses over the network unlike MPI where data is coalesced before it is exchanged. Further, having an integer map makes the vertex map to be processed in the update phase larger by a factor of 32 when compared to the bitmap used in the MPI version. This can also be a limiter in performance for this version. Predecessor information is stored locally like in the case of base-version. There can be conflicts where two PEs discover the same vertex and update the frontier map at the same time. We rely on the system characteristic that a 32-bit write over PCIe completes as one transaction and so the write of one of the PEs persists. During update phase, the owner PE parses its remotely accessible vertex integer map, updates its local frontier array, saves the predecessor information and resets the vertex integer map. We have implemented this to compare the performance of PCIe w.r.t. NVLink, with atomics being possible on NVLink. So, we have not implemented the vertical exchange in this version. Therefore, we limit our runs to 1-D process decomposition in this case. We call this version SHMEM-Put in later sections.

6.3   Using SHMEM over NVLink-Connected GPUs

With NVLink, it is possible to issue CUDA-atomics on peer GPU memory. We have revised our design to take advantage of this feature. Figure 4 shows a high-level summary of this version. The remotely accessible vertex map is a bitmap, with each bit representing a vertex. Newly discovered vertices are directly marked on the vertex bitmap using shmem_atomic_or. The atomic OR API is not available in OpenSHMEM 1.3 specification but has been proposed and accepted into the next revision of the specification. The predecessor information is stored at the discovering processor, like in the MPI version. In order to pass on the predecessor information, each PE maintains a vertex bitmap corresponding to every other PE in the grid row. At the beginning of the update phase, the bitmaps are reduced into a final bitmap which is used to update the local frontier arrays. The processor that had sent a vertex is identified based on the vertex bitmap had been updated. The exchange along the column is fused into the update phase by each PE writing its vertex bitmap to all other PEs in the column, as soon as it reduces each element in the bitmap array. This variant can be run using a 1-D or 2-D processor grid. We refer to this variant as SHMEM-Atomics in later sections.

```
while (frontier not empty) {
    Expand (fused local expansion and exchange among row processors)
    Barrier
    Append (fused local update and exchange among column processors)
    Convergence check (Allreduce on frontier length)
}
```

Fig. 4. High-level summary of the P2P version

7   Results

We have run all our experiments on two types of systems. One of them is a dual-socket Intel Haswell server with 4 K40 GPUs all connected on the same CPU socket. CUDA P2P/IPC can be used among these GPUs, over PCIe. This node has CentOS 7.3.1611 OS and CUDA 8.0. We refer to this system as "K40+PCIe" in this section. The other node is a DGX-1 whose architecture is described in detail in Sect. 5. DGX-1 has Ubuntu 14.04 and CUDA 8.0. When NVLink and PCIe are both available between two GPUs, NVLink is used for all data movement between the GPUs. This is achieved transparently by CUDA IPC (using GPUDirect). Hence, NVLink is used for all communication in our BFS runs on DGX-1 when CUDA-aware MPI is used. We refer to the DGX-1 system as "P100+NVLink" in rest of the section. We use MVAPICH2 2.2 MPI library for both the baseline and cuda-aware MPI runs. NVSHMEM is an implementation of a subset of OpenSHMEM on top of CUDA IPC which allows direct access between GPUs connected via PCIe or NVLink. SHMEM communication operations translate to direct LD/ST/ATOMICS underneath. The graphs are generated with an R-MAT generator and the performance is averaged over 64 BFS operations started from random vertices. This is as specified in the Graph500 specification.

Figure 5 shows a comparison between the baseline and CUDA-aware versions on 4 K40 GPUs connected with PCIe (K40+NVLink) and 4 P100 GPUs connected with NVLink (P100+NVLink). The performance numbers are shown in GTEPS (Giga-Traversed Edges Per Second). We see that CUDA-aware MPI library which takes advantage of direct P2P path between GPUs shows improvement for larger graph sizes where bandwidth becomes important. We see higher improvement on DGX-1 with NVLink compared to the node with PCIe between GPUs.

Figure 6 analyzes these gains by using a split up of the runtime for two scales on DGX-1. For a smaller graph, CUDA-aware MPI removes CUDA memory copies from the application. This shows as a reduction in time spent in CUDA. However, the time in MPI library increases due to the overhead of CUDA memory copies inside the library. For larger sizes, application level copies to and from CPU memory suffer from contention on the PCIe bus to host memory. CUDA-aware MPI uses the direct P2P channel between GPUs, bypassing these

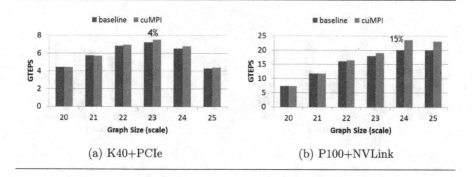

(a) K40+PCIe   (b) P100+NVLink

Fig. 5. Comparison between baseline and CUDA-aware MPI

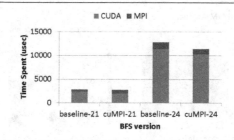

Fig. 6. Time spent in CUDA and MPI for baseline and CUDA-aware MPI versions

bottlenecks. We compare our shmem version against this CUDA-aware MPI version.

Figure 7(a) and (b) compares the CUDA-aware MPI version with the SHMEM version that uses Puts. We see that this version yields significantly lower performance compared to the CUDA-aware MPI version among GPUs connected with PCIe. The SHMEM version directly updates the remote frontier vertex map using writes. This yields a random access pattern over PCIe. We attribute this slowdown to the serialization and poor performance of random accesses over PCIe. On DGX-1, where GPUs are connected with NVLink, we see that SHMEM-Put version achieves better performance than CUDA-aware MPI version, for smaller graph sizes. NVLink has a higher bandwidth and a relaxed ordering for packets. Hence, it yields higher throughput for random accesses. The benefit in BFS comes from fusing communication into the compute kernel. This allows for overlap and reduced latencies by avoiding explicit copies. However, as we go to larger sizes, we are dominated by the overhead of processing the integer map of vertices used in SHMEM-Put variant. The MPI version maintains a bitmap for the same, as explained in Sect. 6.2. Also, the SHMEM-Put version uses a 1D (1×4) decomposition because of the limitation in the implementation. We have used 2D decomposition for MPI as that yields the best performance for it.

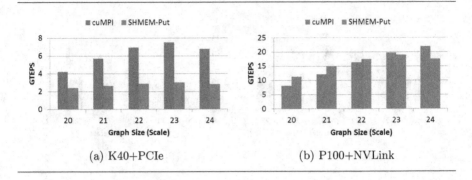

Fig. 7. Comparison between CUDA-aware MPI and SHMEM Put versions

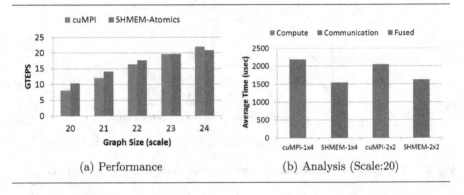

Fig. 8. Comparison between CUDA-aware MPI version and SHMEM-Atomic version, on 4 P100+NVLink

SHMEM-Atomics uses a bitmap instead of integer list to represent the remotely accessible vertex map. This reduces the size of the structure processed to what is used in the baseline version. Both versions use 2D process grids (2×2). Figure 8(a) shows that this achieves a performance gain for a broader set of problem sizes. Figure 8(b) shows the overlap the fused kernel in SHMEM-Atomics achieves for graph scale 20. We see that perfect overlap is achieved with a 1D process grid where there is only horizontal exchange which is fused with the main traversal kernel. With 2D decomposition, the overlap is less than perfect as the communication in the second dimension cannot be hidden completely. The benefits of overlap also diminish for larger graph sizes where the compute time dominates the overall time, as shown in Fig. 6. The 2D process grid was used for results in Fig. 8(a) as it yields better traversal rate for both versions, compared to 1D decomposition. Figure 9(a) and (b) show the performance comparison on 8 nodes in 2×4 and 4×2 process grids, respectively. We see that the improvement with NVSHMEM is greater as we scale from 4 to 8 GPUs due to the reduced overheads (and increased overlap) from fused kernels in the SHMEM version.

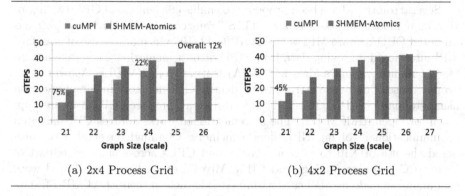

Fig. 9. Comparison between CUDA-aware MPI version and SHMEM-Atomic version, on 8 P100+NVLink

The benefits for smaller graph sizes is higher for the same reason. We limit the smallest graph scale to 21 as performance for smaller graphs does not scale from 4 to 8 GPU. The improvements due to NVSHMEM with a 4×2 grid is lower compared to 2×4 grid as a larger amount of communication happens along the column and there is little compute in the append phase and hence limited scope for overlap.

8 Related Work

There have been a fair number of contributions from vendors and researchers that are geared towards enabling efficient communication from GPUs. NVIDIA's GPUDirect technologies [5,6] have helped reduce communication overheads by removing the need to copy data to CPU memory before it can be moved to other GPUs, within and across nodes. However, the CPU is still involved in initiating communication and synchronizing between computation and communication in the application. This demands a powerful CPU for best performance and incurs overheads that limit strong scaling. GPUDirect Async [7] addresses this by allowing GPU to trigger and synchronize network operations in order with compute kernels that are queued by the CPU. This will allow CPU to be put in low power states as computation and communication is progressed by the GPU. However, communication operations are scheduled only at kernel boundaries. Computation and communication phases have to be defined and queued from the CPU. This will result in multiple kernels and bulk synchronization phases whose overheads can dominate as applications are scaled strongly. In this paper, we consider communication from inside CUDA kernels as an alternative approach to CUDA-aware MPI and show how it can enable better performance. It also improves programmability by being inline with the CUDA programming model and taking advantage of the native GPU execution model.

Several solutions have been proposed to enable efficient use of GPUs with programming models such as MPI and PGAS. Wang et al. and Potluri et al. [8,9] has proposed CUDA-aware MPI with MVAPICH2 [10] which allows use of standard MPI interfaces for moving data from GPU or host memories. They take advantage of unified virtual addressing (UVA) feature from NVIDIA. Ashwin et al. proposed use of datatype attributes to identify GPU memory in communication using standard MPI interfaces [11]. Potluri et al. proposed CUDA-aware approach for OpenSHMEM [12]. The aforementioned works address CPU-initiated communication involving GPU device memory. Cunningham et al. have proposed the use of X10 to program GPUs and CPUs across clusters as part of their APGAS programming model [13]. Miyoshi et al. have contributed work that allows embedding MPI calls within GPU kernels in their FLAT GPU framework [14]. In our approach, we allow the GPU user to rely on the familiar CUDA programming model while using OpenSHMEM to express inter-GPU data movement inline with the CUDA model.

The work of Ueno et al. [15] was among the earliest distributed GPU implementations of BFS at scale attaining over 300 Billions of traversed edges per second (GTEPS) on the TSUBAME [16] supercomputer consisting of 4K GPUs spread across more than 1300 nodes. Our works is based on a more recent distributed BFS implementation proposed by Bisson et al. [17] that has also been shown to scale to all 4K GPUs on the TSUBAME supercomputer. Single node, multi-GPU BFS is available in the Gunrock graph analytics library [18] which has been characterized on dense nodes using latest GPU architectural advances (using Tesla P100 GPUs). Performance results are comparable to what much larger number of GPUs on clusters with lower GPU density per node could achieve and this is due to the significantly faster intra-node bandwidth on dense nodes. The single-node, multi-GPU version of Gunrock relies on CUDA IPC to allow one GPU to directly access the memory of a peer GPU. In this paper, we focus on comparing the performance of using MPI and GPU-side SHMEM for communication in a particular implementation of BFS. We have not focused on optimizing other aspects of the BFS implementation. Hence, we do not compare against other BFS implementations like Gunrock which lack an MPI-based implementations.

9   Conclusion

Clusters with dense GPU nodes are becoming increasingly popular due to better strong scaling characteristics and superior energy efficiency. The memory aperture over which one-sided communication is possible on such platforms, keeps growing. As a result, the SHMEM programming model offers an interesting alternative to MPI as the communication library of choice on such platforms. NVSHMEM is NVIDIA's implementation of SHMEM which enables communication calls to be initiated by GPU threads. This is particularly useful in strong scaling scenarios when the overhead of frequently synchronizing between the CPU and the GPU starts to affect overall performance. Moreover, the possibility to overlap communication with compute goes wasted.

All of these factors contribute to the performance benefits observed in a NVSHMEM-based implementation of BFS compared to the MPI variant, for which, all communication-related control goes through the CPU although the data transfers occur directly between GPUs. As the size of the dataset per GPU decreases (the case with strong scaling), the NVSHMEM version achieves a peak speedup of 75% by eliminating the overheads of synchronizing with the CPU.

Acknowledgments. This research is supported in part by Oak Ridge National Lab, subcontract #4000145249. We would like to thank M. Bisson et al., authors of the multi-GPU implementation of BFS we have used as the baseline in this paper [17]. They have shared their code and have supported this work.

References

1. http://graph500.org: Graph 500 benchmark specification 1.2 (2017). http://www.graph500.org/
2. Merrill, D., Garland, M., Grimshaw, A.: Scalable GPU graph traversal. SIGPLAN Not. **47**, 117–128 (2012)
3. Bisson, M., Bernaschi, M., Mastrostefano, E.: Parallel distributed breadth first search on the Kepler architecture. CoRR abs/1408.1605 (2014)
4. Potluri, S., Rossetti, D., Becker, D., Poole, D., Gorentla Venkata, M., Hernandez, O., Shamis, P., Lopez, M.G., Baker, M., Poole, W.: Exploring openSHMEM model to program GPU-based extreme-scale systems. In: Gorentla Venkata, M., Shamis, P., Imam, N., Lopez, M.G. (eds.) OpenSHMEM 2014. LNCS, vol. 9397, pp. 18–35. Springer, Cham (2015). https://doi.org/10.1007/978-3-319-26428-8_2
5. NVIDIA: GPUDirect (2015). https://developer.nvidia.com/gpudirect
6. NVIDIA: GPUDirect RDMA (2015). http://docs.nvidia.com/cuda/gpudirect-rdma
7. Rossetti, D.: GPUDirect: integrating the GPU with a network interface. In: GPU Technology Conference (2015)
8. Wang, H., Potluri, S., Luo, M., Singh, A.K., Sur, S., Panda, D.K.: MVAPICH2-GPU: optimized GPU to GPU communication for infiniband clusters. Comput. Sci. **26**, 257–266 (2011)
9. Potluri, S., Hamidouche, K., Venkatesh, A., Bureddy, D., Panda, D.K.: Efficient inter-node MPI communication using GPUDirect RDMA for infiniband clusters with NVIDIA GPUs. In: Proceedings of the 2013 42nd International Conference on Parallel Processing, ICPP 2013, Washington, DC, USA, pp. 80–89. IEEE Computer Society (2013)
10. MVAPICH: MPI over infiniband, 10GigE/iWARP and RoCE (2015). http://mvapich.cse.ohio-state.edu
11. Aji, A.M., Dinan, J., Buntinas, D., Balaji, P., Feng, W.C., Bisset, K.R., Thakur, R.: MPI-ACC: an integrated and extensible approach to data movement in accelerator-based systems. In: 14th IEEE International Conference on High Performance Computing and Communications, Liverpool, UK (2012)
12. Potluri, S., Bureddy, D., Wang, H., Subramoni, H., Panda, D.K.: Extending open-SHMEM for GPU computing. In: Proceedings of the 2013 IEEE 27th International Symposium on Parallel and Distributed Processing, IPDPS 2013, Washington, DC, USA, pp. 1001–1012. IEEE Computer Society (2013)

13. Cunningham, D., Bordawekar, R., Saraswat, V.: GPU programming in a high level language: compiling X10 to CUDA. In: Proceedings of the 2011 ACM SIGPLAN X10 Workshop, X10 2011, pp. 8:1–8:10. ACM, New York (2011)
14. Miyoshi, T., Irie, H., Shima, K., Honda, H., Kondo, M., Yoshinaga, T.: Flat: a GPU programming framework to provide embedded MPI. In: Proceedings of the 5th Annual Workshop on General Purpose Processing with Graphics Processing Units, GPGPU-5, pp. 20–29. ACM, New York (2012)
15. Ueno, K., Suzumura, T.: Parallel distributed breadth first search on GPU. In: 20th Annual International Conference on High Performance Computing, HiPC 2013, Bengaluru (Bangalore), Karnataka, India, 18–21 December 2013, pp. 314–323 (2013)
16. Matsuoka, S.: Making TSUBAME2.0, the world's greenest production supercomputer, even greener: challenges to the architects. In: Proceedings of the 2011 International Symposium on Low Power Electronics and Design, Fukuoka, Japan, 1–3 August 2011, pp. 367–368 (2011)
17. Bisson, M., Bernaschi, M., Mastrostefano, E.: Parallel distributed breadth first search on the Kepler architecture. IEEE Trans. Parallel Distrib. Syst. **27**, 2091–2102 (2016)
18. Pan, Y., Wang, Y., Wu, Y., Yang, C., Owens, J.D.: Multi-GPU graph analytics. CoRR abs/1504.04804 (2015)

Evaluation, Implementation and Novel use of OpenSHMEM

Application-Level Optimization of On-Node Communication in OpenSHMEM

Md. Wasi-ur- Rahman[1]([⊠]), David Ozog[2]([⊠]), and James Dinan[2]([⊠])

[1] Intel Corporation, Austin, USA
md.rahman@intel.com
[2] Intel Corporation, Boston, USA
{david.m.ozog,james.dinan}@intel.com

Abstract. The OpenSHMEM community is actively exploring threading support extensions to the OpenSHMEM communication interfaces. Among the motivations for these extensions are the optimization of on-node data sharing and reduction of memory pressure, both of which are problems that hybrid programming has successfully addressed in other programming models. We observe that OpenSHMEM already supports inter-process shared memory for processes within the same node. In this work, we assess the viability of this existing API to address the on-node optimization problem, which is of growing importance. We identify multiple on-node optimizations that are already possible with the existing interface, propose a layered library that extends the functionality of these interfaces, and measure performance improvement when using these techniques.

1 Introduction

High Performance Computing (HPC) system nodes continue to trend toward increasingly powerful and increasingly parallel processors, including many-core processors and accelerators. As a result, HPC application developers are looking beyond conventional parallel programming systems toward hybrid approaches that combine a communication library, such as MPI or OpenSHMEM, with an on-node programming model, such as OpenMP*. The resulting combination enables the application developer to tune for system-level effects, while also efficiently utilizing the capabilities and resources provided by the node-level architecture.

A primary feature that drives the success of Partitioned Global Address Space (PGAS) programming models is their ability to remotely access the memory of other processing elements (PEs) without explicit participation from the target PE. While PGAS programming models, such as OpenSHMEM, conveniently provide such one-sided remote access to the memory of *any* processing element (PE), communication with PEs that share *local* memory may suffer from unnecessary performance overheads. At its core, OpenSHMEM is a data copying library; thus, even when PEs are in the same node, communication via OpenSHMEM can result in the creation of multiple copies of the same data within a shared memory domain. Additional overheads may also arise from various sources: a complex software stack that is capable of supporting general

© Springer International Publishing AG 2018
M. Gorentla Venkata et al. (Eds.): OpenSHMEM 2017, LNCS 10679, pp. 99–113, 2018.
https://doi.org/10.1007/978-3-319-73814-7_7

remote memory access (RMA), the sheer memory replication cost of single process multiple data (SPMD) programming, and the synchronization mechanisms associated with large-scale programming models. As a result, the OpenSHMEM community is actively investigating library extensions to better support node-level optimization, including methods for integrating threading awareness within the library [3,8].

While hybrid programming is of interest to many programmers, maintainers of existing applications may prefer a more evolutionary approach to tuning on-node data sharing. We observe that OpenSHMEM provides a seldom-used function that allows the programmer to query a direct pointer to the remotely accessible memory of another PE within the same shared memory domain. While this functionality is supported by a number of OpenSHMEM implementations, it is challenging to use in its current form because the current OpenSHMEM interfaces don't expose the locality information needed by programmers to effectively utilize this capability.

In this work, we investigate the challenges and opportunities of the OpenSHMEM pointer query API. We develop a portable library, called shnode, that fills the gaps in the current interface and improves the usability of this interface. We believe the results of this work will highlight an evolutionary path for node-level tuning of applications. In addition, we hope that it will provide valuable insights to ongoing efforts to extend OpenSHMEM with new features such as hybrid programming and on-node based teams support. We evaluate the performance impact of our approach using several benchmarks, including a large-scale parallel sorting benchmark and observe that this approach to optimization of on-node communication can yield significant performance improvements.

The rest of the paper is organized as follows. Section 2 presents background on OpenSHMEM and the pointer query API. We highlight some of the key challenges for this work in Sect. 3. Design and implementation details of the shnode library are presented in Sect. 4. We present the details of our experimental evaluation in Sect. 5. Section 6 highlights some of the existing works in the literature and we conclude in Sect. 8.

2   Background

This work investigates shared memory optimizations in the context of OpenSHMEM [15], an HPC communication library that provides a partitioned global address space (PGAS) data model through one-sided read, write, and atomic update routines. In this section, we describe the typical execution models for OpenSHMEM programs and outline various techniques for exploiting on-node memory locality.

One very common use case for OpenSHMEM programs running on HPC clusters is to allocate one or more processing elements (PE) per compute node. Each compute node typically consists of multiple processing units and/or individual cores, so it may be advantageous to assign *multiple* PEs to each compute node to exploit the available parallelism. In the OpenSHMEM programming model, each of these PEs designates a memory region for storing symmetric heap and local variable data.

While the designated memory regions of each PE are *remotely accessible* by any other PE in the application, there is also the possibility that data may *reside locally* with respect to other on-node PEs. However, there is no guarantee that this data locality is exploited by the OpenSHMEM implementation. Even if an implementation does optimize for on-node PE locality, it still may be difficult for an application developer to optimize *outside* of the OpenSHMEM API. Multi-threading within a PE's address space can accomplish on-node parallelism with good data locality, but it is typically not straightforward to accomplish this across the address space of multiple PE's, despite the fact that their memory regions may reside on the same node.

The OpenSHMEM API includes a routine that enables on-node addressing, which may be useful for optimizing applications for memory locality. This routine, called shmem_ptr, returns the specified pointer to a symmetric buffer on the specific PE. Its function signature is:

```
void *shmem_ptr(const void *dest, int pe);
```

where dest is the local pointer to the symmetric data buffer, and pe is the PE id of the desired process. This routine returns a pointer to the "remote" symmetric data object in the local PE's address space. If a program has dest value for all symmetric regions of interest, and knowledge of which PEs are node-local, then shared memory optimizations are possible at the application level. Despite the availability of this function in the API, it is the opinion of these authors that it is underutilized across the OpenSHMEM programs. In Sect. 3 we argue why this underutilization may exist, and Sect. 4 presents how this routine is used in constructing a more user-friendly and general interface for achieving shared memory optimization in OpenSHMEM programs.

3 Challenges and Opportunities

The shmem_ptr routine enables shared memory accesses and optimizations in OpenSHMEM programs. However, there are challenges to using this routine in practice. For example, if an application wants to know which PEs are locally resident, then shmem_ptr gives only very limited information. This routine returns a null pointer whenever the input PE value is off-node. This requires looping over *all* PEs and storing the non-null IDs into a local structure. One goal of this paper is to abstract this procedure into a simpler interface that creates *teams* of processes that group together node-local PE subsets. Such an interface would enable applications to do memory operations within their local teams, which eliminates the overhead of the software stack involved in remote communication.

In addition to the locality knowledge that node-local teams provide, there are other requirements for useful shared memory programming. For instance, consider an algorithm that involves local computation/communication, followed by a collective operation. Instead of having all PEs participate in the collective, the application may only require one PE per *team* to participate. We call this PE a *leader* in our design. Leader election algorithms constitute a well-known topic in distributed systems [2], in part because of their dependence on network topologies and system hierarchy/architecture. Leader election implementations are particularly important in OpenSHMEM, especially for checkpointing applications [1,9]. A goal of our API is to abstract leader selection and to enable customizable *multiple-leader* assignment on a per-node basis.

Perhaps the primary challenge with shared-memory programming lies in developing algorithms that effectively exploit data locality. Often *re-development* is necessary because existing legacy applications rely on algorithms that do not adequately account for locality. Performance improvement for this software is difficult without thoroughly considering data-layout, communication and synchronization strategies, and load balancing. Communication avoiding algorithms show great promise [7], and need to be incorporated to best exploit locality at the node-level. In the following section, we introduce the shnode API based on the shmem_ptr routine to bridge these gaps, enabling application developers to design algorithms that better exploit data locality.

4   Design and Implementation of **shnode**

In this section, we present the design and implementation of our proposed layered library for on-node data sharing, called *shnode*. The purpose of this library is to provide several APIs to application developers with which the application can benefit through avoidance of on-node communication.

As discussed in Sect. 2, we utilize the built-in routine, shmem_ptr, to design shnode. Since shmem_ptr returns the specific memory address for a symmetric data object on an on-node remote PE, it can provide the opportunity for the application developers to store these pointers for direct load and store operations as opposed to invoking remote memory access (e.g. shmem_put). To facilitate this, we propose the APIs listed in Listing 1.1.

To utilize the shnode library, application developers should follow the usual semantics of initialization and termination of shnode functionalities through the OpenSHMEM-like APIs, shnode_init and shnode_finalize. In the future, these functionalities can be incorporated and invoked from the OpenSHMEM initialization and finalize routines based on the input to an environment flag set by the user. After the initialization, the user needs to create the per-node team. Based on the remote data pointers returned by the shmem_ptr routine, shnode creates team of PEs on each node. These data references will be stored so that subsequent remote memory operations can be substituted with direct load and stores to the memory location residing in the on-node PE's symmetric heap. The API shnode_create_team is responsible for creating the team on each node consisting of all those PEs for which a non-NULL value is obtained through shmem_ptr. Figure 1(a) presents the team formation for a two node cluster running with 8 PEs per node. To add more data objects, a user can simply use shmem_add_data for the subsequent shared memory objects. We

Listing 1.1. Proposed fundamental APIs for shnode.

```
/* initialization */
int shnode_init();

/* team creation based on a symmetric data object */
int shnode_create_team(void *data);

/* addition of other symmetric data objects */
int shnode_add_data(void *data);

/* check to see whether the remote pe is a team member */
int shnode_is_team_member(int rem_pe);

/* retrieval of the memory address of an on-node PE */
void *shnode_get_member_remote_addr(int rem_pe, void *data);

/* check to see whether self is the leader of the team */
int shnode_am_team_leader();

/* destroy */ int shnode_finalize();
```

assign the lowest rank PE as the team leader for each node. The purpose of the
leader is further explained in Sect. 4.2.

To store the team information on each PE, we design a simple data structure
mapping each PE to a list of the data object references returned by shmem_ptr.
Figure 1(b) illustrates this for the team presented in Fig. 1(a). To track a specific
data object, we maintain another list that maps the corresponding data object
to the location it is stored in the PE-mapped data structure. This is helpful for
fast retrieval of the requested reference when multiple data objects are stored in
the data structure. The shnode_create_team operation is invoked only once
at the beginning of the application execution; thus, does not incur significant
overheads to the execution time of the application.

After successful team creation, the user can utilize the shnode_get_
member_remote_addr to retrieve the data reference stored in the shnode team
table. Using the remote location address, the user can perform direct load and
store, replacing remote memory operations.

4.1 Better Overlapping Between Communication And Computation

Since shnode provides the memory addresses for symmetric data objects on on-
node PEs, it provides the opportunity to the application developer to replace the
remote memory operations with the direct memory operations, such as memcpy.
Although this eliminates overhead caused by the remote operations, it still has
the drawbacks of invoking memory transfers. One of the alternatives for the
application developers is to perform swapping of the pointers instead of copying
the content. In this way, users can eliminate any software overhead caused by
large memory to memory data transfers. However, in many applications, this
approach might require a significant effort to re-write the application to maintain
correctness.

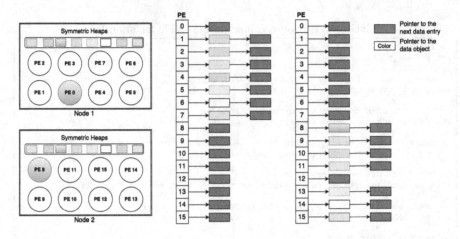

(a) Team formation in shnode

(b) Data structure to store team information on PE 0 (left) and PE 12 (right)

Fig. 1. Design and implementation details of shnode

The other alternative is to customize the remote memory calls in such a way so that the intra-node data transfers are invoked separately from the inter-node ones; thereby optimizing the overlap between communication and computation. Scheduling the intra-node memory operations at the end will ensure better overlap between computation and long-delayed inter-node memory operations. Application developers can utilize the team information from shnode to refine the communication operations in this way.

4.2 Designing **shnode** Collective Helper Routines

With the assignment of a team leader PE per node, we can also optimize the collective communication by designing helper routines for each collective operations. Figure 2 presents one such use case. Our current implementations of these routines assume a power-of-two number of process elements per node and the process launcher launches each of the PEs sequentially from the first node to the last node in the cluster.

As shown in Fig. 2, we can re-design the collective operations considering the hierarchy of nodes achieved from the shnode library. Each collective operation can divide its tasks in three sub-tasks. As an example, we explain here a division of tasks for a reduction operation. In the first sub-task, all the PEs communicate with the on-node leader so that the leaders in each node gets the reduced values from all the PEs on that node. In the second sub-task, a reduce operation is strided over only the leaders across the nodes. This significantly reduces the communication overheads. The stride is calculated from the process per node which is assumed to be a power-of-two value. Finally, all the leaders pass the globally reduced value to the on-node PEs to complete the operation.

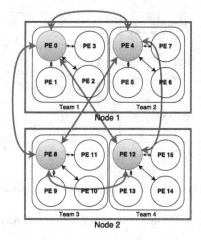

Fig. 2. Multiple leader based collective communication design for shnode

For large collective operations with a higher number of PEs per node, a single leader per node might not yield the maximum benefits possible. In such cases, we create sub-teams within teams and assign the lowest rank of each sub-team as the leader for that team. This reduces the overhead for each leader and thus a balance between the number of teams and the number of PEs per teams is achieved. As an example, Fig. 2 presents two teams per node with different leaders instead of the default one leader. We present evaluations for different numbers of leaders in Sect. 5.3.

5   Performance Evaluation

In this section, we present our evaluation of different benchmarks and applications utilizing the shnode library and compare them with the default approach. We present our evaluations in three different categories: (1) Evaluating shnode with a micro-benchmark, (2) Performance improvement in collectives, (3) Evaluation of applications.

5.1   Experimental Setup

For our evaluation, we have used the NERSC Cori supercomputer, which is the 6th fastest supercomputer on the TOP500 [18] list, published in June, 2017. It is a Cray* XC40 system with 2,388 Intel® Xeon® E5-2698 v3 (Haswell) processor nodes at 2.3 GHz and 9,688 Intel® Xeon Phi™ 7250 (Knights Landing, KNL) processor nodes with 68 cores per node at 1.4 GHz. Each of the KNL nodes have 96 GB of DDR4 memory. All the compute nodes run a light-weight kernel based on the SuSE* Linux* Enterprise Server distribution.

Throughout our experiments, we have used the KNL nodes in Cori. We have implemented shnode on top of Cray* SHMEM v7.5.5 and used the same for our evaluations and comparisons.

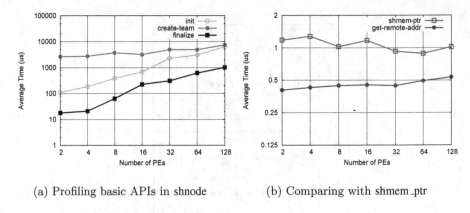

(a) Profiling basic APIs in shnode   (b) Comparing with shmem_ptr

Fig. 3. Profiling analysis for shnode APIs

5.2 Evaluating Shnode with Micro-benchmark

In this section, we evaluate shnode with two different micro-benchmarks. First, we write a micro-benchmark to do a profiling analysis for four of the fundamental APIs that we have proposed in Sect. 4 - shnode_init, shnode_create_team, shnode_get_member_remote_addr, and shnode_finalize. Out of these four APIs, application developers might need to use shnode_get_member_remote_addr multiple times throughout the application execution, whereas, the remaining APIs would only be invoked once during the runtime of the application.

We conduct the profiling analysis in two KNL nodes with a varying number of PEs per node (from 1 to 64). We measure the average execution time for each of these APIs across all PEs. As shown in the Fig. 3(a), with 128 PEs, the initialization, team creation, and finalize routines take only about 0.1 s which does not incur significant overheads. In Fig. 3(b), we compare the shnode_get_member_remote_addr with the default shmem_ptr routine. We can see that with our implementation, we can reduce the query operation cost by 50% on average across different number of PEs. Also, this routine scales well because of the design choices for the data structures in shnode.

We also evaluate the basic put and get performance using micro-benchmark and present these results in Figs. 4 and 5. We modify the OSU micro-benchmarks [17] for shmem_put and shmem_get to incorporate the shnode APIs and compare the modified put and get performances with the default ones. We conduct these experiments on a single node with two PEs.

As shown in Fig. 4(a), shnode can perform 3–4.6x faster compared to shmem_put for small message sizes (up to 2K). For larger message sizes, the benefit reduces to 1.5–2.35x. Similar benefits are observed for shnode based get compared to shmem_get, as shown in Fig. 5. We also measure the message rate for put and present these results in Fig. 4(b). Here, an average benefit of 1.35x is observed for shnode put compared to the shmem_put. Since the shnode implementation of put and get performs a direct memory copy to/from the remote

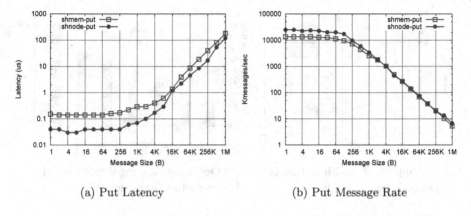

(a) Put Latency   (b) Put Message Rate

Fig. 4. Performance comparison between SHMEM and shnode put operations

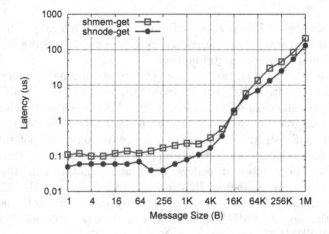

Fig. 5. Performance comparison between SHMEM and shnode get operations

address, this approach obtains significant performance benefits compared to the default ones.

5.3 Performance Improvement in Collective Routines

In this section, we present the performance comparisons between default collective routines and the shnode based helper routines. We implement our shnode based helper collective routines for reduction and collect and present the results here. We also evaluate the impact of multiple leaders per node on each of these collectives.

Figure 6 presents the corresponding experiments on the reduction, specifically a sum based reduction for integer data types (int_sum_to_all). First, we analyze the impact of multiple leaders per node on this reduction and present this result in Fig. 6(a). We conduct this experiment on four KNL nodes where

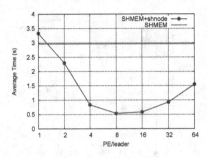 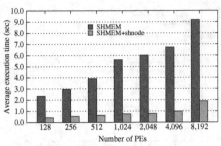

(a) Impact of multiple leaders per node on reductions

(b) Optimization using shnode based helper routine for reduction

Fig. 6. Performance improvement potentials for reductions with shnode

we vary the number of PEs per leader from 1 to 64. We allocate a 10 MB buffer to use as the data source for the reduction. Experimental results presented in this section are averaged over 10 iterations.

As shown in Fig. 6(a), we achieve the most optimal performance for int_sum_to_all with 8 PEs per leader. Thus, with 64 PEs running on each node, we observe the most optimal result with 8 leaders per node, where each of them are responsible for communicating with the 7 other PEs. We also observe that the default SHMEM implementation for reduction could not take advantage of such hierarchical work distribution provided by shnode. With this optimum value for the number of leaders, we conduct another experiment where we increase the total number of PEs from 128 (2 nodes) to 8 K (128 nodes). From the evaluation results presented in Fig. 6(b), we see that with the shnode implementation on top of SHMEM, we can achieve up to 4.87x benefit compared to the default SHMEM approach for int_sum_to_all.

We implement the same for fcollect collective routine and present the results in Fig. 7. We use a similar setup to the reduction experiment.

Unlike int_sum_to_all, we can see in Fig. 7(a) that for fcollect, the optimum performance is achieved with 2 PEs per leader (32 leaders per node for 64 PEs in a node). We also see that the default SHMEM implementation for fcollect performs better compared to the shnode implementation with more PEs per leader. We conduct this experiment on two KNL nodes with 128 total PEs. We also conduct a strong scale experiment for fcollect similar to the int_sum_to_all. For 128 nodes running 8 K PEs, we observe that the shnode implementation out-performs the default SHMEM implementation by 2x.

5.4   Evaluation of Applications

In this section, we evaluate an application, Integer Sort [11] (ISx) to highlight the performance improvements achievable using shnode. ISx represents a class of the bucket sort algorithms which perform an all-to-all communication

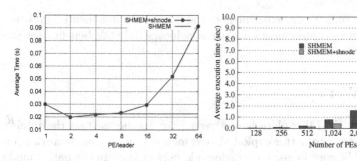

(a) Impact of multiple leaders per node on fcollect

(b) Optimization using shnode based helper routine for fcollect

Fig. 7. Performance improvement potentials for fcollect with shnode

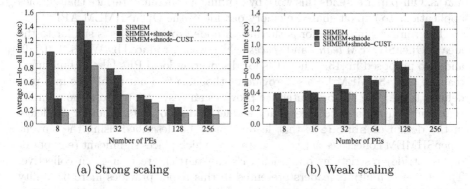

(a) Strong scaling

(b) Weak scaling

Fig. 8. Performance improvement for ISx with SHNODE library and customized communication scheduling

pattern. In this evaluation, we present two different implementations of ISx utilizing shnode, one with no additional changes in the communication pattern (presented as SHMEM+shnode) and the other with customized communication scheduling, where the node-local transfers are separated out and invoked only at the end of the execution (presented as SHMEM+shnode-CUST). We conduct both strong and weak scale experiments for ISx on 4 nodes with varying number of PEs. Figure 8 presents these results.

For strong scale experiment, we use the number of items to sort equal to 1.5 billion and vary the number of PEs from 8 to 256. As shown in Fig. 8(a), with the customized communication pattern, we can achieve 2x benefits compared to the default implementation over SHMEM with 256 PEs. Since ISx overlaps communication with computations, the shnode implementation without the customized communication pattern does not observe much benefit (around 5%) compared to the default implementation. For weak scaling experiments as presented in Fig. 8(b), we observe a performance benefits of 1.5x for 256 PEs. In this experiment, we fix the number of items per PE to 32 M.

Similar to the strong scale experiments, the shnode implementation without customization in communication pattern achieves only 5% benefit over the default implementation.

6   Related Work

Namashivayam et al. [14] explore how shmem_ptr can be used on the Intel® Xeon Phi™ processor to better exploit shared memory and enable vectorization opportunities. This work focuses on single-node performance in the native mode of the Xeon Phi, in which applications run directly on the many-core device. The authors report substantial performance improvements in the latency and bandwidth of one-sided operations, across several reduction algorithms, and in the NAS Integer Sort (IS) and Scalar Penta-diagonal (SP) solver parallel benchmarks. Our paper extends this work by defining a coherent interface that enables applications to exploit shared memory outside of the OpenSHMEM API.

The shnode interface for gathering on-node groups of PEs is similar to the idea of OpenSHMEM *teams* and *spaces*, which was introduced by Welch et al. [19] and also proposed in [13]. The APIs for discovering local PEs [4] and building a team in Cray-SHMEM [5] also provide methods to find out local PEs in a pre-defined team. The shnode interface provides an easy way to store the pointers that can be used later to access the symmetric data objects. Another challenge in the design of shnode is that leaders must be described using the current OpenSHMEM collectives active set notation, which places significant (e.g. power of two stride) restrictions on which PEs can participate in a given collective. The choice of multiple leaders presented in this paper provides more flexibility to utilize shnode team interfaces with additional performance benefits.

There is also analogous work within the Message Passing Interface (MPI) that reflects our interface for shared memory-oriented programming. Hoefler et al. [12] first introduced the (perhaps initially surprising) notion of doing hybrid parallel programming of MPI with *itself* via the MPI+MPI paradigm. This work extends the MPI one-sided interface to include shared memory windows and associated communicators to enable interprocess communication via MPI. Our work in OpenSHMEM similarly enables on-node interprocess communication via the shnode interface, with a relatively simple API built from the shmem_ptr routine. Other work in the PGAS community further builds off the capabilities of shared memory in MPI-3 [10,21].

7   Future Work

Our measurements from Sect. 5 show very promising performance improvements when using the shnode API, yet there remain considerable possibilities for future work. For instance, the shnode concept could (and should) be implemented within the OpenSHMEM software layer for all viable routines, such as collectives and the RMA functions. We present our shnode implementations *outside* the OpenSHMEM layer as a proof-of-concept for what should be implemented *within* an OpenSHMEM library. We have so far only implemented a handle of routines from the OpenSHMEM specification (namely, fcollect, int_sum_to_all, broadcast, and put/get), but many other routines are also compatible.

We believe that shnode will primarily benefit application developers who require processing data across PEs that are grouped into shared-memory teams. Our results from Fig. 8 show a notable performance improvement for a real-world application, ISx. Other applications may also greatly benefit from shnode, but may require restructuring to achieve communication avoidance at the compute node-level. For instance, we observe that the OpenSHMEM stencil algorithm from the Parallel Research Kernels suite [20] may need to be restructured to reduce synchrony between global iterations. This may be possible, for example, by *over-decomposing* the grid domain to avoid starvation due to synchronous iterations.

Due to shnode's performance improvement of reductions (shown in Fig. 6), we believe MapReduce calculations [6] will also greatly benefit because of their heavy use of reduction collectives and the inter-process communication involved in intermediate shuffling operations. For instance, the MapReduce-MPI library [16] centers around several calls to an integer sum reduction, which is the same procedure measured in Fig. 6 above. Future work will quantify the performance gain from reducing and shuffling in shared memory using shnode.

8   Conclusion

This paper has introduced an interface for OpenSHMEM that alleviates the challenges involved with programming in shared-memory. Our implementation, shnode, supports the formation of node-local *teams* within which applications can easily do shared memory operations. We present an API for creating these teams, as well as for nominating a leader process or multiple leader processes. Overall, shnode shows very good performance improvement across RMA microbenchmarks, OpenSHMEM collectives, and the ISx application. Our performance results show that the number of leaders has a substantial impact on performance, depending on the communication algorithm being deployed. Future work for this research will involve shifting shnode capabilities to within the OpenSHMEM software layer, implementing the other variants of collectives and RMA operations, and exploring how to restructure existing applications to better exploit shared memory.

References

1. Arya, K., Garg, R., Polyakov, A.Y., Cooperman, G.: Design and implementation for checkpointing of distributed resources using process-level virtualization. In: 2016 IEEE International Conference on Cluster Computing (CLUSTER), pp. 402–412, September 2016
2. Attiya, H., Welch, J.: Distributed Computing: Fundamentals, Simulations, and Advanced Topics, vol. 19. Wiley, New York (2004)
3. ten Bruggencate, M., Roweth, D., Oyanagi, S.: Thread-safe SHMEM extensions. In: Poole, S., Hernandez, O., Shamis, P. (eds.) OpenSHMEM 2014. LNCS, vol. 8356, pp. 178–185. Springer, Cham (2014). https://doi.org/10.1007/978-3-319-05215-1_13
4. Cray: shmem_local_ptr. http://docs.cray.com/man/xe_libsmam/72/cat3/shmem_local_ptr.3.html
5. Cray: shmem_team_translate_pe. http://docs.cray.com/man/xe_libsmam/72/cat3/shmem_team_translate_pe.3.html
6. Dean, J., Ghemawat, S.: MapReduce: simplified data processing on large clusters. Commun. ACM **51**(1), 107–113 (2008)
7. Demmel, J.: Communication-avoiding algorithms for linear algebra and beyond. In: IPDPS, p. 585 (2013)
8. Dinan, J., Flajslik, M.: Contexts: a mechanism for high throughput communication in OpenSHMEM. In: Proceedings of the 8th International Conference on Partitioned Global Address Space Programming Models, pp. 10:1–10:9. ACM, New York (2014). http://doi.acm.org/10.1145/2676870.2676872
9. Garg, R., Vienne, J., Cooperman, G.: System-level transparent checkpointing for OpenSHMEM. In: Gorentla Venkata, M., Imam, N., Pophale, S., Mintz, T.M. (eds.) OpenSHMEM 2016. LNCS, vol. 10007, pp. 52–65. Springer, Cham (2016). https://doi.org/10.1007/978-3-319-50995-2_4
10. Hammond, J.R., Ghosh, S., Chapman, B.M.: Implementing OpenSHMEM using MPI-3 one-sided communication. In: Poole, S., Hernandez, O., Shamis, P. (eds.) OpenSHMEM 2014. LNCS, vol. 8356, pp. 44–58. Springer, Cham (2014). https://doi.org/10.1007/978-3-319-05215-1_4
11. Hanebutte, U., Hemstad, J.: ISx: a scalable integer sort for co-design in the exascale era. In: 9th International Conference on Partitioned Global Address Space Programming Models, pp. 102–104, September 2015
12. Hoefler, T., Dinan, J., Buntinas, D., Balaji, P., Barrett, B., Brightwell, R., Gropp, W., Kale, V., Thakur, R.: MPI + MPI: a new hybrid approach to parallel programming with MPI plus shared memory. Computing **95**(12), 1121–1136 (2013). http://dx.doi.org/10.1007/s00607-013-0324-2
13. Knaak, D., Namashivayam, N.: Proposing OpenSHMEM extensions towards a future for hybrid programming and heterogeneous computing. In: Gorentla Venkata, M., Shamis, P., Imam, N., Lopez, M.G. (eds.) OpenSHMEM 2014. LNCS, vol. 9397, pp. 53–68. Springer, Cham (2015). https://doi.org/10.1007/978-3-319-26428-8_4
14. Namashivayam, N., Ghosh, S., Khaldi, D., Eachempati, D., Chapman, B.: Native mode-based optimizations of remote memory accesses in OpenSHMEM for Intel Xeon Phi. In: Proceedings of the 8th International Conference on Partitioned Global Address Space Programming Models, pp. 12:1–12:11, PGAS 2014. ACM, New York (2014). http://doi.acm.org/10.1145/2676870.2676881

15. OpenSHMEM Application Programming Interface, Version 1.3, February 2016. http://www.openshmem.org
16. Plimpton, S.J., Devine, K.D.: MapReduce in MPI for large-scale graph algorithms. Parallel Comput. **37**(9), 610–632 (2011). http://dx.doi.org/10.1016/j.parco.2011.02.004
17. The Ohio State University: OSU Microbenchmarks. http://mvapich.cse.ohio-state.edu/benchmarks/
18. Top500 Supercomputing System. http://www.top500.org
19. Welch, A., Pophale, S., Shamis, P., Hernandez, O., Poole, S., Chapman, B.: Extending the OpenSHMEM memory model to support user-defined spaces. In: Proceedings of the 8th International Conference on Partitioned Global Address Space Programming Models, PGAS 2014, pp. 11:1–11:10. ACM, New York (2014). http://doi.acm.org/10.1145/2676870.2676884
20. Van der Wijngaart, R.F., Kayi, A., Hammond, J.R., Jost, G., St. John, T., Sridharan, S., Mattson, T.G., Abercrombie, J., Nelson, J.: Comparing runtime systems with exascale ambitions using the parallel research Kernels. In: Kunkel, J.M., Balaji, P., Dongarra, J. (eds.) ISC High Performance 2016. LNCS, vol. 9697, pp. 321–339. Springer, Cham (2016). https://doi.org/10.1007/978-3-319-41321-1_17
21. Zhou, H., Idrees, K., Gracia, J.: Leveraging MPI-3 shared-memory extensions for efficient PGAS runtime systems. In: Träff, J.L., Hunold, S., Versaci, F. (eds.) Euro-Par 2015. LNCS, vol. 9233, pp. 373–384. Springer, Heidelberg (2015). https://doi.org/10.1007/978-3-662-48096-0_29

Portable SHMEMCache: A High-Performance Key-Value Store on OpenSHMEM and MPI

Huansong Fu[1]($\boxtimes$), Manjunath Gorentla Venkata[2], Neena Imam[2],
and Weikuan Yu[1]

[1] Florida State University, Tallahassee, USA
{fu,yuw}@cs.fsu.edu
[2] Oak Ridge National Laboratory, Oak Ridge, USA
{manjugv,imamn}@ornl.gov

Abstract. The integration of Big Data frameworks and HPC capabilities has drawn enormous interests in recent years. SHMEMCache is a distributed key-value store built on the OpenSHMEM global address space. It has solved several practical issues in leveraging OpenSHMEM's one-sided operations for a distributed key-value store and providing efficient key-value operations on both commodity machines and supercomputers. However, being based solely on OpenSHMEM, SHMEMCache cannot leverage one-sided operations from a variety of software packages. This results in several limitations for SHMEMCache. First, we cannot make SHMEM-Cache available to a wider range of platforms. Second, an opportunity for potential performance improvement is missed. Third, there is a lack of deep understanding about how different one-sided operations can fit in with SHMEMCache and other distributed key-values in general. For example, the one-sided operations in OpenSHMEM and MPI have many differences in their interfaces, memory semantics and synchronization methods, all of which can have distinct implications and also increase the complexity in supporting both OpenSHMEM and MPI for SHMEMCache. Therefore, we have taken on an effort on leveraging different one-sided operations for SHMEMCache and proposed a design of portable SHMEMCache. Based on this new framework, we have supported both OpenSHMEM and MPI for SHMEMCache. We have also conducted an extensive set of experiments to compare the performance of the two versions on both commodity machines and the Titan supercomputer.

1 Introduction

As the capacity of Big Data continues to grow, the attentions from both academia and industry for Big Data also keep expanding. For example, in recent years, distributed key-value (KV) store such as Memcached [1] and Redis [4] have been widely used by social networking websites such as Facebook [28] and Twitter [6] as a caching layer on top of their massive databases. This has fostered a large volume of studies about how to boost the performance of a distributed KV store [13,23,26,32,35]. A common topic of these studies is to use advanced HPC capabilities such as Remote Direct Memory Access (RDMA) to accelerate the

M. Gorentla Venkata et al. (Eds.): OpenSHMEM 2017, LNCS 10679, pp. 114–129, 2018.
https://doi.org/10.1007/978-3-319-73814-7_8

communication in the distributed KV stores. As a result, they can deliver much lower latency and higher throughput compared to original Memcached and Redis where TCP/IP is used.

SHMEMCache [16] is a recent effort on building the KV store on top of the symmetric memory of OpenSHMEM. By doing so, it can leverage the Open-SHMEM one-sided operations such as SHMEM_PUT and SHMEM_GET for the KV operations such as SET and GET. Using OpenSHMEM's one-sided operation will naturally take advantage of RDMA when present. Different from previous related works, SHMEMCache provides novel solutions for data consistency issue, carries out cache management in a coarse-grained and lightweight manner, and scales well to more than one thousand machines. It has been shown that SHMEMCache can deliver very low latency and high throughput KV operations at scale while still ensuring data consistency.

An important factor of SHMEMCache's performant KV operations can be attributed to the performance advantage of OpenSHMEM's one-sided operations. The one-sided communication paradigm, in general, has been popularly supported and implemented by many parallel programming systems such as OpenSHMEM [8], MPI [17] and many others [10,27,29]. However, based solely on OpenSHMEM, SHMEMCache cannot leverage one-sided operations from a variety of one-sided communication libraries. There are several limitations as a result. First, we cannot make SHMEMCache available to a wider range of platforms that OpenSHMEM is not supported or supported well. Second, we miss the opportunity for potential performance improvement as using different one-sided operations can directly affect the performance of KV operations. Third and more importantly, since the one-sided communication libraries are very different in many aspects, they will have distinct suitability for SHMEMCache. The understanding on how they fit in with SHMEMCache can provide a valuable insight on how they fit in with the distributed key-value stores and even other types of systems that leverage one-sided operations, such as the distributed transaction systems [9,14]. Take the one-sided operations in OpenSHMEM and MPI for example, they are different in terms of function interfaces, memory semantics and synchronization methods, all of which can have various implications for SHMEMCache. However, such diversity also results in challenges in realizing SHMEMCache with a wide range of one-sided communication libraries. Simply re-implementing SHMEMCache with different one-sided communication libraries entails a lot of additional efforts.

In this paper, we take on an effort on designing portable SHMEMCache for different one-sided communication libraries. Specifically, we propose a set of communication interfaces for SHMEMCache that brings convenience to the adoption of new one-sided communication libraries. In addition, to illustrate how we implement the interfaces with different one-sided operations, we carry out a detailed analysis that compares the specifications of OpenSHMEM and MPI's one-sided communication. Furthermore, we evaluate and compare SHMEMCache's performance of the two versions, i.e. OpenSHMEM and MPI on both in-house commodity machines and the Titan supercomputer.

The paper is organized as follows. We give a background introduction of this paper in Sect. 2, including SHMEMCache's structure and MPI's one-sided communication. Then, in Sect. 3, we introduce a new software architecture of SHMEMCache, a set of interfaces for portable SHMEMCache and an analysis of OpenSHMEM and MPI's one-sided communications. And we discuss some implementation issues in Sect. 4. Finally, we present our experimental results in Sect. 5.

2 Background

2.1 An Overview of SHMEMCache

As shown in Fig. 1, SHMEMCache leverages the performant one-sided operations of OpenSHMEM to speed up its KV operations. Two main KV operations are supported, namely SET, i.e. inserting a new KV pair or updating an existing KV pair, and GET, i.e. retrieving the value associated with a given key. The server uses symmetric memory of OpenSHMEM to store both hash table and KV pairs so that they are visible to clients. Therefore, SHMEMCache is able to support **Direct KV operations**, where the client can directly access the KV pairs which are located remotely on the server's machine. Besides, it also supports **Active KV operations**, where the client can send messages to the server and let the server complete the KV operation. The messages are directly written to the server's memory using one-sided operations. Similarly, the server can send messages to the client, which serves a purpose such as responding a KV operation or synchronizing cache management information.

2.2 One-Sided Communication in MPI

MPI is the de facto message passing standard nowadays. It strives to provide a rich range of communication abilities such as point-to-point communication and

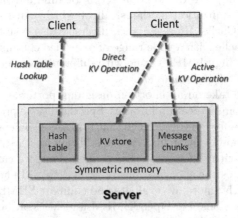

Fig. 1. SHMEMCache structure.

collective communication. As the paradigm of one-sided communication draws much attentions, the MPI standard had started to support it since MPI-2.0. Three types of one-sided operations are supported, i.e. Put (write to remote memory), Get (read from remote memory) and Accumulate (a group of accumulate functions, e.g. SUM).

Later, the MPI standards have further improved its support for one-sided operations. For example, more one-sided Accumulate operations are added such as Compare-And-Swap (CAS) and Fetch-And-Op. More importantly, MPI standard has updated its memory semantics and added the *RMA unified memory* model, where the change made to remote memory can be visible without explicit participation of the remote side, alongside with the existing *RMA separate memory* model, where the remote side needs to call some RMA synchronization functions in order to reflect the updates to its private memory. Although requiring hardware support for memory coherence, the RMA unified model can greatly improve application's performance in many scenarios where the remote side does not need to participate in synchronization. In those scenarios, the model can save a lot of synchronization calls, which are often time consuming. The representative MPI implementations such as MVAPICH [2] and Open MPI [3] have been following up the advancing of MPI standards. For the time being, both MVA-PICH and Open MPI have been fully conformant with the most recent MPI standard (MPI-3.1).

3   Design of Portable SHMEMCache

In this section, we describe our efforts in designing portable SHMEMCache. Firstly, we give an overview to the overall communication architecture of portable SHMEMCache. Then, we introduce the new communication interfaces for portable SHMEMCache. Finally, using OpenSHMEM and MPI as an example, we illustrate how we realize the communication interfaces with regards to the differences in memory semantics and synchronization methods of different one-sided communication libraries.

3.1   Communication Architecture

Figure 2 shows the overall architecture of the communication components of portable SHMEMCache. As mentioned, the client's functions include hash table lookup, direct KV operations and active KV operations. They use the underlying communication interfaces to accomplish their corresponding communication jobs. Among them, both the hash lookup and direct KV operations use the *direct interfaces* which allow the client to directly write or read remote memory of the server. In addition, the active KV operations will use *messaging interfaces* to send or receive messages. Both types of interfaces will leverage the one-sided operations provided by the underlying one-sided communication libraries. On the server side, it only has the messaging interfaces. They are used for responding to the client when the response is requested for an active KV operation, and

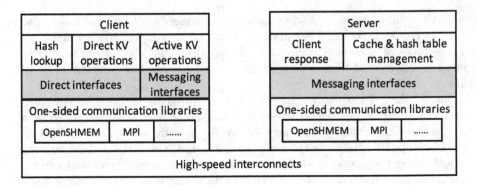

Fig. 2. The communication architecture of portable SHMEMCache.

also for sending cache management and hash table management messages, such as an expiration bar for evicted KV pairs [16]. The one-sided communication libraries will utilize the underlying high-speed interconnect to transfer the data.

3.2 Communication Interfaces

The major difference between the new architecture of portable SHMEMCache and the previous SHMEMCache is the addition of direct and messaging communication interfaces. The realization of SHMEMCache's one-sided communication channel and the implementation of its other components are therefore disentangled from each other, providing convenience in leveraging new one-sided communication libraries.

As shown in Fig. 3, the direct communication interfaces include shmemcache_put and shmemcache_get, which are akin to the put and get operations in common one-sided communication libraries, such as SHMEM_PUT and SHMEM_GET in OpenSHMEM. They have similar input parameters such as the address of local buffer to copy from or copy to. But the direct interfaces in portable SHMEM-Cache abstract the information of remote memory using an ID (dst_mem) and offset (offset). The ID indicates which region of exposed remote memory that the client wants to access. The offset indicates the position in the memory region to access. We find that such abstraction is well suited for most one-sided communication libraries we have studied. The direct interfaces do not include synchronization calls since they can be called inside shmemcache_put or shmemcache_get.

Additionally, the messaging interfaces include shmemcache_send, shmemcache_recv and shmemcache_send_buffered. They are constructed around the Message structure. No dst_mem is needed here since the target memory region is certain, which is an exposed memory buffer on the receiving process dedicated for a specific sending process. The client can choose to use shmemcache_send to directly send the message, which is written to the remote memory and return immediately. The client can also choose to buffer the messages for the same server and use shmemcache_send_buffered to send those

Direct interfaces:

```
int shmemcache_put(void * src_buf, size_t length, ProcessID dst_proc,
                    MemoryID dst_mem, size_t offset);
int shmemcache_get(void * dst_buf, size_t length, ProcessID dst_proc,
                    MemoryID dst_mem, size_t offset);
```

Messaging interfaces:

```
int shmemcache_send(Message * msg, ProcessID dst_proc);
int shmemcache_send_buffered(Message ** msgs, ProcessID dst_proc);
Message * shmemcache_recv(ProcessID dst_proc);
```

Fig. 3. Communication interfaces of portable SHMEMCache.

buffered messages at once. This option is often used when the client does not request the response from the server before its next KV operation. A window size (e.g. 8) is predetermined as a parameter to indicate how many buffered messages to send at once. Note that, for direct interfaces we do not enable the buffering because unlike messaging, the client needs to indicate further actions according to the return value of the direct interfaces. For example, when a SET does not succeed because it fails to lock the target memory (see Sect. 2), it is up to the client to choose to either wait longer or abort the operation.

3.3 Comparison of Memory Semantics and Synchronization of One-Sided Operations

There can be many differences in the memory semantics and synchronization methods between different one-sided communication libraries. Here we only discuss OpenSHMEM and MPI regarding their suitability for SHMEMCache, but similar principles can be followed when trying to use other one-sided communication libraries. Essentially being a PGAS model, OpenSHMEM allows a PE to use non-blocking one-sided operation to directly access the data objects in remote symmetric memory without any specific synchronization call from the corresponding target PE. Such semantics suits SHMEMCache well as it alleviate the burden of the server, which often becomes a bottleneck serving millions of requests per second. There are, however, some synchronization routines for the target PE to block until observing the updates to its data objects, such as SHMEM_WAIT. But the source PE does not need to wait until the synchronization is done by the target PE in order to complete its one-sided operation. The target PE can poll its symmetric memory in a lightweight manner without blocking to receive the data. For SHMEMCache's messaging interfaces, such method will be used. The source PE has additional synchronization routines to ensure the delivery and ordering of data, e.g. SHMEM_QUIET for assuring delivery of all outstanding one-sided operations and SHMEM_FENCE for assuring the ordering of the delivery.

As for MPI, as previously mentioned, there are two memory models for MPI one-sided operations which are RMA separate and RMA unified models. In the RMA separate model, a remote update can be visible in the target private memory only after an ensuring call from the target process. In the RMA unified model, such update can be visible without the additional calls from the target process. We can see that the RMA separate model is not desired by SHMEM-Cache and the RMA unified model better resembles OpenSHMEM's memory semantics. Therefore, system support for the RMA unified model is needed.

Moreover, MPI also has more synchronization methods for its one-sided operations. There are two categories of synchronization methods. One is called *active target communication* and another is called *passive target communication*. In the active target communication, both source and target process explicitly form a *synchronization epoch*, during which the one-sided operations can be conducted and completed. In comparison, in the passive target communication, only the source process needs to form the epoch but the target process does needs that. Three synchronization methods in MPI are available, i.e. *fence*, *post-and-wait* and *lock-unlock*, each of which works for one of the two categories. Both the fence and post-and-wait methods work for the active target communication and the lock-unlock works for the passive target communication. SHMEMCache needs the passive target communication because both direct and messaging communication interfaces preclude the help from the target process. Therefore, the lock-unlock method should be the choice for SHMEMCache.

Note that, it is not impossible to use RMA separate model or active target communication for SHMEMCache. For example, we can use a concept of "universal epoch" in SHMEMCache. That is, every PE repeatedly and collectively starts and closes an epoch. Only in the epoch, each PE can conduct one-sided operations. However, there is a big difficulty in deciding the duration of the epoch in that approach. If the duration is too short, there will be too much synchronization overheads, especially for the PEs that do not have any operation to carry out in that epoch, so the universal synchronization will significantly delay their following operations. It the duration is too long, since the data delivery cannot be guaranteed until the epoch finishes, the completion of many KV operations will be prolonged, hence the increased KV operation latency, which is very undesirable for SHMEMCache. However, this approach could be much more desirable by some bulk synchronous scenarios such as running a graph processing application on in-memory KV store, which could be one of the future endeavors.

4   Implementation

We have implemented the new communication interfaces using both OpenSH-MEM and MPI's one-sided operations with about 110 lines of code. All code is written in C. In this section, we report some implementation issues.

4.1   Difference Between OpenSHMEM and MPI Implementations

Unlike OpenSHMEM, to expose the memory, there is an additional step to associate it with an MPI window to make it remotely accessible. The association is built as follows to better fit in with the communication interfaces: the hash table is associated with one window, the KV store is associated with one window, each group of the message chunks that receive messages from one PE gets associated with one window.

In addition, the one-sided operations in MPI needs different input parameters as those in OpenSHMEM. MPI one-sided operations need the displacement from start position of the window of the address it wants to access, while OpenSHMEM only needs the address. Therefore, for OpenSHMEM, we need to calculate the address and use it for OpenSHMEM one-sided operations. While for MPI, the offset is directly used for its one-sided operations. In addition, despite being universal applicable for different one-sided operations, the use of offset instead of address requires the pointer directory to change accordingly.

4.2   Alternative MPI Implementation Options

MPI has lighter-weight synchronization calls for its one-sided operations, such as lock-all and unlock-all. They are lighter-weight in the sense that they need fewer synchronization calls when a process needs to communicate with a group of processes. However, we do not have such scenarios in SHMEMCache to exploit this benefit. For direct KV operations and non-buffered active KV operations, a client only writes to or read from one server at a certain time. Even for buffered active KV operations, the messages are buffered and sent to only one target process. Our test result backs this assessment, showing that replacing lock and unlock with lock-all and unlock-all operations in SHMEMCache does not give us any performance improvement.

In addition, one may consider using the non-blocking MPI Isend/Irecv routines to implement the messaging interfaces. However, they do not fit in with SHMEMCache as well because we will need exact matching of Isend and Irecv calls, which is not feasible in SHMEMCache's scenarios.

For MPI, the globally visible memory is allocated by `MPI_Alloc_mem`. Although in our experiments, there is no performance difference resulted from using `MPI_Alloc_mem` or common memory allocation function in C such as `malloc`, it is still preferred to use `MPI_Alloc_mem` for potential improvement on a system that can provide optimization.

5   Evaluation

Our experiments are conducted on two systems. The first one is an in-house cluster of 21 server nodes called *Innovation*. Each machine is equipped with 10 dual-socket Intel Xeon(R) cores and 64 GB memory. All nodes are connected through an FDR Infiniband interconnect with the ConnectX-3 NIC.

The second is the *Titan* supercomputer at Oak Ridge National Laboratory [5]. Titan is a hybrid-architecture Cray XK7 system, which consists of 18,688 nodes and each node is equipped with a 16-core AMD Opteron CPU and 32 GB of DDR3 memory. We use Open MPI version 2.1.0 for both OpenSHMEM and MPI implementations. Unless otherwise specified, on each machine we run only one client or server, without collocating them.

We use the YCSB benchmark suite [11] to generate our workload. It is a tool that can generate workloads based on real-world statistics. Our workload contains 1 million KV operations that operate on 1 million records, each of which has a 16 Byte key and 128 Byte value. The distribution of KV pairs follows the Zipfian distribution. The proportion of SET and GET in the workload varies depending on the experiment types: for KV operation latency test, only one of SET/GET is included and for throughput test, the workload consists of 95% GET and 5% SET. To avoid the impact of initialization and data ingress, we load all the KV pairs in memory before starting the time measuring.

5.1   Operation Latency

Active Operation. Figure 4 shows the average operation latency when using the active KV operation. In this experiment, the client does not buffer the messages and also requires a response from the server before proceeding to next KV operation. We can see that on both Innovation and Titan, the OpenSHMEM version consistently outperforms the MPI version for different value sizes. The main reason behind this is the difference in synchronization overheads. The MPI's

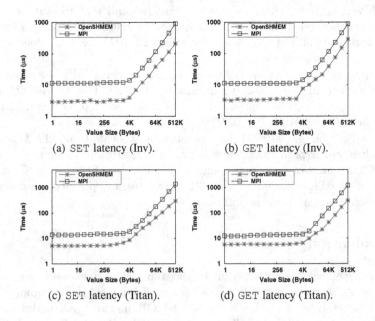

(a) SET latency (Inv).   (b) GET latency (Inv).

(c) SET latency (Titan).   (d) GET latency (Titan).

Fig. 4. Active operation latency.

lock and unlock steps for each sending message cost much more than OpenSH-MEM's only one synchronization call, i.e. shmem_quiet. Moreover, as the value size increases, there will be more messages to send, hence the increasing number of synchronization calls. Therefore, the OpenSHMEM version continues to show performance advantage for larger value sizes.

Direct Operation. Figure 5 shows the average operation latency when using the direct KV operation. We can see that the OpenSHMEM version still has generally more competitive performance than the MPI version. However, the advantage of OpenSHMEM version over MPI version is less pronounced than that in Fig. 4, especially for large value size. This is because the number of synchronization calls does not increase as much as the value size when conducting direct KV operations. Only one synchronization call is needed for every direct KV operation. For some larger value sizes, performance of the MPI version becomes comparable or even better than the OpenSHMEM version. In addition, SET on Titan has higher latency than that on Innovation, which is mainly because on Innovation we opt to use the RDMA compare-and-swap for more competitive performance on the Linux cluster of Innovation.

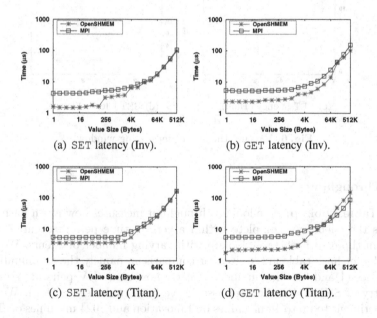

(a) SET latency (Inv).   (b) GET latency (Inv).

(c) SET latency (Titan).   (d) GET latency (Titan).

Fig. 5. Direct operation latency.

Effect of Messaging Window Size. To further investigate the impact of synchronization overheads that affect the performance of MPI version, we vary the messaging window size, which is the number of buffered messages to send in the active KV operation latency experiment. Figure 6 shows the average operation latency with difference messaging window sizes. It can be seen that both the OpenSHMEM and MPI versions have better performance if window size is more than one. Among the two, the MPI version has a larger improvement when window size continues to increase, because that helps saturate its relatively large synchronization overheads. But both will cease to deliver noticeable improvement when the window size reaches certain number.

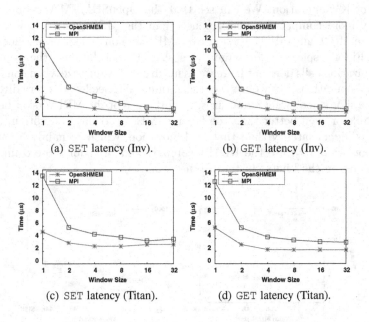

(a) SET latency (Inv).   (b) GET latency (Inv).

(c) SET latency (Titan).   (d) GET latency (Titan).

Fig. 6. Varying the size of messaging window.

5.2   Throughput

Hash Table Lookup. The lookup throughput measures how much hash table lookups the client can complete within a certain time period. Figure 7 shows the throughput of hash table lookup with varying number of clients. We show two different hash table entry sizes for comparison, namely the two numbers of sub-entries (1 and 8). The number indicates how many KV pairs are stored in one entry of SHMEMCache's set-associative hash table (see Sect. 2). We scale the experiment to up to 16 machines on Innovation and 1024 machines on Titan. From the results we can see that, the performance of the two versions are comparable on both Innovation and Titan. However, the OpenSHMEM version still outperforms the MPI version slightly and consistently. The results also demonstrate that both the OpenSHMEM and MPI versions have achieved good scalability with 1024 clients from different machines accessing the hash table of only one same server.

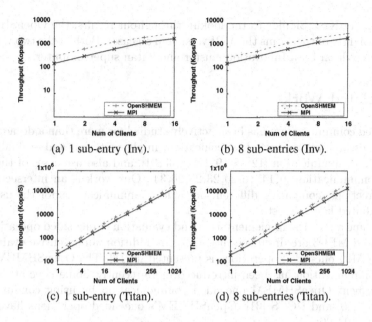

(a) 1 sub-entry (Inv).

(b) 8 sub-entries (Inv).

(c) 1 sub-entry (Titan).

(d) 8 sub-entries (Titan).

Fig. 7. Lookup throughput with varying number of clients.

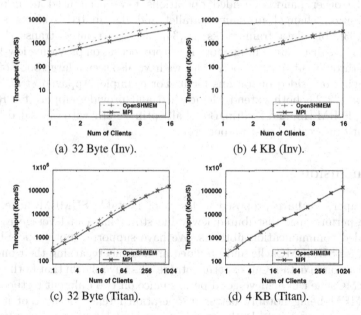

(a) 32 Byte (Inv).

(b) 4 KB (Inv).

(c) 32 Byte (Titan).

(d) 4 KB (Titan).

Fig. 8. KV operation throughput with varying number of clients.

KV Operations. We also evaluate the throughput for KV operations with the mixed workload introduced before. Figure 8 shows results with varying number of clients. We depict the results for two value sizes, a smaller one (32 Byte) and a larger one (4 KB). Similar to the lookup throughput results, the OpenSHMEM version slightly outperforms the MPI version in all cases. Both of the two versions can scale well on both Innovation cluster and Titan supercomputer.

6   Related Works

One-sided communication has been actively studied for more than a decade. The related research efforts include specification, implementation and evaluation of one-sided communication [12,18,19,21,24,30,31], and also use cases of the one-sided communication [9,14–16,20,23,25,26,34]. Our work is an intersection of both directions, comparing different one-sided communications for the use case of distributed key-value store.

To name a few, the implementation and evaluation of one-sided operations in MPI-2 and MPI-3 are discussed in [12,21]. In addition, an extensive evaluation study of MPI one-sided operations is presented in [18]. The OpenSHMEM one-sided communication has been introduced more recently. Some have attempted to implement OpenSHMEM one-sided communication by using conduit such as MPI-3 [19] and UCCS [31]. OpenSHMEM's one-sided operations have been studied in [24,30].

On the other hand, one-sided operations have been used to implement communication channel in many parallel and distributed systems such as MPI [25,33], big data frameworks [20,34], and distributed transaction systems [9,14]. As distributed in-memory KV store focuses on providing low-latency and high-throughput remote operations, we have also seen a large body of works on leveraging one-sided operations for it. For example, Appavoo *et al.* [7] and Jose *et al.* [22,23] both extend Memcached and provide support for RDMA. Pilaf [26], FaRM [13] and HydraDB [35] all optimize GET with one-sided RDMA reads that can greatly boost its performance.

7   Conclusion

In this paper, we have proposed a design of portable SHMEMCache, which is a high-performance distributed key-value store that can leverage a variety of one-sided communication libraries. We have supported both OpenSHMEM and MPI for SHMEMCache and provided an analysis regarding their one-sided communication in detail. Our experimental results have shown that both versions of SHMEMCache can achieve good performance on two different testbeds, with OpenSHMEM being notably better in operation latency because of its lower synchronization overheads. Both can achieve good scalability towards more than 1000 machines on the Titan supercomputer. In future, we will support more one-sided communication libraries and compare their performance. We will also explore more use cases for the one-sided communication such as graph processing applications.

Acknowledgment. This work was supported in part by a contract from Oak Ridge National Laboratory and the National Science Foundation awards 1561041 and 1564647.

This research used resources of the Oak Ridge Leadership Computing Facility, which is a DOE Office of Science User Facility supported under Contract DE-AC05-00OR22725.

References

1. Memcached. https://memcached.org/downloads
2. MVAPICH. http://mvapich.cse.ohio-state.edu/
3. OpenMPI. https://www.open-mpi.org/
4. Redis. http://redis.io/
5. Titan Supercomputer. https://www.olcf.ornl.gov/titan/
6. Aniszczyk, C.: Caching with twemcache (2012)
7. Appavoo, J., Waterland, A., Da Silva, D., Uhlig, V., Rosenburg, B., Van Hensbergen, E., Stoess, J., Wisniewski, R., Steinberg, U.: Providing a cloud network infrastructure on a supercomputer. In: Proceedings of the 19th ACM International Symposium on High Performance Distributed Computing, pp. 385–394. ACM (2010)
8. Chapman, B., Curtis, T., Pophale, S., Poole, S., Kuehn, J., Koelbel, C., Smith, L.: Introducing OpenSHMEM: SHMEM for the PGAS community. In: Proceedings of the Fourth Conference on Partitioned Global Address Space Programming Model, p. 2. ACM (2010)
9. Chen, Y., Wei, X., Shi, J., Chen, R., Chen, H.: Fast and general distributed transactions using RDMA and HTM. In: Proceedings of the Eleventh European Conference on Computer Systems, p. 26. ACM (2016)
10. UPC Consortium: UPC language specifications v1. 2. Lawrence Berkeley National Laboratory (2005)
11. Cooper, B.F., Silberstein, A., Tam, E., Ramakrishnan, R., Sears, R.: Benchmarking cloud serving systems with YCSB. In: Proceedings of the 1st ACM Symposium on Cloud Computing, pp. 143–154. ACM (2010)
12. Dinan, J., Balaji, P., Buntinas, D., Goodell, D., Gropp, W., Thakur, R.: An implementation and evaluation of the MPI 3.0 one-sided communication interface. Concurr. Comput. Pract. Exp. **28**, 4385–4404 (2016)
13. Dragojević, A., Narayanan, D., Castro, M., Hodson, O.: Farm: fast remote memory. In: 11th USENIX Symposium on Networked Systems Design and Implementation (NSDI 14), pp. 401–414 (2014)
14. Dragojević, A., Narayanan, D., Nightingale, E.B., Renzelmann, M., Shamis, A., Badam, A., Castro, M.: No compromises: distributed transactions with consistency, availability, and performance. In: Proceedings of the 25th Symposium on Operating Systems Principles, pp. 54–70. ACM (2015)
15. Fu, H., SinghaRoy, K., Venkata, M.G., Zhu, Y., Yu, W.: SHMemCache: enabling memcached on the OpenSHMEM global address model. In: Gorentla Venkata, M., Imam, N., Pophale, S., Mintz, T.M. (eds.) OpenSHMEM 2016. LNCS, vol. 10007, pp. 131–145. Springer, Cham (2016). https://doi.org/10.1007/978-3-319-50995-2_9
16. Fu, H., Venkata, M.G., Choudhury, A.R., Imam, N., Yu, W.: High-performance key-value store on OpenSHMEM. In: Proceedings of the 17th IEEE/ACM International Symposium on Cluster, Cloud and Grid Computing, pp. 559–568. IEEE Press (2017)

17. Geist, A., Gropp, W., Huss-Lederman, S., Lumsdaine, A., Lusk, E., Saphir, W., Skjellum, T., Snir, M.: MPI-2: extending the message-passing interface. In: Bougé, L., Fraigniaud, P., Mignotte, A., Robert, Y. (eds.) Euro-Par 1996. LNCS, vol. 1123, pp. 128–135. Springer, Heidelberg (1996). https://doi.org/10.1007/3-540-61626-8_16

18. Gropp, W., Thakur, R.: An evaluation of implementation options for MPI one-sided communication. In: Di Martino, B., Kranzlmüller, D., Dongarra, J. (eds.) EuroPVM/MPI 2005. LNCS, vol. 3666, pp. 415–424. Springer, Heidelberg (2005). https://doi.org/10.1007/11557265_53

19. Hammond, J.R., Ghosh, S., Chapman, B.M.: Implementing OpenSHMEM using MPI-3 one-sided communication. In: Poole, S., Hernandez, O., Shamis, P. (eds.) OpenSHMEM 2014. LNCS, vol. 8356, pp. 44–58. Springer, Cham (2014). https://doi.org/10.1007/978-3-319-05215-1_4

20. Huang, J., Ouyang, X., Jose, J., Wasi-ur Rahman, M., Wang, H., Luo, M., Subramoni, H., Murthy, C., Panda, D.K.: High-performance design of HBase with RDMA over infiniband. In: 2012 IEEE 26th International Parallel & Distributed Processing Symposium (IPDPS), pp. 774–785. IEEE (2012)

21. Jiang, W., Liu, J., Jin, H.-W., Panda, D.K., Gropp, W., Thakur, R.: High performance MPI-2 one-sided communication over infiniband. In: IEEE International Symposium on Cluster Computing and the Grid, CCGrid 2004, pp. 531–538. IEEE (2004)

22. Jose, J., Subramoni, H., Kandalla, K., Wasi-ur Rahman, M., Wang, H., Narravula, S., Panda, D.K.: Scalable memcached design for infiniband clusters using hybrid transports. In: 2012 12th IEEE/ACM International Symposium on Cluster, Cloud and Grid Computing (CCGrid), pp. 236–243. IEEE (2012)

23. Jose, J., Subramoni, H., Luo, M., Zhang, M., Huang, J., Wasi-ur Rahman, M., Islam, N.S., Ouyang, X., Wang, H., Sur, S., et al.: Memcached design on high performance RDMA capable interconnects. In: 2011 International Conference on Parallel Processing (ICPP), pp. 743–752. IEEE (2011)

24. Jose, J., Zhang, J., Venkatesh, A., Potluri, S., Panda, D.K.: A comprehensive performance evaluation of OpenSHMEM libraries on InfiniBand clusters. In: Poole, S., Hernandez, O., Shamis, P. (eds.) OpenSHMEM 2014. LNCS, vol. 8356, pp. 14–28. Springer, Cham (2014). https://doi.org/10.1007/978-3-319-05215-1_2

25. Liu, J., Wu, J., Panda, D.K.: High performance RDMA-based MPI implementation over infiniband. Int. J. Parallel Prog. 32(3), 167–198 (2004)

26. Mitchell, C., Geng, Y., Li, J.: Using one-sided RDMA reads to build a fast, CPU-efficient key-value store. In: USENIX Annual Technical Conference, pp. 103–114 (2013)

27. Nieplocha, J., Palmer, B., Tipparaju, V., Krishnan, M., Trease, H., Aprà, E.: Advances, applications and performance of the global arrays shared memory programming toolkit. Int. J. High Perform. Comput. Appl. 20(2), 203–231 (2006)

28. Nishtala, R., Fugal, H., Grimm, S., Kwiatkowski, M., Lee, H., Li, H.C., McElroy, R., Paleczny, M., Peek, D., Saab, P., et al.: Scaling memcache at facebook. In: Presented as Part of the 10th USENIX Symposium on Networked Systems Design and Implementation (NSDI 13), pp. 385–398 (2013)

29. Numrich, R.W., Reid, J.: Co-array Fortran for parallel programming. ACM SIG-PLAN Fortran Forum 17, 1–31 (1998). ACM

30. Pophale, S., Nanjegowda, R., Curtis, T., Chapman, B., Jin, H., Poole, S., Kuehn, J.: OpenSHMEM performance and potential: a NPB experimental study. In: The 6th Conference on Partitioned Global Address Space Programming Models (PGAS12). Citeseer (2012)

31. Shamis, P., Venkata, M.G., Poole, S., Welch, A., Curtis, T.: Designing a high performance OpenSHMEM implementation using universal common communication substrate as a communication middleware. In: Poole, S., Hernandez, O., Shamis, P. (eds.) OpenSHMEM 2014. LNCS, vol. 8356, pp. 1–13. Springer, Cham (2014). https://doi.org/10.1007/978-3-319-05215-1_1

32. Shankar, D., Lu, X., Islam, N., Wasi-Ur-Rahman, M., Panda, D.K.: High-performance hybrid key-value store on modern clusters with RDMA interconnects and SSDs: non-blocking extensions, designs, and benefits. In: 2016 IEEE International Parallel and Distributed Processing Symposium, pp. 393–402. IEEE (2016)

33. Shipman, G.M., Woodall, T.S., Graham, R.L., Maccabe, A.B., Bridges, P.G.: Infiniband scalability in Open MPI. In: Proceedings 20th IEEE International Parallel & Distributed Processing Symposium, p. 10-pp. IEEE (2006)

34. Wang, Y., Que, X., Yu, W., Goldenberg, D., Sehgal, D.: Hadoop acceleration through network levitated merge. In: Proceedings of 2011 International Conference for High Performance Computing, Networking, Storage and Analysis, p. 57. ACM (2011)

35. Wang, Y., Zhang, L., Tan, J., Li, M., Gao, Y., Guerin, X., Meng, X., Meng, S.: HydraDB: a resilient RDMA-driven key-value middleware for in-memory cluster computing. In: SC 2015, p. 22. ACM (2015)

Balancing Performance and Portability
with Containers in HPC:
An OpenSHMEM Example

Thomas Naughton[1]([✉]), Lawrence Sorrillo[2], Adam Simpson[2], and Neena Imam[3]

[1] Computer Science and Mathematics Division, Oak Ridge National Laboratory,
Oak Ridge, TN 37831, USA
naughtont@ornl.gov
[2] Center for Computational Sciences, Oak Ridge National Laboratory,
Oak Ridge, TN 37831, USA
[3] Computing and Computational Sciences Directorate,
Oak Ridge National Laboratory, Oak Ridge, TN 37831, USA

Abstract. There is a growing interest in using Linux containers to streamline software development and application deployment. A container enables the user to bundle the salient elements of the software stack from an application's perspective. In this paper, we discuss initial experiences in using the Open MPI implementation of OpenSHMEM with containers on HPC resources. We provide a brief overview of two container runtimes, Docker & Singularity, highlighting elements that are of interest for HPC users. The Docker platform offers a rich set of services that are widely used in enterprise environments, whereas Singularity is an emerging container runtime that is specifically written for use on HPC systems. We describe our procedure for container assembly and deployment that strives to maintain the portability of the container-based application. We show performance results for the Graph500 benchmark running along the typical continuum of development testbed up to full production supercomputer (ORNL's *Titan*). The results show consistent performance between the native and Singularity (container) tests. The results also showed an unexplained drop in performance when using the Cray Gemini network with Open MPI's OpenSHMEM, which was unrelated to the container usage.

This work was sponsored by the U.S. Department of Energy's Office of Advanced Scientific Computing Research. This manuscript has been authored by UT-Battelle, LLC under Contract No. DE-AC05-00OR22725 with the U.S. Department of Energy. The United States Government retains and the publisher, by accepting the article for publication, acknowledges that the United States Government retains a non-exclusive, paid-up, irrevocable, world-wide license to publish or reproduce the published form of this manuscript, or allow others to do so, for United States Government purposes. The Department of Energy will provide public access to these results of federally sponsored research in accordance with the DOE Public Access Plan (http://energy.gov/downloads/doe-public-access-plan). This research used resources of the Oak Ridge Leadership Computing Facility, which is a DOE Office of Science User Facility supported under Contract DE-AC05-00OR22725.

M. Gorentla Venkata et al. (Eds.): OpenSHMEM 2017, LNCS 10679, pp. 130–142, 2018.
https://doi.org/10.1007/978-3-319-73814-7_9

1   Introduction

There is much interest in the emerging use of Linux containers to streamline software development and application deployment. This is primarily due to the rich set of tools that have appeared for web and commodity based workloads. These new capabilities offer users the ability to quickly customize their execution environment and offer improved user productivity by providing "portable" applications. These container-based approaches also offer potential benefits for reproducibility of computational experiments by capturing the salient elements of the software stack from an application's perspective. However, there are some challenges when trying to employ containers in high performance computing (HPC). For example, integration of new tools/methods into existing HPC services and security policies. Additionally, there may be performance issues if the underlying resources are not properly leveraged, e.g., using tuned communication libraries and HPC network drivers.

In general, the container runtime environments that exist today are primarily focused on enterprise systems like Docker. This leads to assumptions and priorities that are not fully aligned with an HPC context. A very basic difference is that HPC systems generally use batch allocations where a single user is given exclusive access to a set of nodes that are attached to a high speed interconnect. There is little need to add additional network isolation layers that reduce direct access to the high speed interconnect. Other examples of inconsistencies due to choices associated with an enterprise setting include assumptions about user access controls and local storage and filesystems.

In this paper, we discuss our initial experience in using the Open MPI [3] implementation of OpenSHMEM with containers on HPC resources. We describe the procedure for container assembly and deployment that attempts to maintain the portability of the container-based application. This methodology is evaluated from the perspectives of portability and performance. We show performance results for the Graph500 benchmark running along the typical continuum of development testbed up to full production supercomputer (ORNL's *Titan*).

2   Background

A container is a method for encapsulating an execution environment. Linux containers leverage two operating system (OS) isolation mechanisms: resource namespaces and control groups (cgroups). These mechanisms extend the classic UNIX fork/exec model to allow for further refinements to the sharing (or restricting) of resources viewable by processes. A *container runtime* is the software tool that coordinates the use of these low-level mechanisms to provide simplified access for managing the setup and execution of containers. The container runtime drives the initialization of a container and offers convenient interfaces to attach and interact with "container-ized" applications. A *container image* is the software bundle that contains the application and its dependent files and data.

There are several emerging tools for running containers and managing the work-flow of image creation and sharing. Docker is a popular enterprise solution and Singularity is an emerging solution specifically targeting HPC environments.

2.1 Docker

The Docker [2] tool is actually comprised of several separate pieces. The Docker Engine includes the user interface, storage drivers, network overlays and container runtime. The Docker Registry is an image server, which can be used to provide both public and private shares with a central community registry hosted at Docker Hub (https://hub.docker.com). There is also an orchestration interface and specification called Docker Compose. These tools all use a similar specification format so there is consistency between the tools/layers. Docker also includes support for linking the control daemons on different hosts into a grouping called a *Swarm*. In Docker Swarm mode, a user can perform distributed computing with containers spanning multiple hosts. An overlay network is typically used to provide seamless interaction between container-ized processes running on different physical hosts.

2.2 Singularity

Singularity [5] is a container runtime created for use in HPC environments. The focus is on providing a user with "compute mobility", while following expected practices for HPC sites. The runtime follows common practices for user permission management, whereby a user has the same access in the container environment as they do outside the container. This limits some actions that the user can perform on the HPC resource directly, which mainly involves operations associated with image management. Singularity supports building images via a definition file or by importing Docker images. A new Singularity Hub is coming online for sharing images and managing image creation. Singularity does not setup any network isolation, nor does it provide any distributed control capability. Instead, Singularity expects the user to use the existing HPC network directly and leverage available parallel resource management/launch capabilities that are standard in managed HPC environments.

3 Approach

A major motivation for using containers is to streamline the deployment of applications by providing a consistent execution environment that is carried to each machine. This environment is defined in the container image and allows a user to install software and configure their application as they choose. However, there are some aspects that require special attention, namely those pieces that interface with the system. For example, there must be proper compatibility between the C runtime library (libc) that exports the interface to the kernel via system calls.

Similarly, the interface to network devices and graphics processing units (GPUs) also require special attention to ensure correct and efficient access.

There are different methods for coping with these host specific elements. In general, they involve either exporting elements to dynamically access the proper software interfaces (libraries) or embedding all possible interfaces (libraries) into the image. However, the latter is not always an option as some software is not freely redistributable (e.g., network drivers) and it may simply be outside the user's purview.

The following describes our considerations and methodology for creating a container image to deploy the OpenSHMEM enhanced version of the Graph500 benchmark. We used a typical development life-cycle as the basis for our approach: (1) develop on a small testbed (Docker & Singularity); and, (2) run on a production machine (Singularity).

3.1 Container Deployment

As mentioned above, there are two general approaches for dealing with host specific elements: (a) customize the image with the requisite software, or (b) dynamically load the requisite software. The customized option can potentially break the portability of the container image, and potentially adds to the complexity of the image creation process. The dynamic load option avoids problems with portability, but may not be fully realizable. To better understand this process, we deployed a version of the Graph500 benchmark that uses OpenSHMEM [1]. We attempted to keep the image as generic as possible and customize only when necessary.

OpenSHMEM. There are several emerging implementations of OpenSHMEM, but very few are pre-packaged with standard Linux distributions. When preparing our OpenSHMEM based benchmark, we identified that Open MPI includes an implementation of OpenSHMEM. The Open MPI shipped with Ubuntu 17.04 enables OSHMEM support by default, which meant we could install the distribution version of Open MPI (`openmpi`) in the image to have a working OSHMEM.

"Split Level" Launch. A key element of the Singularity approach to containers is that you avoid recreating pieces that are already available in HPC for launching parallel applications. This includes the system process management interface. For example, HPC systems have remote process launching services on all compute nodes and the parallel runtime environments are setup to use these services for remote process startup. The notion of a "split level" launch is where the host's process management interfaces are used to startup the container-ized application on the parallel platform, i.e., the parallel application is split between host and container during launch. In the case of Open MPI, the runtime layer is enhanced to understand how to properly launch a process using Singularity. The runtime is on the host. The application is in the container. The host runtime starts up the containers-ized parallel application. The communication libraries from the host can also be injected into the container for use at execution time. The injection is accomplished by sharing the host communication libraries with the container and pre-pending this path to the LD_LIBRARY_PATH used in the container. Note, this assumes that the libraries maintain proper Application Binary Interface (ABI) compatibility if the host/container versioning is not exactly identical.

3.2   Container Image Setup

We created a Docker image for Graph500-oshmem, which was useful for initial testing on the development machine. The Docker image was then used to create a Singularity image for Graph500-oshmem. We tested using a direct import of the Docker image with Singularity and using a Singularity bootstrap definition file (much like a Dockerfile). There was no significant difference when working on the development system, but on production machines the Singularity import method might be more useful as it can be used without root permissions (nor a local Docker installation).

A few image customizations were required in order to run the container on the production machine. We had to add a few directories for bind mounts (Fig. 1) that are setup at runtime for use on the Titan machine, e.g., ALPS scheduler information, Lustre, parallel filesystem mounts. A few changes were made to the environment for the container by editing the /environment file in the Singularity container[1] (Fig. 2). We also had to add the *Munge* authentication library, which had not been installed in the image, and was needed at execution time on the production system (Fig. 3).

```
1     mkdir -p /opt/cray
2     mkdir -p /var/spool/alps
3     mkdir -p /var/opt/cray
4     mkdir -p /lustre/atlas
5     mkdir -p /lustre/atlas1
6     mkdir -p /lustre/atlas2
7
8     if [ "x${MY_TITAN_USERNAME}" != "x" ] ; then
9         mkdir -p /ccs/home/${MY_TITAN_USERNAME}
10    fi
```

Fig. 1. Directories to create in image to support required bind mounts for use on Titan.

---

[1] In Singularity-2.3, we should be able to make the environment changes dynamically without having to directly edit the "/environment" file by using SINGULARITYENV_ prefixes.

```
1    # Appended to /environment file in container image
2
3    # On Cray, extend LD_LIBRARY_PATH with host CRAYLibs
4    if test -n "$CRAY_LD_LIBRARY_PATH"; then
5        export PATH=$PATH:/usr/local/cuda/bin
6        # Add Cray specific library paths
7        export LD_LIBRARY_PATH=${CRAY_LD_LIBRARY_PATH}:/opt/cray/sysutils
         /1.0-1.0502.60492.1.1.gem/lib64:/opt/cray/wlm_detect/1.0-1.0502.64649.2.2.gem
         /lib64:/usr/local/lib:/lib64/usr/lib/x86_64-linux-gnu:/usr/local/cuda/lib:/
         usr/local/cuda/lib64:${LD_LIBRARY_PATH}
8    fi
9
10   # On Cray, Also add the host OMPI Libs
11   if test -n "$CRAY_OMPI_LD_LIBRARY_PATH"; then
12       # Add OpenMPI/2.0.2 libraries
13       export LD_LIBRARY_PATH=${CRAY_OMPI_LD_LIBRARY_PATH}:${LD_LIBRARY_PATH}
14       # Apparently these are needed on Titan
15       OMPI_MCA_mpi_leave_pinned=0
16       OMPI_MCA_mpi_leave_pinned_pipeline=0
17   fi
```

Fig. 2. Additions for the "/environment" file in the Singularity image, appended to the end of file.

```
1    apt-get update \
2        && apt-get install -y \
3            libmunge2 \
4            munge \
5        && apt-get clean
```

Fig. 3. Additional packages to add to the container image for use on production machine (Titan).

4   Evaluation

The motivation for containers is to have a portable "bundle" (image) to allow an application to be self-sufficient. The intent of our experiment is to have a consistent image that can be transferred between the testbed and production environments, while achieving the potential performance for each machine. We ran the Graph500-oshmem [1] and OSU [6] benchmarks to identify any performance differences when running with and without a container.

4.1   Testing Environment

The *UB4* development cluster is a small four node testbed of Dell C6220 machines connected via a dedicated 10GigE interconnect. The machines have dual Intel(R) Xeon(R) 2.0 GHz CPU with 8 cores per processor (16 cores per node) and 64 GB of physical memory. The nodes have a Mellanox MT26428 ConnectX interface that is configured to run in 10GigE mode using the mlx4_en device driver. The nodes are running Ubuntu 16.04.1 at the host level with a Linux 4.4.0-75-generic kernel. The nodes are installed with Docker v1.13 and Singularity v2.2.1.

The *Titan* supercomputer is housed at the Oak Ridge Leadership Computing Facility (OLCF) [7]. Titan is a 200 cabinet Cray XK7 comprised of 18,688 nodes with an AMD Opteron 6274 (Interlagos) CPU and a NVidia Kepler K20X GPU, for a total theoretical peak performance of 27 PFlops. The CPUs have 16 cores and 32 GB of memory per node, plus 6 GB of memory for each GPU. The nodes are connected via a 3D Torus Cray Gemini network. The system runs the Cray Linux Environment (CLE), which is currently CLE 5.2.82. During our tests, the nodes were installed with Singularity v2.2.1.

4.2 OpenSHMEM/Graph500

We used the Graph500 benchmark that had been enhanced to use OpenSH-MEM [1]. The benchmark takes two input parameters, Scale and EdgeFactor, which determine the size of the graph used for the problem. Based on these two parameters, the benchmark generates a list of edges and constructs a graph, which is subsequently used in a breadth first search (BFS) from 64 randomly selected points [4]. The BFS searches are timed with the mean time for each search reported in the closing benchmark statistics. The benchmark also reports the time to construct the graph and generate the edge list.

All tests used the default edge factor, `edges = 16`. The graph scale was varied to identify a reasonable running time to help expedite testing. Also, we disabled validation (`SKIP_VALIDATION = 1`) to reduce the running time for the Graph500 benchmark.

We used the Open MPI implementation of OpenSHMEM, specifically Open MPI v2.0.2. The OpenSHMEM framework was configured to use the `spml/yoda` component. The tests were run in a native mode (no container) to establish a baseline for comparison when running the tests from a Singularity container. The GNU toolchain was used for all tests, with GCC 5.4.0 on the UB4 development cluster, and GCC 5.3.0 on Titan.

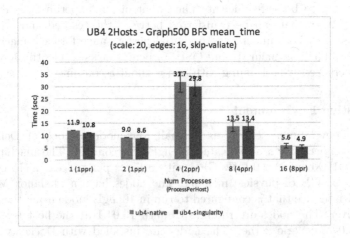

Fig. 4. Graph500 at scale = 20 (edges = 16) with TCP, running on 2 nodes of UB4 cluster.

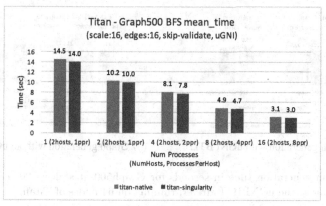

(a) BFS scale=16 hosts=2

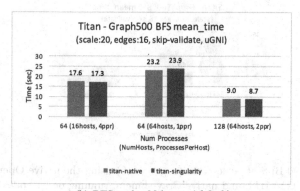

(b) BFS scale=20 hosts=16 & 64

Fig. 5. Graph500 BFS comparison with and without a Singularity container using the uGNI BTL from Open MPI OpenSHMEM. Figure 5(a) is at scale = 16 using 2 hosts. Figure 5(b) is at scale = 20 using 16 and 64 hosts as indicated in the x-axis.

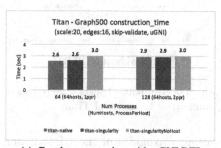

(a) Graph construction with uGNI BTL   (b) Graph construction without uGNI BTL

Fig. 6. Graph construction time in seconds for Graph500 at scale = 20 (edges = 16), with and without the uGNI BTL driver, running on 64 nodes of Titan.

138   T. Naughton et al.

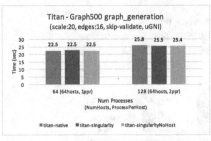

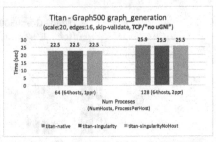

(a) Graph generation with uGNI BTL   (b) Graph generation without uGNI BTL

Fig. 7. Graph generation time in seconds for Graph500 at scale = 20 (edges = 16), with and without the uGNI BTL driver, running on 64 nodes of Titan.

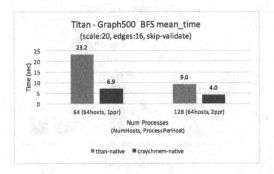

Fig. 8. Graph500 BFS at scale = 20 (edges = 16) using the native Open MPI Open-SHMEM with uGNI BTL and native Cray-shmem, running on 64 nodes of Titan.

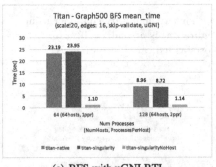

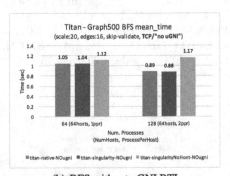

(a) BFS with uGNI BTL   (b) BFS without uGNI BTL

Fig. 9. Mean time in seconds for breadth first search of Graph500 at scale = 20 (edges = 16), with and without the uGNI BTL driver, running on 64 nodes of Titan.

Figure 4 shows the times for the BFS using two nodes in the UB4 cluster with scale = 20 and edges = 16. There is a slight decrease in performance for the container case, but overall the results are very similar. The 4 processes case (2 per node) shows some variability.

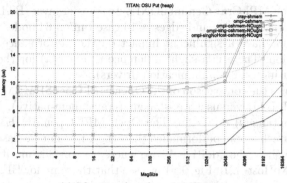

(a) Message sizes from 1-16K bytes.

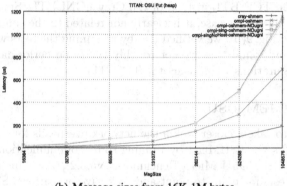

(b) Message sizes from 16K-1M bytes.

Fig. 10. Latency in microseconds (μsec) for OSU `shmem_putmem()` (heap) test running on 2 nodes of Titan for CraySHMEM, Open MPI OpenSHMEM with, and without, the uGNI BTL.

In the next set of tests we check to see if any additional overheads are encountered when using Singularity on the production system (*Titan*), which uses a host provided installation of Open MPI to obtain optimized transport drivers for the Cray Gemini interconnect. The tests show native (no-container) and Singularity with host drivers passed via `LD_LIBRARY_PATH` (injected into container via host bind mount). In later tests we also include the "NoHost" container case, which eliminates use of the host's communication libraries and instead uses the communication libraries contained within the Singularity image.

Figure 5 shows the mean time for the Graph500 BFS running natively (no container) and within a Singularity container on Titan. The tests were run using different problems scales (scale = 16 and scale = 20) and numbers of hosts (2, 16, and 64 hosts). All of the runs showed roughly the same performance with and without the container.

In Figs. 6 and 7, we show the time for graph construction and generation using all three scenarios (Native, Singularity, and Singularity-NoHost) with and without the Open MPI Cray Gemini uGNI byte transfer layer (BTL). The results shown are for the scale = 20 and edges = 16 case run on 64 nodes of Titan. The container did not have a significant impact on the performance for construction or generation. There is a slight difference in Fig. 6(a) for the "Singularity NoHost" (not using host communication drivers).

Figure 8 shows the comparison of the Open MPI OpenSHMEM (titan-native) with the uGNI BTL versus Cray-shmem (crayshmem-native), both running natively (no containers) on Titan. The Open MPI OpenSHMEM case (titan-native) shows much worse performance than the Cray-shmem case.

In Fig. 9 we show the additional case where we run Singularity without the host drivers ("NoHost"). In Fig. 9(a), we see that the time for BFS is effectively the same when running with or without the container and using the uGNI BTL. However, the "NoHost" case performs much better, which is unexpected as this will be using the TCP BTL instead of the Cray uGNI BTL. Since we get this performance in the native case, it is clearly not related to the container runtime (Singularity). In Fig. 9(b), we verified this by rerunning the tests with the uGNI BTL disabled and found that we got roughly the same performance across all three test configurations when using the TCP BTL.

4.3   OpenSHMEM/OSU

We attempted to take a closer look a the network overheads for the uGNI BTL with Open MPI's OpenSHMEM by running some communication microbenchmarks. We used the OSU Micro Benchmarks v5.3.2, which include OpenSHMEM specific tests for point-to-point and collective operations. Since these are at the OpenSHMEM level, this uses the same communication libraries as the Graph500 test but is focused strictly on the network elements. However, there were some errors in the Open MPI v2.0.2 implementation of OpenSHMEM that caused tests to fail when using uGNI. These were experienced in the native (non-container) case.

In Fig. 10, we show the results of the OSU put (heap) benchmark, which tests `shmem_putmem()` for varying message sizes. Figure 10(a) shows that the native Cray SHMEM performs slightly better for smaller messages than the Open MPI OpenSHMEM with uGNI, and both do significantly better than the TCP ("No uGNI") case. Figure 10(b) shows the scale-up for the three configurations, with Cray SHMEM scaling much better than the Open MPI OpenSHMEM. As expected, the Singularity cases follow the same curve as the native TCP ("No uGNI") case. The Singularity test with uGNI are not included because the tests failed to complete with this configuration of Open MPI's OpenSHMEM.

4.4   Observations

It was very convenient to have the Open MPI v2.0.2 release with OpenSHMEM support directly from the Ubuntu 17.04 Linux distribution. The general TCP BTL was stable for testing and showed decent performance in our Graph500 tests at scale = 20 on 64 nodes. However, the uGNI BTL was not stable with the

OpenSHMEM interface, i.e., via spml/yoda component. The Graph500 results for Native and Singularity had the same performance for both uGNI and TCP BTLs. Unexpectedly, the non-uGNI case (Singularity-NoHost) had better performance in our tests due to bad performance/problems with the Open MPI-2.0.2 OSHMEM with uGNI. The only OSU OpenSHMEM tests that ran successfully were the 'put' based tests. The native Open MPI OSHMEM had higher latency than native CraySHMEM.

Regarding Singularity, on the production machine we were unable to make edits to the container image directly. This was somewhat inconvenient as we iterated through changes to the image and had to push a full image for each edit. For example, a single change to the `/environment` file required a full upload of the entire image. This is likely to be resolved in the next release of Singularity (v2.3), which allows write operations without needing privileged (`sudo`) access for some operations, e.g., "copy". Also, we could push changes to the environment via `SINGULARITYENV_xxx`. We do have to customize the image with directories for bind mounts, since we do not have an overlay filesystem (e.g., OverlayFS) on the system. The performance was consistent between native and Singularity.

We are not able to use CraySHMEM for the container case, which is because we cannot create an image on the system, and partly because that defeats the purpose of a "portable container" (CraySHMEM is only for Cray). This limits the comparison tests we could perform with containers.

On Titan, we discovered that the current setup does not allow access to the project directories. We were not able to pass these as user-defined bind mounts because that feature is disabled[2]. The fix would be to add a site configuration to the Singularity installation that would allow the project directories to be bind mounted in like the other host level directories, e.g., `/lustre/atlas`.

5   Conclusion

We used the Graph500 benchmark to investigate the performance of an OpenSH-MEM application with Singularity-based containers in a production environment (Titan). We described our experience and setup methodology for taking containers from a development machine up to a production system. We identified a basic set of image edits for use on Titan. We also identified unexpected slowness in Open MPI's OpenSHMEM with uGNI BTL, but consistent performance was obtained between the native and Singularity case.

While the work is still ongoing, a few things stood out in our initial experiences with OpenSHMEM and containers on Titan. Singularity itself did not introduce any significant overheads for our tests. An OpenSHMEM that is directly included in Linux distributions is convenient, and simplifies the procedures for users packaging their applications. However, in the absence of this, a set of publicly available container images that users can customize may also be useful. CraySHMEM is not really interesting for "compute mobility" as it cannot

---

[2] The older Linux kernel (3.0.x) used in CLE does not support `PR_SET_NO_NEW_PRIVS`, which is used to avoid possible privilege escalation.

142   T. Naughton et al.

be deployed outside of Cray and eliminates the primary motivation (portability) for containers; but may be useful for reproducibility across Cray instances/sites.

The HPC site will need to provide a few setup pieces for end-users to ensure they tailor their containers to include necessary elements for running on HPC machines. This mainly involves directories for bind mounts to map host paths into the container, e.g., parallel file systems shares. Additionally, creating images on service/login nodes is not currently viable since it requires the user to have write access to their image, but as of Singularity-2.2.1 that feature requires escalated privileges. The fact that users are expected to build their images in their local environment and ship the results to the HPC system potentially restricts their access to site features like advanced compilers and other commercial software. It would be useful to provide users some ability to build containers on service nodes that have access to the commercial tools.

5.1 Future Work

While testing the Open MPI implementation of OpenSHMEM we became aware that the Unified Communication X (UCX) implementation (spml/ucx) may be a better option than the configuration we tested[3]. It would be good to rerun these tests with a more recent version of Open MPI using UCX to see if we encountered the same stability problems on Titan. We would also like to look more closely at the precise cause of the discrepancy in performance between the uGNI and TCP cases on Titan with the Graph500-oshmem benchmark. This would also be helpful to see if containers add any additional challenges when using HPC profiling tools.

References

1. D'Azevedo, E.F., Imam, N.: Graph 500 in OpenSHMEM. In: Gorentla Venkata, M., Shamis, P., Imam, N., Lopez, M.G. (eds.) OpenSHMEM 2014. LNCS, vol. 9397, pp. 154–163. Springer, Cham (2015). https://doi.org/10.1007/978-3-319-26428-8_10
2. Docker: An open platform for distributed applications for developers and sysadmins. https://www.docker.com
3. Gabriel, E., et al.: Open MPI: goals, concept, and design of a next generation MPI implementation. In: Kranzlmüller, D., Kacsuk, P., Dongarra, J. (eds.) EuroPVM/MPI 2004. LNCS, vol. 3241, pp. 97–104. Springer, Heidelberg (2004). https://doi.org/10.1007/978-3-540-30218-6_19
4. Graph500 Benchmark Specification. http://graph500.org/?page_id=12
5. Kurtzer, G.M., Sochat, V., Bauer, M.W.: Singularity: scientific containers for mobility of compute. PLoS ONE 12(5), e0177459 (2017). https://doi.org/10.1371/journal.pone.0177459
6. OSU Micro-Benchmarks. http://mvapich.cse.ohio-state.edu/benchmarks
7. Titan Cray XK7. https://www.olcf.ornl.gov/computing-resources/titan-cray-xk7

[3] Our tests were configured to use the spml/yoda component for Open MPI-2.0.2's OpenSHMEM framework and not the spml/ucx component.

Exploiting and Evaluating OpenSHMEM
on KNL Architecture

Jahanzeb Maqbool Hashmi[(✉)], Mingzhe Li, Hari Subramoni,
and Dhabaleswar K. Panda

Department of Computer Science and Engineering,
The Ohio State University, Columbus, USA
{hashmi.29,li.2192,subramoni.1,panda.2}@osu.edu

Abstract. Manycore processors such as Intel Xeon Phi (KNL) with
on-package Multi-Channel DRAM (MCDRAM) are making a paradigm
shift in the High Performance Computing (HPC) industry. PGAS programming models such as OpenSHMEM due to its lightweight synchronization primitives and shared memory abstractions are considered a
good fit for irregular communication patterns. While regular programming models such as MPI/OpenMP have started utilizing systems with
KNL processors, it is still not clear whether PGAS models can easily adopt and fully utilize such systems. In this paper, we conduct a
comprehensive performance evaluation of the OpenSHMEM runtime on
many-/multi-core processors. We also explore the performance benefits
offered by the highly multithreaded KNL along with the AVX-512 extensions and MCDRAM for OpenSHMEM programming model. We evaluate Intra- and Inter-node performance of OpenSHMEM primitives on
different application kernels. Our evaluation of application kernels such
as NAS Parallel Benchmark and 3D-Stencil kernels show that OpenSH-
MEM with MVPAICH2-X runtime is able to take advantage of AVX-512
extensions and MCDRAM to exploit the architectural features provided
by KNL processors.

Keywords: PGAS model · OpenSHMEM · MVAPICH2-X · KNL
MCDRAM

1 Introduction

Emerging Manycore processors such as second generation Intel Xeon Phi namely
Knights Landing (KNL) provide a high degree of parallelism. In order to increase
the compute capabilities of the scientific applications, High Performance Computing (HPC) clusters are employing manycores due to their concurrency benefits. This trend is evident from the Top500 list where one of the largest multi-
petaflop supercomputers in the US is employing KNL manycores [2].

This research is supported in part by National Science Foundation grants #CNS-
1419123, #CNS-1513120, #ACI-1450440 and #CCF-1565414.

© Springer International Publishing AG 2018
M. Gorentla Venkata et al. (Eds.): OpenSHMEM 2017, LNCS 10679, pp. 143–158, 2018.
https://doi.org/10.1007/978-3-319-73814-7_10

Intel Xeon Phi (KNL) processor comes equipped with up to 68 cores that can be configured in different modes depending on the usage scenario. Further, Each core of the mesh employs 4-way hardware multi-threading totaling up to 272 hardware threads. In addition to the highly multi-threaded cores and multi-level parallelism, KNL also comes equipped with 512-bit vector registers. With the AXV-512 extension, a single KNL node can achieve 3TFlops of double-precision and 6TFlops of single-precision performance. Furthermore, KNL also offers a new memory sub-system by integrating an on-package Multi-Channel DRAM (MCDRAM) that provides up to 5X improved memory bandwidth compared to normal off-package DDR4 memory. The on-package MCDRAM can be configured in three different modes: Flat mode, Cache mode, and Hybrid mode.

On the other hand, PGAS programming models such as OpenSHMEM due to their lightweight synchronization and one-sided semantics provide a good alternative to Message Passing models for irregular data-driven applications. Past studies show that irregular applications have demonstrated improved programmability and performance when using PGAS programming models [5,11]. The adoption of manycore processors, particularly KNL by modern high-performance computing systems lead us to a broad question: *Can PGAS models, specifically OpenSHMEM, benefit from the architectural features of KNL processors?*

1.1 Motivation

Optimizing HPC runtimes and applications on such manycore systems with high bandwidth memories is full of challenges and attracts lots of research interests. Past studies [10] have analyzed the challenges and effects of running regular programming models such as MPI/OpenMP over emerging heterogeneous systems. However, PGAS programming models, such as OpenSHMEM, have not been studied well enough on KNL platform. This paper mainly explores the performance characteristics of OpenSHMEM on KNL architecture. It presents a detailed evaluation using micro-benchmarks and application kernels and exploits architectural features such as AVX-512 extensions and MCDRAM.

1.2 Contributions

In this paper, we provide a comprehensive evaluation study of OpenSHMEM runtime on KNL, involving intra- and inter-node performance analysis. We also investigate the potential benefits of AVX-512 and MCDRAM usage for micro-benchmark as well as applications. We use MVAPICH2-X based high-performance implementation of OpenSHMEM. Specifically, we use the Unified Communication Runtime (UCR) of MVAPICH2-X. The findings of this paper provide a baseline for the future studies of PGAS programming models on KNL-like manycore architectures.

The main contributions of this paper are summarized as below:

- Discuss different architectural modes of Intel KNL processor.
- Evaluate OpenSHMEM point-to-point, collectives, and atomic operations on KNL processor in comparison to Intel Broadwell based systems.
- Evaluate scientific application kernels using MVAPICH2-X communication runtime for intra-node and inter-node configurations.
- Investigate the potential benefits of KNL's architectural features such as AVX-512 extensions and MCDRAM for the OpenSHMEM application kernels.
- Discuss different design approaches to fully exploit the concurrency benefits of KNL with AVX-512 vectorization and MCDRAM usage.

The rest of the paper is organized as follows: Relevant background information is provided in Sect. 2. Evaluation methodology are discussed in Sect. 3. The comprehensive evaluation results are discussed in Sect. 4. Section 5 discusses the overall insights. Section 6 surveys the literature work. Section 7 contains the conclusion and future work.

2   Background

In this section, we provide details of the relevant background required for this paper.

2.1   Intel Knights Landing - Architectural Overview

Intel Knights Landing (KNL) is a self-booting processor which packs up to six Teraflops of compute throughput. KNL comes equipped with 68–72 cores located on 34–36 active tiles. Each tile has a single 1-megabyte L2 cache that is shared between the two cores and further each core comprises of four threads. Two major architectural features provided by KNL are highly multi-threaded cores and on-package MCDRAM. An overview of these features is given below.

Mesh Interconnect: A 2D-mesh interconnect is used for on-die communication by the cores, memory and I/O controllers, and other agents. This 2D-mesh can be configured in following ways:

1. *All to All*: In this mode, memory addresses are uniformly distributed across all tag directories on the chip. It is not recommended to use this mode for performance purposes as its main use is for debugging and troubleshooting.
2. *Quadrant/Hemisphere*: In this mode, the tiles are divided into four groups called quadrants, which are spatially local to four groups of memory controllers. The division into quadrants is hidden from the operating system and the memory appears as a contiguous block from user's perspective.
3. *SNC2/SNC4*: In sub-NUMA cluster modes SNC-2 and SNC-4 the chip is also partitioned into two hemispheres or four quadrants. However, unlike Quadrant/Hemisphere mode, SNC mode exposes these quadrants to OS as separate NUMA nodes.

In this paper, we only focus on Quadrant mode for our evaluations.

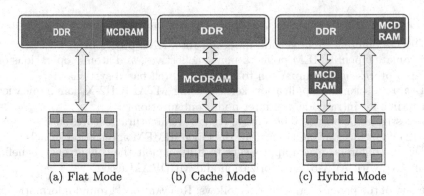

Fig. 1. MCDRAM configuration modes on KNL

High Bandwidth Memory (MCDRAM): KNL comprises of six DDR4 channels and eight MCDRAM (multi-channel DRAM) channels. The MCDRAM memory can yield an aggregate bandwidth of 450 GB/s in contrast with DDR4 memory which can yield 90 GB/s. MCDRAM on a single KNL can be configured in three different ways, as shown in Fig. 1.

(1) Flat Mode — provides full control over the MCDRAM allocations and it is mainly used for performance oriented runs. In this mode, both the DDR4 and MCDRAM are exposed as two distinct NUMA nodes. The application can have access to 96 GB of DDR memory along with 16 GB of MCDRAM. The default allocation happens on DDR, however, one can directly use MCDRAM through the use Linux NUMA library or through the memkind [4] library.

(2) Cache Mode — where the fast MCDRAM is configured as an L3 cache. The operating system transparently uses the MCDRAM to move data from main memory. The application can only access 96 GB of DDR for direct allocations while MCDRAM allocation happens transparently.

(3) Hybrid Mode — In this mode, the part of MCDRAM acts as the L3 cache while remaining MCDRAM is exposed as the second NUMA alongside DDR. This is not as widely used as other modes.

2.2   MVAPICH2-X OpenSHMEM Runtime

MVAPICH2-X (MV2-X), provides a unified high-performance communication runtime — UCR, that supports both MPI and PGAS programming models on InfiniBand clusters. It enables developers to port parts of large MPI applications that are suited for the PGAS programming model. This minimizes the development overheads that have been a substantial deterrent in porting MPI applications to PGAS models. MV2-X provides support for the reference implementation of OpenSHMEM. Currently, it is based on the University of Houston OpenSHMEM version 1.2.

3   Evaluation Methodology

We first start with different OpenSHMEM primitives (data-movement, Atomics, Collectives) using OpenSHMEM micro-benchmarks from OSU Micro-benchmark Suite (OMB) version 5.3.2. The evaluations performed in this paper, use KNL nodes configured in Flat-Quadrant mode. We use several application kernels to compare the performance of KNL and Broadwell nodes.

For application evaluations, we use three configurations of KNL. First, we do a default run without any of the KNL specific optimization. Second, we compile the applications with AVX-512 vectorization support. Third, we allow the memory allocations to be performed on MCDRAM. We perform a core-by-core comparison of KNL and Broadwell nodes for varying number of processes. However, for the sake of a fair comparison, we also provide a node-by-node comparison with both systems running at full-subscription. Since KNL has 4-way hardware multithreaded cores, we ensure that we bind different PEs to different cores so that they do not share the same core (running on different hardware threads of the same core). We also disable the Hyper-threading on Broadwell nodes.

4   Performance Evaluation

This section describes the experimental setup used to conduct our performance evaluation. An in-depth analysis of the results is also provided. All results reported here are averages of multiple (10) runs to discard the effect of system noise. For micro-benchmark evaluations, the communication buffers are allocated on DDR memory while the application kernels evaluation shows the performance trends on DDR as well as MCDRAM.

4.1   Experimental Setup

For the evaluation, we use second generation Intel Xeon Phi nodes. Each node comprises a 68-core KNL processor with 16 GB of MCDRAM memory and 96 gigabytes of DDR4 memory. Further, Each node is equipped with MT4115 EDR ConnectX HCAs with PCI-Ex Gen3 interfaces. In our experiments, we configure the KNL nodes in Flat-Quadrant mode. The operating system used is CentOS Linux release 7.2.1511 (Core) with kernel version 3.10.0-327.36.2.el7.x86_64. We use MVAPICH2-X version 2.2 combined with the unified runtime support. We used GCC v5.4.0 for all the compilation and KNL specific optimization. Specifically, we use -O3 -mavx512f to generate AVX-512 vectorized code for application kernels.

For the sake of providing a baseline comparison, we also use an Intel Broadwell based cluster for all the experiments. Each node of this cluster consists of a Xeon E5 2680 v4 processor with 128 GB of RAM. The nodes are connected with EDR ConnectX HCA model MT5115 with PCI-Ex Gen3 interfaces. The operating system used is CentOS Linux release 7.2.1511 (Core) with kernel version 3.10.0-327.10.1.el7.x86_64. The detailed specifications are shown in Table 1.

Table 1. Hardware specification of the clusters used

Specifications	Broadwell	Xeon Phi (KNL)
Processor family	Intel Broadwell	Knights Landing
Processor model	E5 2680 v4	KNL 7250
Clock speed	2.4 GHz	1.4 GHz
No. of sockets	2	1
Cores per socket	14	68
Threads per core	1	4
Mesh config	NUMA	Flat-Quadrant
RAM (DDR)	128 GB	96 GB
MCDRAM	-	16 GB
Interconnect	IB-EDR(100 G)	IB-EDR(100 G)

4.2 Data Movement Operations

In this section, we evaluate the performance of OpenSHMEM point-to-point data movement (shmem_put and shmem_get) operations. We use OSU OpenSH-MEM micro-benchmarks [1] for these evaluations. The osu_oshm_put benchmark measures the latency of shmem_putmem operation for varying message sizes. In this microbenchmark, PE-0 issues a shmem_put operation and writes the data at PE-1, followed by a call to shmem_quiet. On the other hand, PE-1 goes into shmem_barrier. This operations is repeated for multiple iterations. Similarly, in osu_oshm_get benchmark PE-0 performs a shmem_getmem operation to read data from PE-1.

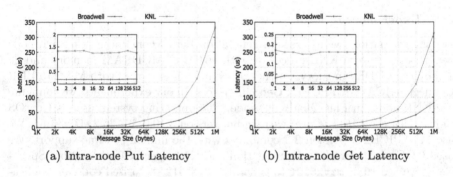

(a) Intra-node Put Latency   (b) Intra-node Get Latency

Fig. 2. Intra-node evaluation of OpenSHMEM put and get operations

The performance evaluation of shmem_put and shmem_get are reported in Fig. 2. We compare the latency achieved on KNL with our baseline Broadwell system. For shmem_put operation, at 1-byte message, the reported latency on KNL is 1.34 us as compared to 0.18 us on Broadwell. A similar trend is observed on large message ranges where KNL latency is about 3X worse than that of Broadwell. However, for shmem_get operation, the 1-byte latency at KNL is 0.17 us and 0.03 us on Broadwell. For intra-node transfers, MVAPICH2-X based OpenSHMEM implements symmetric heap as the shared-memory. The small message transfers use shared-memory schemes while medium to large messages use Linux's Cross Memory Attach (CMA) based zero-copy transfers for performance reasons. Due to the lower clock speed and smaller cache of KNL, the performance of memcpy operation suffers significantly resulting in the lower raw performance relative to the Broadwell cores.

4.3   Atomic Operations

In order to evaluate the performance of OpenSHMEM atomic operations, we again use OSU microbenchmark (OMB). The relevant benchmark in OMB is osu_oshm_atomic which measures the performance of OpenSHMEM atomic operations for different data types. In this benchmark, the first PE issues several atomic operations one after the other to its peer PE. The average latency of each atomic operation is reported. The benchmark reports the performance of up to 14 operations, however, for the sake of brevity, in this paper, we only report three operations with 32-bit and 64-bit types.

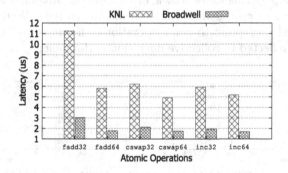

Fig. 3. OpenSHMEM atomics performance on KNL and broadwell cluster on 128 processes

Figure 3 shows the performance of fetching and non-fetching atomics on KNL and Broadwell system using 128 processes. We observe that the overall latency of these operations on KNL remains about 3X higher than that of Broadwell. Similar to the point-to-point performance, the lower clock speed and a smaller cache of KNL affect the performance.

4.4   Collectives Operations

In this section, we evaluate different OpenSHMEM collectives such as shmem_broadcast and shmem_reduce on KNL and Broadwell cluster. Similar to the prior evaluation, we also use OSU OpenSHMEM collective benchmarks. These benchmarks measure the average latency of the collective operation for different message sizes and process counts. Multiple iterations of the benchmark are executed and in the end, the average latency across all the iterations is reported. In our evaluation of collective operations, we vary the process count from 2 to 128. For the sake of brevity, we show three different graphs indicating small, medium, and large messages for each collective benchmark.

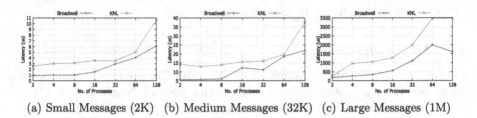

(a) Small Messages (2K)   (b) Medium Messages (32K)   (c) Large Messages (1M)

Fig. 4. OpenSHMEM broadcast performance at varying scale

Figures 4(a), (b), and (c) show the performance of shmem_broadcast operation on small (2 KB), medium (32 KB), and large (1M) messages respectively. We see that the performance of shmem_broadcast on Broadwell is higher than KNL for all message ranges and process counts. Since the collective operations are implemented over point-to-point operations, the impact of point-to-point performance is reflected in collective operation performance.

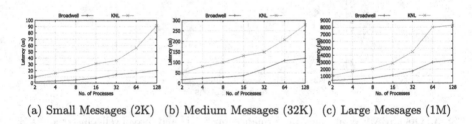

(a) Small Messages (2K)   (b) Medium Messages (32K)   (c) Large Messages (1M)

Fig. 5. OpenSHMEM reduce performance at varying scale

Similarly, the performance of shmem_reduce is shown in Figs. 5(a), (b), and (c). We observe the similar trend as of shmem_broadcast that the raw latency of reduce on KNL is also about 3X higher than that of Broadwell due to the slower point-to-point performance.

4.5   NAS Parallel Benchmark

The NAS Parallel Benchmarks (NPB) are a set of programs that are designed to be typical of several HPC applications. In our evaluation, we use Class 'B' problem size. We run MG, EP, BT, and SP in the experiments.

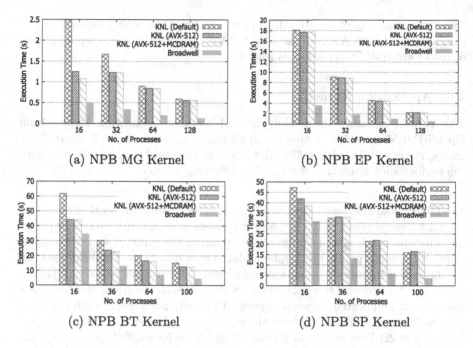

(a) NPB MG Kernel

(b) NPB EP Kernel

(c) NPB BT Kernel

(d) NPB SP Kernel

Fig. 6. OpenSHMEM NAS parallel benchmark performance

Figure 6 shows the execution time of four kernels of NAS Parallel Benchmark. In the experiments, the Broadwell and KNL nodes are fully occupied with OpenSHMEM PEs. For MG results with 16 PEs on KNL, we see that the KNL with AVX-512 enabled is able to reduce the total execution time by more than 2X. The performance benefits come from vectorization. However, as the number of PEs keep increasing, the benefits of AVX-512 tend to decrease. The reason is that the ratio of communication and computation is increasing with more number of PEs. When MG is running with MCDRAM, the total execution time could be reduced by up to 18% compared to running with DDR. Although both AVX-512 and MCDRAM are able to reduce the total execution time of MG on KNL, Broadwell still performs better than KNL. With 128 PEs, KNL only delivers 20% performance as of Broadwell. For the EP benchmark, we see that KNL with AVX-512 enabled achieves similar performance with KNL default scheme. The reason is that the computation kernel in EP could not directly benefit from the vectorization. EP running with 128 PEs on KNL delivers around 20% performance as of 128 PEs on Broadwell. For the BT benchmark with 16 PEs, the total execution time for KNL-Default, KNL-AVX-512, KNL-AVX-512-MCDRAM, and Broadwell is 61.2, 42.3, 42.2, and 34.8 s, respectively. KNL with MCDRAM and AVX-512 extension enabled could deliver 90% performance as of Broadwell. Since BT benchmark is not memory bound, so MCDRAM does not bring performance benefits. For the SP benchmark with 16 PEs, we see that KNL-Default, KNL-AVX-512, KNL-AVX-512-MCDRAM can deliver 63%, 75%,

78% performance as of Broadwell, respectively. From the NAS numbers, we can clearly see that both AVX-512 and MCDRAM could benefit the compute phases of the OpenSHMEM applications kernels.

4.6   Application Kernels

This section discusses the performance of different application kernels from OpenSHMEM test suite. We use five applications kernels namely, 2D-Heat, Heat Image, Matrix Multiply, DAXPY, and ISx. The details of each kernel along with the performance results are discussed in following sections.

2D-Heat: The 2D-Heat kernel is a type of stencil computation that simulates the heat distribution in a 2D domain. It consists of a grid with boundary points and inner points. Boundary points have an initial temperature and the temperature of the inner points need to be updated over iterations. The heat equation can be solved iteratively by various numerical methods such as Jacobi, Gauss-seidel and Successive Over-relaxation (SOR). In each iteration, the boundary rows are communicated between adjacent PEs and at the end of each iteration, a reduction is performed to check the convergence. Figure 7(a) shows the performance of 2D-Heat kernel on Broadwell and KNL for multiple processes using $2\,K \times 2\,K$ size grid. As discussed in Sect. 3, we report evaluation results for different KNL optimizations and compare the results against baseline Broadwell. As we can see that the default KNL performs around 3X worse than the AVX-512 optimized execution. However, we do not see much benefit when MCDRAM is used. The reason is that MCDRAM does not help in reducing the latency under less system load. The benchmark spends most of the time in computation and communication makes up only a small portion of the overall execution.

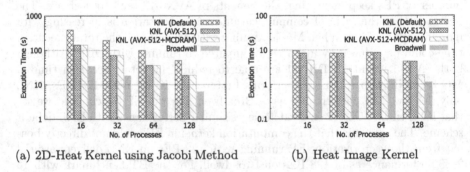

(a) 2D-Heat Kernel using Jacobi Method   (b) Heat Image Kernel

Fig. 7. OpenSHMEM heat diffusion kernels performance

Heat Image: This application kernel also solves the heat conduction task based on row-based distribution of the matrix. The application distributes the matrix in rows among PEs and then exchanges the result of the computation. The major communication operation is the data transfer across the matrix rows/ columns (using shmem_put) and the synchronization operations (using shmem_barrier_all.) Finally, after doing all the transfers, the output is written to a file in an image format. The matrix size is specified as input. In our experiments, we used an input matrix of size 2K × 2K bytes.

The performance results of the Heat Image kernel is presented in Fig. 7(b). In these experiments, we kept the input size constant (2K × 2K) and varied the system scale from 16 processes to 128 processes. We plot the execution time (in seconds) on the Y-axis and the system-scale is plotted on X-axis. In this result, we see that allocating the matrix on MCDRAM achieves up to 2X increased performance as compared to unoptimized executions. Although the vectorization shows up to 20% improvement for 16 processes, this improvement diminished on a larger scale. However, the MCDRAM benefits are more pronounced on larger scale. This behavior shows that in a more bandwidth bound application scenario where memory accesses happen too frequently, MCDRAM can accelerate the overall execution.

Matrix Multiplication: This is a simple matrix multiplication kernel implemented in OpenSHMEM. Two matrices with double precision floating point elements are multiplied and the result is stored in a third matrix. The performance results are presented in Fig. 8(a). The execution time (in seconds) is plotted in the Y-axis and the system size is plotted against X-axis. The performance trend shows that AVX-512 optimized run achieves 2.5X improvement in total execution time since most of the application time is spent in computation. For MCDRAM, we observe a rather interesting trend. From 16 to 64 processes, we see no difference in performance when using MCDRAM over DDR. However, on 128 processes, a 25% degradation is observed. As we've discussed earlier that the benefits of MCDRAM are pronounced when there is more system load (high concurrency). However, in applications where minimal communication is involved (embarrassingly parallel), MCDRAM performance is even worse than DDR. This has also been reported by Intel [9].

DAXPY: This kernel is a simple DAXPY like kernel with computation and communication. It simulates a typical application that uses a one-dimensional array for local computation and does a reduction collective operation of the result. The data transfer is done using shmem_put operation, synchronization using shmem_barrier_all, and reduction using shmem_reduce operations. The execution time reported by the benchmark involves the OpenSHMEM initialization time also. The performance results are presented in Fig. 8(b). The execution time (in seconds) is plotted in the Y-axis and the system size is presented in the X-axis. In this benchmark, the problem size increases with the increase in the system size. We see that the AVX-512 vectorization reduces the execution time

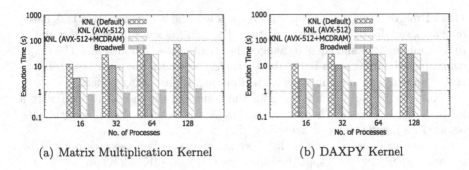

(a) Matrix Multiplication Kernel   (b) DAXPY Kernel

Fig. 8. OpenSHMEM matrix multiplication and DAXPY performance

of the benchmark by half on KNL, however, MCDRAM does not show any significant improvement over vectorized run. Nevertheless, the performance of Broadwell still remains significantly higher than the optimized KNL run (Fig. 9).

Scalable Integer Sort (ISx) Kernel: This kernel is an improved version of original NAS Integer Sort kernel and is scalable to a large number of nodes. We use its OpenSHMEM implementation obtained from https://github.com/ParRes/ISx.git. IS belongs to the bucket sort algorithms that perform all-to-all communications. It has support for both strong and weak scaling, however, we only use strong scaling in this experiments. Figure 10 shows the performance of OpenSHMEM ISx kernel on Broadwell and KNL with various optimizations. Similar to prior results, we observe up to 3X improvement in overall performance when using AVX-512 vectorization. In all the executions, Broadwell remains 2X better than optimized KNL while MCDRAM does not show much improvement over DDR.

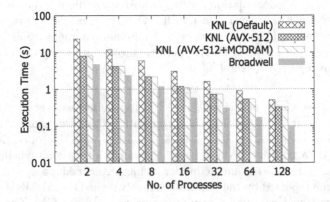

Fig. 9. OpenSHMEM scalable integer sort kernel performance

4.7   Summary of Node-Level Comparison Using Application Kernels

We discussed the core-by-core comparison using application kernels in Sect. 4.6. Here, we provide a node-level comparison of a single KNL node with a Broadwell node. We use KNL optimized (AVX-512 with MCDRAM) version of the application kernels for comparison. Figure 10 presents a summary of the aforementioned application kernels using node-by-node comparison on KNL and Broadwell systems. Both the systems utilize all the available cores while threading is disabled. We observe that while Broadwell shows better performance on 2D-Heat, Matrix Multiplication, and DAXPY kernels, KNL shows up to 30% increased performance for Heat Image kernel. On ISx kernel with strong scaling, KNL remains on par with Broadwell.

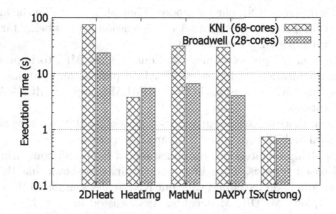

Fig. 10. Node-by-Node comparison of KNL and Broadwell.

5   Discussion of Performance Results

We summarize the comparison between Broadwell and KNL performance in Fig. 11. On KNL architecture, when the AVX-512 extension is enabled, the execution time of applications could be reduced significantly. While the performance of micro-benchmarks and application kernels on Broadwell remains higher than KNL for core-by-core comparison, KNL shows some improvement over Broadwell for node-by-node comparison. The lower clock speed and a smaller cache of KNL have significant impact on the performance of memcpy operation that leads to about 3X degradation on KNL when compared to Broadwell on a core-by-core comparison. We also observed that MCDRAM did not help much in most of the application kernels. The reason is that the application kernels are mostly latency bound while MCDRAM has shown to have additional latency overheads when there is not enough concurrency available.

6 Related Work

Several studies have explored and taken advantage of the scalability and programmability that OpenSHMEM offers. Lin et al. [8] proposed a group of alternative hybrid MPI+OpenSHMEM designs to improve the performance of the classification and regression algorithm k-NN on the large-scale environment with InfiniBand.

Zhao and Marsman presented the HBM performance analysis on the VASP code, a widely used materials science code, using Intel's development tools, Memkind and AutoHBW, and a dual-socket Ivy Bridge processor node on Edison, as a proxy to the MCDRAM on KNL [12]. Doerfler et al. determined the Roofline for the Intel KNL processor, determining the sustained peak memory bandwidth and floating-point performance for all levels of the memory hierarchy, in all the different KNL cluster modes. They also determine the arithmetic intensity and the performance for a set of application kernels being targeted for the KNL based supercomputer Cori [6].

Kandalla et al. [7] proposed new solutions in Cray MPI to improve multithreaded communication performance of hybrid parallel applications. Further, they discussed new API extensions in Cray SHMEM to support MCDRAM based memory allocations.

In [3], the authors presented early case-studies of NERSC workloads on KNL and Xeon based architecture. They compared the performance of 20 application kernels by applying architectural optimizations of KNL and comparing it with the Haswell based systems. Their intra-node evaluation shows that the Haswell system has overall lower execution time but KNL scales well for all the clustering modes and exploits MCDRAM benefits. As discussed in Sect. 4, we have also witnessed similar trends while evaluating OpenSHMEM application kernels.

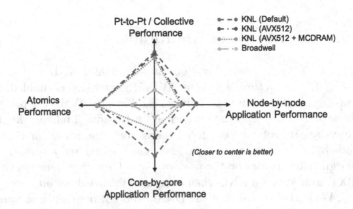

Fig. 11. Evaluation results

7   Conclusion and Future Work

In this paper, we provided a comprehensive performance evaluation of OpenSH-MEM over the KNL architecture. We presented a detailed comparison of the performance of different OpenSHMEM primitives (data-movement, Atomics, Collectives) on CPU and KNL architectures. We also provided a detailed analysis of core-by-core and node-by-node comparison of the performance trends observed in five applications with AVX-512 extension and MCDRAM. The study indicates that AVX-512 extension and MCDRAM can benefit OpenSHMEM applications on the KNL architecture. In the future, we plan to co-design applications on KNL systems and demonstrate the impact of KNL on the execution time of applications.

References

1. OSU Micro-Benchmarks (2015)
2. TACC Stampede KNL Cluster (2017). https://portal.tacc.utexas.edu/user-guides/stampede
3. Barnes, T., Cook, B., Deslippe, J., Doerfler, D., Friesen, B., He, Y., Kurth, T., Koskela, T., Lobet, M., Malas, T., et al.: Evaluating and optimizing the NERSC workload on knights landing. In: International Workshop on Performance Modeling, Benchmarking and Simulation of High Performance Computer Systems (PMBS), pp. 43–53. IEEE (2016)
4. Cantalupo, C., Venkatesan, V., Hammond, J., Czurlyo, K., Hammond, S.D.: Memkind: An Extensible Heap Memory Manager for Heterogeneous Memory Platforms and Mixed Memory Policies. Technical report, Sandia National Laboratories (SNL-NM), Albuquerque, NM (United States) (2015)
5. Cong, G., Almasi, G., Saraswat, V.: Fast PGAS implementation of distributed graph algorithms. In: Proceedings of the 2010 ACM/IEEE International Conference for High Performance Computing, Networking, Storage and Analysis, SC 2010, pp. 1–11. IEEE Computer Society, Washington, DC (2010)
6. Doerfler, D., Deslippe, J., Williams, S., Oliker, L., Cook, B., Kurth, T., Lobet, M., Malas, T., Vay, J.-L., Vincenti, H.: Applying the roofline performance model to the intel xeon phi knights landing processor. In: Intel Xeon Phi User's Group (IXPUG 2016) (2016)
7. Kandalla, K., Mendygral, P., Radcliffe, N., Cernohous, B., Knaak, D., McMahon, K., Pagel, M.: Optimizing Cray MPI and SHMEM Software Stacks for Cray-XC Supercomputers based on Intel KNL Processors (2016)
8. Lin, J., Hamidouche, K., Zhang, J., Lu, X., Vishnu, A., Panda, D.: Accelerating k-NN algorithm with hybrid MPI and OpenSHMEM. In: Gorentla Venkata, M., Shamis, P., Imam, N., Lopez, M.G. (eds.) OpenSHMEM 2014. LNCS, vol. 9397, pp. 164–177. Springer, Cham (2015). https://doi.org/10.1007/978-3-319-26428-8_11
9. Memory Latency on the Intel Xeon Phi x200 Knights Landing processor. https://sites.utexas.edu/jdm4372/2016/12/06/memory-latency-on-the-intel-xeon-phi-x200-knights-landing-processor/
10. Potluri, S., Venkatesh, A., Bureddy, D., Kandalla, K., Panda, D.K.: Efficient intra-node communication on intel-MIC clusters. In: 13th IEEE International Symposium on Cluster Computing and the Grid (CCGrid 2013) (2013)

11. Zhang, J., Behzad, B., Snir, M.: Optimizing the Barnes-Hut algorithm in UPC. In: Proceedings of 2011 International Conference for High Performance Computing, Networking, Storage and Analysis, SC 2011, pp. 75:1–75:11. ACM, New York (2011)
12. Zhao, Z., Marsman, M.: Estimating the performance impact of the MCDRAM on KNL using dual-socket Ivy bridge nodes on Cray XC30. In: Cray User Group Meeting (CUG 2016) (2016)

OpenSHMEM Tools

Performance Analysis of OpenSHMEM Applications with TAU Commander

John C. Linford[1]([✉]), Samuel Khuvis[1], Sameer Shende[1], Allen Malony[1],
Neena Imam[2], and Manjunath Gorentla Venkata[2]

[1] ParaTools, Inc., 2836 Kincaid St., Eugene, OR 97405, USA
{jlinford,skhuvis,sameer,malony}@paratools.com
[2] Oak Ridge National Laboratory, 1 Bethel Valley Rd,
Oak Ridge, TN 37831, USA
{imamn,manjugv}@ornl.gov
http://www.paratools.com/
http://ut-battelle.org/

Abstract. The TAU Performance System® (TAU) is a powerful and highly versatile profiling and tracing tool ecosystem for performance engineering of parallel programs. Developed over the last twenty years, TAU has evolved with each new generation of HPC systems and scales efficiently to hundreds of thousands of cores. TAU's organic growth has resulted in a loosely coupled software toolbox such that novice users first encountering TAU's complexity and vast array of features are often intimidated and easily frustrated. To lower the barrier to entry for novice TAU users, Para-Tools and the US Department of Energy have developed "TAU Commander," a performance engineering workflow manager that facilitates a systematic approach to performance engineering, guides users through common profiling and tracing workflows, and offers constructive feedback in case of error. This work compares TAU and TAU Commander workflows for common performance engineering tasks in OpenSHMEM applications and demonstrates workflows targeting two different SHMEM implementations, Intel Xeon "Haswell" and "Knights Landing" processors, direct and indirect measurement methods, callsite, profiles, and traces.

Keywords: TAU Commander · TAU Performance System
Performance engineering · Profiling · Tracing · Callsite

1 Introduction

The TAU Performance System® (TAU) is a powerful and highly versatile profiling and tracing tool ecosystem for performance analysis of parallel programs developed in part by Department of Energy (DOE) and National Science Foundation (NSF) research funding granted to the University of Oregon [12,13,18]. Developed over the last twenty years, TAU has evolved with each new generation of HPC systems and presently scales efficiently to hundreds of thousands of cores on the largest machines in the world. TAU can be applied in a portable way to

© Springer International Publishing AG 2018
M. Gorentla Venkata et al. (Eds.): OpenSHMEM 2017, LNCS 10679, pp. 161–179, 2018.
https://doi.org/10.1007/978-3-319-73814-7_11

codes written in Fortran, C, C++, Java, and Python, which utilize MPI message communication and/or multi-threading (e.g., pthread, OpenMP) for execution across different parallel machines. TAU also supports partitioned global address space (PGAS) languages and libraries like Universal Parallel C (UPC), vendor SHMEM implementations, and implementations of the OpenSHMEM standard [4]. TAU has helped several DOE Innovative and Novel Computational Impact on Theory and Experiment (INCITE) [1] projects scale up successfully on systems at Oak Ridge Leadership Computing Facility (OLCF), the National Energy Research Scientific Computing Center (NERSC), and the Argonne Leadership Computing Facility (ALCF). For example, TAU helped reduce the runtime of the IRMHD INCITE code from 528 h to 70 h on BlueGene/P and BlueGene/Q systems [5,15].

TAU's organic growth over many years has resulted in a loosely coupled software toolbox. While many experts use TAU on a daily basis, novice users first encountering TAU's complexity and vast array of features can be intimidated or easily frustrated. TAU offers an abundance of choice with no obvious defaults and little or no feedback in case of user or system error. The user interface to TAU is now at a point where it is neither consistent nor unified, forcing users to learn several different workflows and understand a variety of command line options and environment variables to be effective.

To simplify TAU usage and facilitate more effective production of application performance data, ParaTools has developed a "production-grade" performance engineering solution called *TAU Commander* [14]. This new tool lowers the barrier to entry for novice TAU users by presenting a simple, intuitive, and systematic user interface that guides users through performance engineering workflows and offers constructive feedback in case of error. TAU Commander has measurably improved productivity and software performance in government and industry HPC applications. For example, TAU Commander enabled a 30% runtime reduction in extreme-scale computational fluid dynamics (CFD) simulation with NASA's FUN3D [11].

TAU Commander's design arises from years of TAU user feedback and a study of 124 TAU workflows that identified a common workflow, shown in Fig. 1. It targets specific "pain points" that are a source of discouragement for novice TAU users. The most frequently reported pain point is the requirement to reconfigure TAU or select a different TAU configuration when the desired metrics are not measured. The red path in Fig. 1 illustrates why this complaint is so pronounced: it is possible for the user to reach the second-from-last step in the workflow before they become aware of the incorrect TAU configuration and are sent back to the beginning of the workflow. The earliest they could have been informed of the misconfiguration is during their application compilation, several steps into the workflow. TAU Commander resolves this pain point by allowing the user to concisely state their end goal at the beginning of the workflow so that errors are rapidly detected and resolved. It also unifies the user interface so that all configuration options are specified in the same way, are checked for correctness, and can be enumerated, listed, and searched. The user interface, online help,

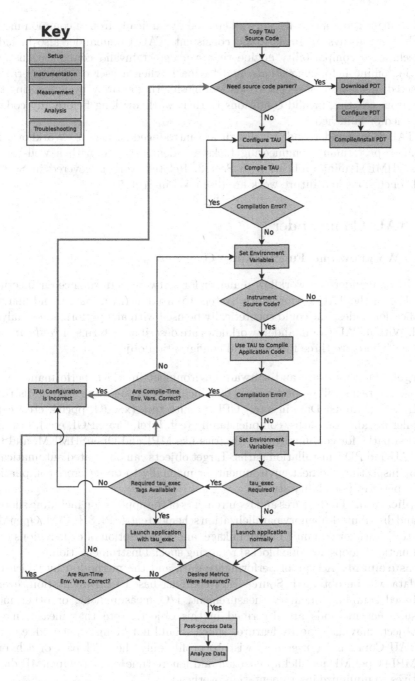

Fig. 1. The TAU performance analysis workflow providing instrumentation at compile time and run time. The red path shows the most commonly reported "pain point" in the workflow. TAU Commander simplifies the workflow as described in Sect. 2. (Color figure online)

and configuration option lists are all created dynamically from a common model so they are always up to date and consistent. TAU Commander also includes a declarative compatibility engine that can detect invalid configurations and provide online help, suggestions, and feedback when a user or system error is detected. In many cases, this avoids troubleshooting entirely by preventing the user from creating invalid conditions in their workflow long before any code is compiled or launched.

TAU Commander and it's design are introduced in Sect. 2. Workflows for common performance engineering tasks are demonstrated with a well-known OpenSHMEM mini-application in Sect. 3. Related work is covered in Sect. 4, and conclusions and future work are discussed in Sect. 5.

2   TAU Commander

2.1   Workflow and Functionality Overview

TAU Commander is a workflow manager for software performance engineering. It relies on the TAU Performance System to instrument, measure, and analyze application codes, but could theoretically be used with any performance analysis tool. Within TAU Commander, workflows are described in terms of *configuration objects*. There are three fundamental configuration object types:

Target. The hardware and software environment in which performance engineering tasks will be performed. This includes the operating system distribution (e.g. Linux, Darwin, etc.) CPU architecture (x86_64, ppc64, etc.) compiler installation paths, compiler family (e.g. Intel, Cray, PGI, etc.), installation paths for communication libraries like MPI and OpenSHMEM, and the TAU and PDT installation paths. Target objects can be created automatically by inspecting the host environment, or manually to target cross-compilation or perform portability studies.

Application. The features and requirements of the application including shared- and distributed-memory parallelization schemes (e.g. MPI, SHMEM, OpenMP, etc.), static or dynamic binary linkage, and a description of code regions (e.g. functions, loops, or code blocks) requiring special instrumentation.

Measurement. A type of performance data and the method(s) by which the data will be obtained. Source- and compiler-based instrumentation, event-based sampling, memory measurement, I/O measurement, or other measurement methods are described in this object. Note that measurements objects may also specify features which should not be instrumented, e.g. the TAU Commander user may wish to profile only the MPI part of a hybrid MPI+OpenMP parallel application and ignore time spent in OpenMP directives to minimize instrumentation overhead.

Users define workflows by composing sets of targets, applications, and measurements. We call this approach the *TAM Model*. Selecting one target, application, and measurement each concisely and completely defines the task at hand so that the workflow manager can determine the necessary actions to achieve the desired result. This also enables detection of user or system error by monitoring for actions or program outputs that conflict with the specified end goal. For example, the task of application performance analysis is described in the TAM model by one target, one application, and many measurements. By holding the target and application constant while varying the measurement configuration, we explore the different performance characteristics of the application when executing in a well-defined hardware/software environment. This is demonstrated in Sect. 3. Similarly, system benchmarking is defined as one target, many applications, one measurement. Holding the target and measurement constant while varying the application explores how well a particular hardware/software combination executes different workloads. Environment tuning and hardware evaluation or purchasing tasks are described as many targets, one application, and one measurement. By holding the application and measurement constant while varying the target, we discover which hardware/software combination achieves the optimal performance characteristics for a specific application. Although TAU Commander is the first tool to implement this model, TAM is a generic and portable approach to describing and organizing performance engineering workflows and could theoretically be used by any tool to elucidate the nature of software performance problems.

A combination of exactly one target, application, and measurement forms an *experiment*. The experiment configuration object completely describes the all hardware and software factors that produced a set of performance data, hence experiments enable provenance.[1] Each time the selected application is executed, a new *trial* of that experiment is recorded. TAU Commander maintains the resulting performance data, a record of the user's runtime environment (e.g. PATH), and timestamps marking the start and end of the trial. Users may perform many trials to minimize variance in the dataset or, by changing runtime parameters, explore scalability. TAU Commander maintains all configuration objects and performance datasets in a *project*, which is simply a container for grouping objects and data that relate to a common objective. A project may contain any number of target, application, or measurement objects.

The TAM model dramatically simplifies the TAU workflow by providing context to a user's actions and enabling users to clearly and concisely define their goals and working environment at the start of the workflow. The TAU Commander workflow is shown in Fig. 2. The information provided in the selected experiment enables TAU Commander to automatically configure and install TAU as needed, dramatically shortening the setup step. Under TAU Commander, software troubleshooting is only required in the case of a software bug and is no longer a regular part of the workflow. Simply launching the application under TAU Commander constitutes the entire measurement step since the tool is able to automatically determine the necessary environment variables and command line options to produce a desired dataset.

---

[1] Note that not producing any data is a valid experimental result, i.e. this particular experiment raises a fault in the application and the end goal is to use post-mortem debugging to determine the cause of the fault [19].

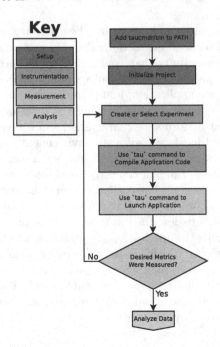

Fig. 2. The TAU Commander workflow.

2.2 Command Line Interface for Configuration, Compilation, Measurement, and Analysis

```
1 $ oshcc *.c -o a.out
2 $ oshrun -np 4 ./a.out
```

Listing 1.1. Compile and run a simple SHMEM code.

```
1 $ tau oshcc *.c -o a.out
2 $ tau oshrun -np 4 ./a.out
3 $ tau show
```

Listing 1.2. Generate performance data for a simple SHMEM code.

The TAU Commander user interface is a single command called tau that may be prepended to any command line. The tau command is used to create, modify, query, and delete configuration objects and performance data alike. It is also used to perform any task required by the performance analysis workflow including configuring and installing the TAU Performance System and all its dependencies (e.g. PDT), instrumenting application source code, preloading library wrappers, launching instrumented applications, and visualizing performance data. Its usage is similar to the popular git command, which provides subcommands for various tasks and provides online help through the --help command line option. Listing 1.1 shows how a simple SHMEM application might be compiled and executed on four processing elements (PEs). Listing 1.2 shows how performance data for that application may be generated with TAU Commander. The tau command parses its command line options to detect if it is being used during a compilation, application launch, or data analysis task. The target, application, and measurement configuration objects selected by the user – the current experiment – determine the actions the tau command will take according to the situation. If an appropriate TAU configuration (sometimes called a TAU Makefile) does not already exist, TAU Commander will automatically acquire TAU and all its dependencies via network download or file copy, configure all software packages appropriately, and install the packages in a filesystem location that permits future TAU Commander users to reuse the TAU configuration. These configuration and installation tasks are performed by the command shown on Line 1 of Listing 1.2. When the application is launched under TAU Commander (Line 2 of Listing 1.2), the tool will automatically determine the required values of all TAU-specific environment variables and command line options to tau_exec (if any). The generated performance data will be collected automatically and stored in a local performance database. The tau show command on Line 3 of Listing 1.2 displays the most recently generated profile or trace data in the most appropriate performance analysis tool (ParaProf, Jumpshot, or Vampir). In all cases, the tau command receives input from the command line only; environment variables or configuration files are not used by TAU Commander. The command also makes extensive use of default values and strives to provide sensible defaults based on the current system configuration.

2.3   Implementation Challenges

The challenges in implementing TAU Commander lie primarily in developing an intuitive user interface and an extensible model for generating and selecting TAU configurations. We addressed the user interface challenge by following the command/subcommand design popular with tools like "git". This user interface organization is both intuitive and easily extended by creating new subcommands or adding command line options to existing commands. Each TAU configuration generates a TAU Makefile, header and module files, dynamic and static libraries, and files containing compiler and linker command line options. TAU's configure script creates a new configuration. Many of this script's options are deprecated, activate experimental code, depend or conflict with other options, or are not well documented. Manually specifying every valid combination of options is impossible. Also, some configurations are mutually exclusive within the same TAU installation, e.g. configurations targeting different versions of the same compiler. Furthermore, new features are constantly added to TAU so TAU Commander must be able to recalculate all valid configurations when new configuration options are implemented. We addressed these problems by creating a declarative compatibility engine in TAU Commander that uses a system of requirements specified on certain target, application, or measurement properties. The details of this system are beyond the scope of the paper, but can be found in the TAU Commander developer documentation [10].

3   OpenSHMEM Usage and Examples

TAU Commander supports all SHMEM implementations that are supported by the TAU Performance System®, including OpenSHMEM reference implementations [4], Sandia OpenSHMEM (SOS) [17], and Cray SHMEM. Here we demonstrate TAU Commander usage with SOS 1.3.3 and Cray SHMEM 7.4.4 on the Cori supercomputer at NERSC, using either Intel Xeon "Haswell" or Intel Xeon Phi "Knight's Landing" (KNL) compute nodes. Cori is a heterogeneous Cray XC40 comprised of 2,388 Haswell compute nodes and 9,688 KNL compute nodes. Each Haswell node has two 16-core Intel Xeon E5-2698 processors at 2.3 GHz and 128 GB DDR4 memory. Each KNL node has one 68-core Intel Xeon Phi 7250 processor at 1.4 GHz, 16 GB MCDRAM, and 96 GB DDR4 memory.

Our example application is ISx [7], an open source, parallel, integer sort miniapplication implementing in-memory bucket sort written in C. It supports both strong and weak scaling studies, making it a useful tool for testing and comparing the performance of OpenSHMEM implementations. No pre-installation or preparation of TAU was performed so that TAU Commander's ability to "bootstrap" a fully functional TAU installation in a unique supercomputing environment is demonstrated. The only action taken to set up TAU Commander was to add the directory containing the tau command to our PATH environment variable. We configured SOS 1.3.3 to use libfabric's GNI provider library and Intel 17.0.2 compilers.

3.1   Event-Based Sampling with Callsites

The first step in using TAU Commander is to create a new project. The initialize subcommand creates a skeleton project containing target, application, and measurement configuration objects initialized from defaults discovered by probing the host system. Figure 3 shows the result of executing this command on Cori. The --shmem command line option indicates that our application uses SHMEM. Since Cori is a Cray system, TAU Commander will assume Cray SHMEM by default and probe the cray-shmem module to discover the location of the SHMEM installation. Because each TAU configuration is closely tied to a particular combination of compilers and MPI or SHMEM libraries, TAU Commander probes the current environment to discover C, C++, and Fortran compilers for serial, MPI, and SHMEM codes. A hash uniquely identifying that particular combination of compilers and libraries is used as a tag on the new software installation so that changes in compiler or library versions will trigger a rebuild of TAU and possibly its dependencies.

Callsite profiling allows a user to observe how much time is being spent in OpenSHMEM calls and where the call was invoked in the source code. TAU utilizes debugging information to resolve callsite addresses to source code file names and line numbers. TAU Commander will automatically add the appropriate command line options (e.g. -g) to ensure that debugging symbols are available. We updated TAU's measurement layer to support OpenSHMEM callsites in both

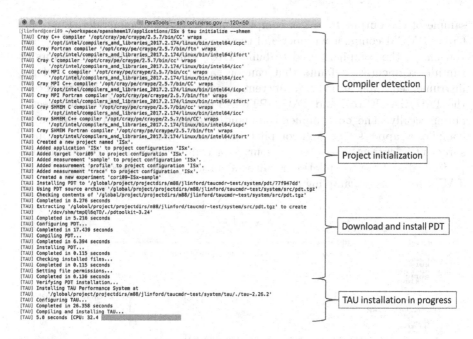

Fig. 3. Creating a new project for performance analysis of a SHMEM application via TAU Commander's `initialize` subcommand.

profiles and traces. The primary challenge was to insert the appropriate calls to libunwind and related libraries such that TAU's own callstack did not interfere with callsite resolution. We determined a callstack offset that achieved this for profiles and traces and modified TAU's trace generation library to generate the required callsite data. Once callsites were supported in TAU, we added a new attribute to TAU Commander's measurement model describing the TAU environment variables that must be set to activate callsite profiling and the required dependencies. Callsite profiling may be activated in TAU Commander by passing the `--callsite` flag when creating or editing a measurement.

```
●●●                ParaTools — ssh cori.nersc.gov — 120×44
[jlinford@cori09 ~/workspace/openshmem17/applications/ISx/SHMEM $ make optimized
tau cc -Wall -Wextra -std=c99  -O3 -DNDEBUG -xCORE-AVX2 -D SCALING_OPTION=1 -c pcg_basic.c -o obj/pcg_basic.o_s
[TAU] Cray SHMEM C compiler '/opt/cray/pe/craype/2.5.7/bin/cc' wraps
[TAU]      '/opt/intel/compilers_and_libraries_2017.2.174/linux/bin/intel64/icc'
[TAU] TAU_MAKEFILE=/global/project/projectdirs/m88/jlinford/taucmdr-test/system/tau/./tau-2.26.2/craycnl/lib/Makefile.ta
u-intel-3f5a233a-shmem-pdt
[TAU] TAU_OPTIONS=-optNoCompInst -optLinkOnly -optQuiet
[TAU] tau_cc.sh -g -Wall -Wextra -std=c99 -O3 -DNDEBUG -xCORE-AVX2 -D SCALING_OPTION=1 -c pcg_basic.c -o
[TAU]      obj/pcg_basic.o_s
```

Fig. 4. ISx compilation with TAU Commander.

To instrument ISx, the makefile must be modified to prepend the `tau` command to the compiler command. This is easily accomplished by changing Line 1 of the makefile from "CC = cc" to simply "CC = tau cc". Figure 4 shows a

sample of the output from ISx compilation with TAU Commander. First, the
Cray SHMEM compiler wrapper and the compiler it wraps are checked against
versions of the compilers used to build TAU. This avoids the linker errors or
runtime segmentation faults that can be caused by compiling TAU and the
instrumented application with different compilers. Next, appropriate values for
the TAU_MAKEFILE and TAU_OPTIONS environment variables are selected
automatically. The cc compiler command is replaced with TAU's tau_cc.sh
compiler wrapper script, and compilation proceeds. Because the sampling measurement is currently selected no source- or compiler-based instrumentation is
performed and the compilation result is a statically linked executable including
TAU's event-based sampling code.

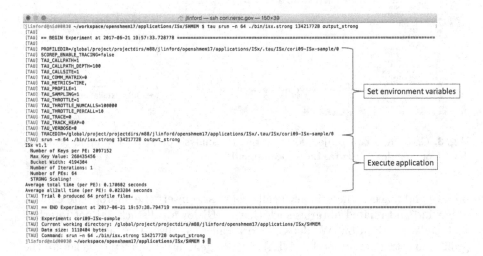

Fig. 5. Gathering event-based sampling performance data from ISx.

To gather performance data from ISx with TAU Commander, simply prepend
the tau command to the usual command line. This forms a new trial of the
selected experiment. Figure 5 shows the result of executing ISx on 64 PEs on
two Haswell compute nodes of Cori. Fifteen TAU environment variables are
configured automatically before ISx is executed. The measurement configuration specifies that event callsites should be recorded, so the TAU_CALLSITE
environment variable has been set to "1". When ISx completes, the resulting
performance data (906 KB) are stored in the project database. The tau show
command will display the data directly from the database, or the data can be
exported in a portable file format via the tau trial export command to be
viewed on another system. In that case, the path to the exported file is passed to
tau show on the command line. TAU Commander will configure and install TAU
on that system as well and finally display the exported data. Figure 6 shows ISx
performance data gathered via event-based sampling. Calls to the OpenSHMEM
API are visible and Line 497 of isx.c is highlighted as a performance hotspot.
Callsite information is also visible for OpenSHMEM.

Name	Exclusive TIME	Inclusive TIME ▽	Calls	Child Calls
▼ ■ .TAU application	0.306	1.347	1	326
■ void shmem_init(void) C	0.498	0.498	1	0
■ void shmem_finalize(void) C	0.462	0.462	1	0
▼ ■ [CONTEXT] .TAU application	0	0.32	6.406	0
▼ ■ [SUMMARY] main [{/global/project/projectdirs/m88/jlinford/openshmem17/applications/ISx/SHMEM/isx.c}]	0.262	0.262	5.172	0
■ [SAMPLE] main [{/global/project/projectdirs/m88/jlinford/openshmem17/applications/ISx/SHMEM/isx.c} {497}]	0.149	0.149	2.922	0
■ [SAMPLE] main [{/global/project/projectdirs/m88/jlinford/openshmem17/applications/ISx/SHMEM/isx.c} {374}]	0.041	0.041	0.812	0
■ [SAMPLE] main [{/global/project/projectdirs/m88/jlinford/openshmem17/applications/ISx/SHMEM/isx.c} {376}]	0.036	0.036	0.719	0
■ [SAMPLE] main [{/global/project/projectdirs/m88/jlinford/openshmem17/applications/ISx/SHMEM/isx.c} {378}]	0.011	0.011	0.219	0
■ [SAMPLE] main [{/global/project/projectdirs/m88/jlinford/openshmem17/applications/ISx/SHMEM/isx.c} {260}]	0.008	0.008	0.172	0
■ [SAMPLE] main [{/global/project/projectdirs/m88/jlinford/openshmem17/applications/ISx/SHMEM/isx.c} {381}]	0.005	0.005	0.094	0
■ [SAMPLE] main [{/global/project/projectdirs/m88/jlinford/openshmem17/applications/ISx/SHMEM/isx.c} {476}]	0.004	0.004	0.078	0
■ [SAMPLE] main [{/global/project/projectdirs/m88/jlinford/openshmem17/applications/ISx/SHMEM/isx.c} {379}]	0.004	0.004	0.078	0
■ [SAMPLE] main [{/global/project/projectdirs/m88/jlinford/openshmem17/applications/ISx/SHMEM/isx.c} {380}]	0.004	0.004	0.078	0
▶ ■ [SUMMARY] pcg32_boundedrand_r [{/global/project/projectdirs/m88/jlinford/openshmem17/applications/ISx/SHMEM/pcg_basic.c}]	0.057	0.057	1.203	0
■ [SAMPLE] __close_nocancel [{/home/abuild/rpmbuild/BUILD/glibc-2.19/npt/../sysdeps/unix/syscall-template.S} {81}]	0.001	0.001	0.016	0
■ [SAMPLE] __wrap_shmem_n_pes [{/global/project/projectdirs/m88/jlinford/openshmem17/applications/ISx/SHMEM/bin/isx.strong} {0}]	0.001	0.001	0.016	0
■ void shmem_int_put(int *, const int *, size_t, int) C	0.037	0.037	126	0
■ long long shmem_longlong_fadd(long long *, long long, int) C	0.018	0.018	128	0
■ void *shmem_malloc(size_t) C	0.015	0.015	16	0
■ void shmem_barrier_all(void) C	0.009	0.009	27	0
■ void shmem_fcollect64(void *, const void *, size_t, int, int, int, long *) C	0.001	0.001	7	0
■ void shmem_collect32(void *, const void *, size_t, int, int, int, long *) C	0	0	1	0
■ void shmem_longlong_sum_to_all(long long *, const long long *, size_t, int, int, int, long long *, long *) C	0	0	1	0
■ int shmem_my_pe(void) C	0	0	9	0
■ void shmem_free(void *) C	0	0	8	0
■ int shmem_n_pes(void) C	0	0	1	0
▼ ■ [CALLSITE] void shmem_init(void) C	0.996	0.996	2	0
▼ ■ [CONTEXT] [CALLSITE] void shmem_init(void) C	0	0.481	1.688	0
■ [SAMPLE] __ioctl [{/home/abuild/rpmbuild/BUILD/glibc-2.19/misc/.../sysdeps/unix/syscall-template.S} {81}]	0.473	0.473	1.344	0
■ [SAMPLE] _pmi_smp_barrier_join [{/usr/src/packages/BUILD/cray-pmi-5.0.10/src/pmi_core/smp_barrier.c} {70}]	0.006	0.006	0.281	0
■ [SAMPLE] Tau_lite_stop_timer [{/global/project/projectdirs/m88/jlinford/taucmdr-test/system/tau/tau-2.26.2/src/Profile/TauCAPI.cpp} i	0.002	0.002	0.047	0
■ [SAMPLE] _dmappi_sheap_alloc [{/home/abuild/rpmbuild/BUILD/cray-dmapp-7.1.1/src/dmapp_sheap.c} {318}]	0.001	0.001	0.016	0

Fig. 6. ISx profile with callsite information gathered via event-based sampling.

3.2   Source-Based Instrumentation

Event-based sampling can highlight performance hot spots at the source line
level, but it is inherently inaccurate since it is an indirect measurement method.
Direct measurement via source- or compiler-based instrumentation usually pro-
duces cleaner, more accurate profiles at the cost of increased runtime overhead.
Source-based instrumentation is enabled in TAU Commander by selecting a measurement configuration that specifies automatic or manual source-based instrumentation. This is done via the select subcommand as shown in Fig. 7. The
arguments to select are configuration objects that are to be composed into a
new experiment, or an existing experiment object. In Fig. 7, we have specified the
"profile" measurement object. The ISx project contains only one target and one
application, so the desired target and application can be implied. Upon forming
the new experiment, TAU Commander checks for TAU configurations that can
generate the specified performance data for the particular target and application.
In this case, a new TAU configuration supporting source-based instrumentation
is required so TAU is reconfigured and recompiled. Finally, the user is advised
that the application must be recompiled.

With the new experiment selected, ISx may be profiled and the resulting
data visualized using exactly the same workflow as described in Sect. 3.1. In
summary, ISx is recompiled via make optimized as shown in Fig. 4 and executed
with the tau command as shown in Fig. 5. Changing the selected experiment has
changed the context in which these actions are performed, resulting in different
performance data. Figure 8 shows the exclusive time profile of ISx code regions
measured via source-based instrumentation.

The data shown in Figs. 6 and 8 are taken from *profiles* of ISx. Source-based
instrumentation may also be used to generate *traces*. Profiles do not contain temporal data but rather aggregate performance events to form summary statistics.

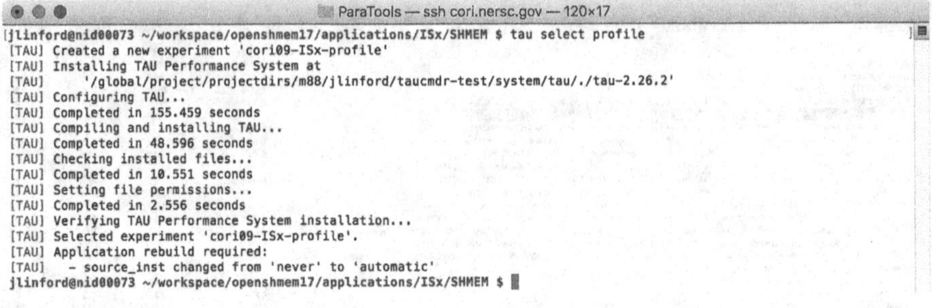

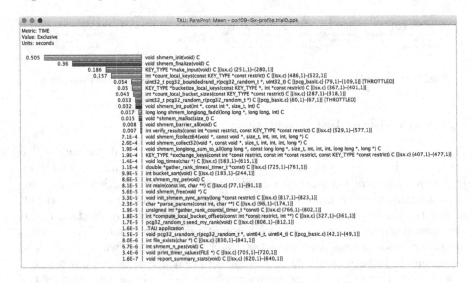

Fig. 7. Selecting the "profile" measurement configuration to form a new experiment.

Fig. 8. ISx profile gathered via source-based instrumentation.

Traces however, preserve the timestamp of each performance event so that the order of events may be observed. The storage requirement of traces is typically many orders of magnitude larger than that of profiles. To generate traces of ISx with TAU Commander we select the "trace" measurement configuration as shown in Fig. 9. In this case, a TAU configuration supporting source-based instrumentation already exists from when the "profile" measurement was selected so TAU is not recompiled. TAU Commander has also detected that switching from profiles to traces does not require the application to be recompiled so no message advising recompilation is printed. ISx may now be executed via the `tau` command and traces are generated instead of profiles (Fig. 10).

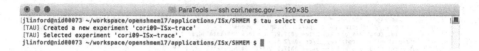

Fig. 9. Selecting the "trace" measurement configuration to form a new experiment.

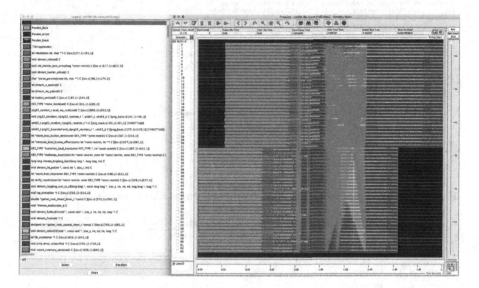

Fig. 10. ISx trace gathered via source-based instrumentation.

3.3 ISx with Sandia OpenSHMEM

To compare SHMEM implementations in TAU Commander we create target configurations for each SHMEM installation. The `target create` subcommand creates a new target. Figure 11 shows how this command is used to create a new target configuration called "cori.SOS" that uses SOS compilers instead of the default Cray SHMEM compilers. The `select` subcommand may then be used to select the new target configuration as shown in Fig. 12. TAU Commander will detect the change in compilers and reconfigure TAU as needed. It will also notify the user that their application must be recompiled to reflect the change in Open-SHMEM implementation. Compilation and execution then proceed similarly to Figs. 4 and 5.

Creating new measurement configurations enables new views of the application's performance. For example, an application's communication matrix can reveal communication patterns and highlight load imbalance or congestion. The `measurement create` subcommand can be used, or existing measurements may be copied and modified via the `measurement copy` subcommand. Figure 13 shows how we create a new measurement configuration called "comm" that is a copy of the "profile" configuration, but with an additional `--comm-matrix` flag. This flag indicates that point-to-point communication should be tracked

Fig. 11. Creating a new target called "cori.SOS" to profile Sandia OpenSHMEM.

```
● ○ ●                    Terminal — ssh cori.nersc.gov — 120×22
[jlinford@cori09 ~/workspace/openshmem17/applications/ISx $ tau select cori.SOS ISx profile
[TAU] Created a new experiment 'cori.SOS-ISx-profile'
[TAU] Installing TAU Performance System at
[TAU]      '/global/project/projectdirs/m88/jlinford/taucmdr-test/system/tau/./tau-2.26.2'
[TAU] Configuring TAU...
[TAU] Completed in 26.045 seconds
[TAU] Compiling and installing TAU...
[TAU] Completed in 32.441 seconds
[TAU] Checking installed files...
[TAU] Completed in 1.974 seconds
[TAU] Setting file permissions...
[TAU] Completed in 1.337 seconds
[TAU] Verifying TAU Performance System installation...
[TAU] Selected experiment 'cori.SOS-ISx-profile'.
[TAU] Application rebuild required:
[TAU]    - SHMEM_CC changed from '/opt/cray/pe/craype/2.5.7/bin/cc' to
[TAU]      '/global/homes/j/jlinford/opt/sos-4f5f8192/bin/oshcc'
[TAU]    - SHMEM_CXX changed from '/opt/cray/pe/craype/2.5.7/bin/CC' to
[TAU]      '/global/homes/j/jlinford/opt/sos-4f5f8192/bin/oshc++'
[TAU]    - SHMEM_FC changed from '/opt/cray/pe/craype/2.5.7/bin/ftn' to
[TAU]      '/global/homes/j/jlinford/opt/sos-4f5f8192/bin/oshfort'
jlinford@cori09 ~/workspace/openshmem17/applications/ISx $ ▊
```

Fig. 12. Selecting the "cori.SOS" target, "ISx" application, and "profile" measurement to form a new "cori.SOS-ISx-profile" experiment.

at runtime so the communication matrix may be recorded. Copying configuration objects in this way is purely a convenience feature; configuration objects may always be created from scratch. The `select` subcommand is used to select the new "comm" configuration, and ISx is executed as before to generate the communication matrix shown in Fig. 14.

3.4 Intel Xeon Phi "Knights Landing"

TAU Commander can be used with SHMEM applications executing on the Intel Xeon Phi "Knight's Landing" (KNL). To explore ISx performance on Cori's KNL nodes, we create and select a new target configuration that specifies the host architecture as KNL as shown in Fig. 15. TAU Commander will detect the

```
● ● ●                          Terminal — ssh cori.nersc.gov — 120×19
[jlinford@nid00010 ~/workspace/openshmem17/applications/ISx/SHMEM $ tau measurement copy profile comm --comm-matrix
[TAU] Added measurement 'comm' to project configuration 'ISx'.
[jlinford@nid00010 ~/workspace/openshmem17/applications/ISx/SHMEM $ tau measurement list
== Measurement Configurations (/global/project/projectdirs/m88/jlinford/openshmem17/applications/ISx/.tau/project.json)
==

+--------+---------+-------+--------+-------------+----------------+--------+------+------+------+--------+
|  Name  | Profile | Trace | Sample | Source Inst.| Compiler Inst. | OpenMP | CUDA | I/O  | MPI  | SHMEM  |
+--------+---------+-------+--------+-------------+----------------+--------+------+------+------+--------+
| sample |   tau   | none  |  Yes   |    never    |     never      | ignore |  No  |  No  |  No  |  Yes   |
+--------+---------+-------+--------+-------------+----------------+--------+------+------+------+--------+
| profile|   tau   | none  |   No   |  automatic  |     never      | ignore |  No  |  No  |  No  |  Yes   |
+--------+---------+-------+--------+-------------+----------------+--------+------+------+------+--------+
|  trace |  none   | slog2 |   No   |  automatic  |     never      | ignore |  No  |  No  |  No  |  Yes   |
+--------+---------+-------+--------+-------------+----------------+--------+------+------+------+--------+
|  comm  |   tau   | none  |   No   |  automatic  |     never      | ignore |  No  |  No  |  No  |  Yes   |
+--------+---------+-------+--------+-------------+----------------+--------+------+------+------+--------+

jlinford@nid00010 ~/workspace/openshmem17/applications/ISx/SHMEM $ █
```

Fig. 13. Using the `tau measurement copy` command to create a new measurement called "comm" that is a modified copy of the "profile" measurement.

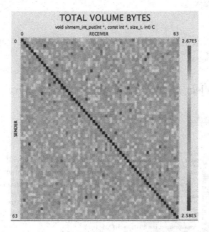

Fig. 14. Communication matrix of ISx executing on Cori with Sandia OpenSHMEM.

change in host architecture and recompile TAU and dependencies as needed. All performance analysis tasks demonstrated in Sect. 3 may be performed on KNL exactly as they are on Haswell. For example, Fig. 16 shows the mean exclusive time profile of ISx while executing on 136 KNL cores as measured by source-based instrumentation. With a KNL target configuration selected, TAU Commander manages all KNL-specific details so that the workflow is identical to the workflows we have demonstrated on Haswell CPUs.

Supporting KNL-based Cray systems in TAU Commander required a new platform architecture configuration so that additional, KNL-specific flags are passed when configuring TAU. In most cases, configuring TAU for KNL requires only one new configuration flag: `-useropt=-DTAU_MAX_THREADS=512`. However, on Cray systems additional flags like `-arch=craycnl` must be passed, even though KNL is an x86_64 architecture and most KNL systems are configured with `-arch=x86_64`. We implemented new platform architecture in TAU Commander that specifically indicates KNL-based Cray systems such that all the required flags are selected automatically.

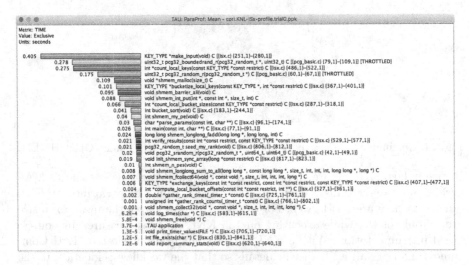

Fig. 15. Creating and selecting a target configuration for Cori's KNL compute nodes.

Fig. 16. Mean exclusive time profile of ISx while executing om 136 KNL cores of Cori as measured by source-based instrumentation.

4   Related Work

OpenSHMEM [4,8] has emerged as an effort to join the disparate SHMEM implementations into a common, portable and high performance standard. Bader and Cong have demonstrated fast data structures for distributed shared memory [2]. Pophale et al. defined the performance bounds of OpenSHMEM [16].

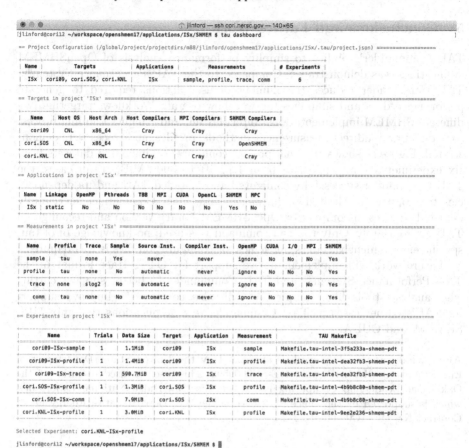

Fig. 17. ISx project showing all configuration objects and dataset sizes.

Both profiling and tracing are relevant to better understanding the performance characteristics of an application. While profiling shows summary statistics, tracing can reveal the temporal variation in application performance. Among tools that use the direct measurement approach, the VampirTrace [9] package provides a wrapper interposition library that can capture the traces of I/O operations. Scalasca [6] is a portable and scalable profiling and tracing system that can automate the detection of performance bottlenecks in message passing and shared memory programs. TAU, VampirTrace, and Scalasca use the PAPI [3] library to access hardware performance counters.

5   Conclusions and Future Work

TAU Commander's ability to simplify performance analysis of OpenSHMEM applications was demonstrated. Compared to the TAU Performance System®, TAU Commander reduces the number of user actions required to generate performance data and simplifies the workflow overall. Workflows targeting two different SHMEM implementations, Intel Haswell and Knights Landing processors, direct and indirect measurement methods, profiles, and traces were demonstrated. Figure 17 shows the final project configuration including datasets from six experiments ranging in size from 1.1 MiB to 590.7 MiB. In all cases, the TAU Commander successfully configured and installed TAU and its dependencies to produce the desired performance data. TAU Commander successfully detected changes in compiler or OpenSHMEM library version and reconfigured TAU appropriately. Only the `tau` command was used; no knowledge of of tau-specific environment variables, makefiles, or configuration files is was required.

Future work will implement native support for OTF2 trace format in the TAU Performance System® and TAU Commander to better support cutting edge analysis tools like Vampir. We will also continue to improve support for TAU's corner cases in TAU Commander, e.g. applications that mix MPI, SHMEM, and CUDA.

Acknowledgments. This work is supported by the United States Department of Energy under DOE SBIR grant DE-SC0009593. This research used resources of the Oak Ridge Leadership Computing Facility at the Oak Ridge National Laboratory, which is supported by the Office of Science of the U.S. Department of Energy under Contract No. DE-AC05-00OR22725.

References

1. U.S. Department of Energy INCITE leadership computing, December 2015. http://www.doeleadershipcomputing.org/
2. Bader, D.A., Cong, G.: Fast shared-memory algorithms for computing the minimum spanning forest of sparse graphs. J. Par. Distrib. Comp. **66**(11), 1366–1378 (2006). http://dx.doi.org/10.1016/j.jpdc.2006.06.001
3. Browne, S., Dongarra, J., Garner, N., Ho, G., Mucci, P.: A portable programming interface for performance evaluation on modern processors. Int. J. High Perform. Comput. Appl. **3**(14), 189–204 (2000)
4. Chapman, B., Curtis, T., Pophale, S., Poole, S., Kuehn, J., Koelbel, C., Smith, L.: Introducing OpenSHMEM: SHMEM for the PGAS community. In: Proceedings of the Fourth Conference on Partitioned Global Address Space Programming Model, PGAS 2010, pp. 2:1–2:3. ACM, New York (2010). http://doi.acm.org/10.1145/2020373.2020375
5. Francis, I., Drugan, C.: Groundbreaking astrophysics accelerated. HPC Source, February 2013
6. Geimer, M., Wolf, F., Wylie, B.J.N., Mohr, B.: Scalable parallel trace-based performance analysis. In: Mohr, B., Träff, J.L., Worringen, J., Dongarra, J. (eds.) EuroPVM/MPI 2006. LNCS, vol. 4192, pp. 303–312. Springer, Heidelberg (2006). https://doi.org/10.1007/11846802_43

7. Hemstad, J., Hanebutte, U.R.: ISx: An integer sort mini-application for the exas-cale era (2015). Partitioned Global Address Space SC'15 Booth
8. Jose, J., Kandalla, K., Luo, M., Panda, D.: Supporting hybrid MPI and OpenSH-MEM over infiniband: design and performance evaluation. In: The 41st Interna-tional Conference on Parallel Processing (ICPP), pp. 219–228 (2012)
9. Knupfer, A., Brunst, H., Nagel, W.: High performance event trace visualization. In: Proceedings of Parallel and Distributed Processing (PDP). IEEE (2005)
10. Linford, J.C.: TAU commander developer documentation, June 2017. http://paratoolsinc.github.io/taucmdr/
11. Linford, J.C., Vadlamani, S., Shende, S., Malony, A.D., Jones, W., Anderson, W.K., Nielsen, E.: Performance engineering FUN3D at scale with TAU Comman-der. In: Proceedings of the ACM/IEEE The International Conference for High Performance Computing, Networking, Storage and Analysis (SC 2016), November 2016. To Appear
12. Malony, A., Biersdorff, S., Shende, S., Jagode, H., Tomov, S., Juckeland, G., Dietrich, R., Poole, D., Lamb, C.: Parallel performance measurement of hetero-geneous parallel systems with GPUs. In: 2011 International Conference on Parallel Processing (ICPP), pp. 176–185, September 2011
13. Malony, A.D., Mellor-Crummey, J., Shende, S.S.: Measurement and analysis of parallel program performance using TAU and HPCToolkit. In: Performance Tuning of Scientific Applications. CRC Press, New York, November 2010
14. ParaTools, Inc.: TAU Commander: An intuitive interface for the TAU Performance Analysis System (2014). https://www.sbir.gov/sbirsearch/detail/687037
15. Perez, J., Shende, S.: Furthering the understanding of coronal heating and solar wind origin. Technical report, Argonne National Labs, January 2013
16. Pophale, S., Nanjegowda, R., Curtis, T., Chapman, B., Jin, H., Poole, S., Kuehn, J.: OpenSHMEM performance and potential: a NPB experimental study. In: The 6th Conference on Partitioned Global Address Space Programming Models (PGAS 2012) (2012)
17. Seager, K., Choi, S.-E., Dinan, J., Pritchard, H., Sur, S.: Design and implemen-tation of OpenSHMEM using OFI on the aries interconnect. In: Venkata, M.G., Imam, N., Pophale, S., Mintz, T.M. (eds.) OpenSHMEM 2016. LNCS, vol. 10007, pp. 97–113. Springer, Cham (2016). https://doi.org/10.1007/978-3-319-50995-2_7
18. Shende, S., Malony, A.: The TAU Parallel Performance System. Int. J. High Per-form. Comput. Appl. 20(2), 287–311 (2006)
19. Shende, S., Malony, A., Linford, J., Wissink, A., Adamec, S.: Isolating runtime faults with callstack debugging using TAU. In: Proceedings of the HPEC 2012 Conference (2012)

Author Index

Printed in the United States
By Bookmasters